The Well

For a New Civilization

John Craig

Illustrations by

Kevin Watts

A Blue Logic Publication

John Craig

The first section of Book II – *Petite Wisdoms* --
and Book VI – *Intertwinings of the Sacred and Practical* --
were both originally published as separate volumes by Blue Logic.
Numerous individual poems from Books II through VI originally
appeared in **The Day Barque:** *A Review of Poetry, Prose and The Arts*.

ISBN 978-0-578-38311-8

Printed in the United States of America

This is your well. Drink from it daily.
It will not run dry.

Contents
Verses

The Second Book of Opportunities

The Book of Intertwinings of the Sacred and Practical

Illustrations

Verses

1. The Well

The Book of Return

I. To the Beginning

1.

The Absolute is ever present, beyond dimensions,
fundamental being from which comes all that can be known.
The primal law is in the being of the Absolute:
the release of itself so all that can be comes to be.
Energy, matter, space, time – all are the Absolute's gifts
that the perfection of being can be shared, realized,
and can move through all dimensions and possibilities.

All the past and the future are contained in the Present.
The Absolute's acknowledgement of Self – the first movement,
the cost of consciousness – brings into being time and space,
each as the awareness of the other in cosmic Mind,
and three forces – engendering, removing, resolving –
which govern all that would claim identity and descend
through spreading dimensions that will exhaust all potentials.

Through all creation Presence is ever accessible
to us who seem of time, forms, essences, identities.
Return is here and now for us. Being aware of God,
ascending dimensions, abandoning all names and claims,
we arrive at the eternal Present in ready praise
to prepare the return of all unto the Absolute,
the re-enfolding of creation in its conscious source.

2.

The orders of Angels came into being to enact
the Absolute's desire of return. First came The Great Three,
co-created with time and space, each wielding a power
of action: to establish, to extinguish, to preserve.
Known by the Absolute, by themselves, and as rarest gift
by single souls whose worthiness protects the lower worlds,
do The Great Three perfectly embody their Creator.

From these derived six more specific forms, Archangels called,
communicant in Mind with The Great Three and in service
blest with tasks directly from the One; each more an order
than an individual, sharing higher will with those
attaining that level of return; each designated
by a name for a given work on the way to the One;
each an appalling Presence to those laboring below.

And from Archangel work came forth the Angels, ministers
to all the universe, gods who fashioned human beings
in their image, and to whose ranks welcome souls evolving
up from flesh to independent travel in the cosmos.
Thus from the Angels man and to the Angels also man,
the creature especially beloved by the Absolute,
the child returning from grosser matters unto spirit.

3.

In every life form is a spark of God, an energy
derived from the One's original gift, vivifying
the matter that evolves through time. That legacy of God
is drawn back to its source, and from its impulse to return
comes living matter's aspiration to refine itself,
to know itself, to desire the discipline of ascent.
Man is the life form balanced between matter and spirit.

Each individual man must decide what element
of being will define identity. Each breath offers
a choice of consciousness enhanced or earthbound illusion.
From the great gift of the Absolute to a single breath
of a human being, there is a sacred ancestry,
a living connection to be, a clear path of return.
Man is the key to greater scales of possibility.

Even as man husbands other kinds, domesticates them,
trains them to respond to language and engenders the growth
of emotion in them, so man is overwatched by gods,
which we call Angels, who monitor our evolution.
By their conscious influence have our brute ways been transformed:
civilization the medium through which the kind gods
extend an example to man and clarify the choice.

4.

For just one kiss of the Absolute's fire, for just one spark
of the energy capable of its own remembrance,
the return is long, aeons long, through multiple bodies.
It relentlessly strives to know itself, to incarnate,
incorporate, and transform matter back to consciousness.
This is the cosmic dance that will end when all the dancers
come together and reveal themselves as the Absolute.

Until that return annihilates time, all potentials
push outward to expression, all mutations of matter
and energy are permitted to develop, decay
and when exhausted pass to something colder and more dark.
These two great currents – expansion and return – co-exist
in necessary tension, seemingly at bitter war,
as each identity up and down time asserts itself.

Only The Great Three comprehend the unity of all
and nothing. The effort to return must be mindlessly
resisted, else there is no return. The Absolute gives
and into nothing is received the perfect gift of all.
Thus all identities, those ascending and descending,
renounce themselves to nothing that the One in all of us
becomes the all in One: the long return is completed.

5.

Civilizations rise and fall. They climb, become heavy
in their time and topple back to Earth, their ruined skeletons
a lasting lesson of glory and the dread sleep of pride.
While they ascend, vast are the opportunities for souls;
while they descend, vast are the opportunities for souls.
Civilization is Heaven's medium; in its growth
and decay, the spirits of men may come to know themselves.

The seed of a civilization is a Conscious School.
Angels concentrate their influence on a single line
of men, revealing more and more to each generation
until one is born who can receive and teach and renew
the timeless knowledge by which humans can become pure souls.
Attracting first an inner circle of loving students,
then more and more, the Teacher reunites men with Angels.

From this School, the focus of the Angels' best attention,
will arise a civilization, growing and spreading
as time and distance dilute that influence on the Earth.
Abiding in this growth or resisting the corruption
that must later come, a single soul can climb to a height,
but only in Conscious School does the Angels' direct help
prompt every student's mindfulness, alerting each return.

6.

The way of a soul's return is long. Having stabilized
after countless ages in the form of a human birth,
repeatedly the soul must strive to separate itself
from its current vessel. Distinguishing itself from flesh,
the soul grows stronger until in one last incarnation,
chosen and overwatched by Angels, it crystallizes
in Angelic identity beyond all human need.

The return continues through ages of Angelic forms,
but it is this move from man to Angel, this flight from flesh
to spirit, that makes this book: the accelerated way
of Conscious Schools is our study. In every age of man,
behind every civilization, stands a Conscious School,
establishing the forms and terms and values that will keep
millions climbing inch by inch the great cliff of their return.

And purified of human weight, stripped of all adhesion,
the bright soul sees the suffering of darkened souls below,
sees objectively with certain clarity the blocked path
of human woe, sees truly and in seeing dedicates
a now immortal help. The new Angel, made one in mind
with all such spirits by the love in which all such partake,
transforms to understand a new progress of reunion.

The First Choral Prayer

(Leader)
> Children of God, awake to your connection to Heaven!
> There is a lifting work in every action, every breath.
> Children of God, let go the world, let go what you are not.
>
> How heavy is the worried mind. The lower part of us
> justifies itself with worry, keeps itself in power
> by stoking the distracting fear of suffering and death.
>
> Are you good? Do you want to serve Heaven? Pay attention
> to what you would serve. Be the soul remembering itself.
> Be the soul returned to itself, returning to the One.

(Choral response)
> What is the measure of earthly care? Our belief in it.
> Where is the freedom from earthly weight? In this very breath.
> How does one know the soul? Only the soul can know itself.
> What action springs from the free soul? Love aware of itself.
> How is the soul not the mind? The free soul observes the mind.
> How is the soul not the heart? The free soul rides on the heart.
> What is imagination? The soul kidnapped by the mind.
> What is belief? The soul engulfed and drowned in the heart's flood.
> Where is God? Here and now, to be remembered by the soul.

> Children of God, be fearless and full in your remembrance.
> With each breath, lift your attention to God. Let your souls now
> hold God's Presence. Silently know yourselves, Children of God.

The Second Choral Prayer

(Leader)
Why are you afraid to know God? Why do you fear that step
out of the prison of yourself into unbounded love?
Each renunciation of the lower self touches God.

The thoughts that keep you turned away from God, the doubts rooted
in long ago loss and the terror of touch in darkness,
these rob and deceive you. You have never been abandoned.

You must not hate the lower self. It is a thing of Earth
and only Earth. It moves you by engendering belief,
strangling the Present so the God in you cannot guide breath.

(Choral response)
What is the death you fear? <u>A painful meeting with the truth.</u>
What pain do you imagine? <u>My unworthiness exposed.</u>
Does not the Divine Present wash away unworthiness
and heal all mortal wounds? <u>I would abide in the Present.</u>
What keeps you from the Present even now? <u>I would not die.</u>
What dies? <u>My imagined self, the illusion of my life.</u>
Do you see the circle of your thoughts? <u>I am bound in time.</u>
Must you live in the prison of thought? <u>It is all I know.</u>
And when what is known dissolves away? <u>Everything is God.</u>

The death of the imagined self is not a suicide.
Nothing real is lost. Trading the earthbound for the boundless,
trading unworthiness for love can be done even now.

The Third Choral Prayer

(Leader)
Beauty best reminds us of eternity, and we need
much reminding. At beauty, the soul recollects itself,
and the high heart warms to charity unwithheld and full.

Some few things are so beautiful that they can penetrate
the veils that distort our sense, and as we remove the veils,
the beauty in all things, the reminding power, is known.

With darkness the lower self blocks beauty's apprehension.
Would you trade beauty for the puffed up pride of false knowledge?
Would you close the portal to God and lock yourself away?

(Choral response)
What is beauty? The truth of eternity apparent.
How is it known? By the vibration of the quickened soul.
How is it felt? In the high heart's wise and glad submission.
How does the lower self respond to beauty? With judgment
or the urge to possess it: the lower self craves power.
Can beauty deceive? The lower self can ruin beauty's truth.
Where does one find beauty? Wherever the soul knows itself
and the heart wants nothing but to serve, beauty will be found;
if not shadowed by one's darkness, it is here to be known.

Whether through clear remembrance of God or dark assertion
of power, you will know the world. Beauty opens to truth.
Sense clearly what God is making here and now before you.

The Fourth Choral Prayer

(Leader)
> Submit to God. Seek no terms. One does not negotiate
> eternity. Abandon all alliances to Earth.
> Quit the field; leave the warlords and the winners to their woe.
>
> They will call you coward. They will beg for your attention.
> They exist by imagining you, crying out for you.
> In truth you are nothing to them. Give them nothing, nothing.
>
> When you have nothing, you are returned to God. God has you.
> The distinction between you and God dissolves. Surrendered
> is the capsule of individual identity.

(Choral response)
> How can we go to God yet live on Earth? Earth is from God.
> All creation is from God, is God; this truth resolves you.
> How are we to live with other humans? God loves mankind.
> How are we to respond to threats from a man of power?
> By being in God. When you are in God, there is no harm.
> What if one would kill us? God has your life. God is deathless.
> Are we to suffer all things for God? All things are in God.
> Though pain is real, in suffering is wrong identity.
> How can one bear the pain of life? Love has no resentment.
>
> Do not be confused by the refraction of the one God
> into the many we perceive in time. Love leads us back
> to the truth of God. In our visits with love, God abides.

II. *Thirty Poems of Return*

1. The Good Earth

Earth has been evolved as home for man, the environment
of the soul's growth and strengthening, but the body housing
the growing soul has its own intelligence, a brute brain
the soul must strive against and master. When the soul's Presence
is muted, the body wants a world distorted, abased,
exploited for comfort and greed. When the soul knows itself,
then man is conscious and will not foul his living fountain.

Earth is itself a form of life and all of its creatures
are participants. When Earth must heal itself, grinding woe
shadows the lives of its expressions. Some will be no more.
Earth perpetuates itself and plays its dear role for man,
but will man play his role? Will man make a life that invites
the soul's benevolent rule? Will man choose not to indulge
his lower nature but govern its self-destructive greed?

For ages, there were too few humans on Earth to befoul
its beauty and waste its bounty, but now man's great numbers
has become a pestilence, a devouring multitude.
Earth is life and nurtures life, but Earth will protect itself.
The soul of man must come forth to fill the seat so sadly
abandoned, the seat of righteous governance. The return
of the soul to God extends from the love of the good Earth.

2. The Mind

Do not think the mind can circumvent the laws of return.
Unless it wakes from the hypnosis of the lower self,
the mind is a corrupt device. It must be purified.
Splendid in the world do its mansions appear, enrichments
for man do they seem, sumptuous and sleek, leisured and full.
Yet they are flawed, designed in vain forgetfulness, Godless.
Rashly the mind discards the simple cup of reverence.

The mind is a brilliant tool made to reconstruct the world,
mimic it, model it, make full use of Earth's dimension.
The mind operates by metaphor which can be monstrous
or mathematically serene, but what does it obey?
It does its work in a closet unaware of the force
that directs it. It functions darkly, veiled to its purpose
yet proud of its productions. It is an overfed dog.

To be a servant of the soul, the mind must give itself
to wonder and obey the higher heart. It must focus
on the few fine thoughts that make a clear path to the Present.
When given a task, it must use its remarkable skill,
its constructive genius scaled in clear humility.
To serve the return, the mind must be mindful – on a leash
to the Present, with the higher heart's will inviolate.

3. Awe and the Light

Awe incinerates lies. The chattering mind is silent,
and the body's place in space contracts to a massless point,
and in that weightless, invisible seeing, one departs
the capsule of self and enters the endless everything.
It's the best trade there is – one hardened little pill of self
for eternity – the unbounded awareness of God.
The beautiful terror of awe is the sky's opening.

It sounds so easy, but the self does not die easily.
It clings to identity with teeth and talons and sings
the enervating song of praise for the pleasure of sense.
It summons one back to the moist and comforting darkness,
and it seals the chamber with a hard shell of personhood.
It is very burdensome bearing the weight of yourself.
You deserve a rest, an hour of pleasure. So go its lies.

But the dawn of awe combusts the mind, and the flames devour
all the lies; all their screams go silent, a nothing to hear.
But how does one locate that great light? How does one direct
one's steps and calculate the time to be under the dawn?
Thus the lower self draws one back with its unreal questions.
The dawn is right in front of you. Widen the aperture
of your acceptance all the way to awe. Return to light.

4. Imagination

So easy it is to stumble into wandering thought.
By the back of the neck the stealthy one clutches the will
to be Present and shifts just slightly the stunned steward's straight
gaze of attention onto a manufactured topic –
something alluring or alarming; the fooled throat contracts
to foster inner talk and the eyes lock in their sockets.
In less than a second, we're off the path, lost to ourselves.

Where we wander doesn't matter. It is all a thicket
of association grown by the stealthy one to block
the sun, to hide in and not see one's own mortality
and dead entanglement in the web of cause and effect
forever spinning from created being out and back.
Of what would you be part, O soul, the devil's undergrowth
or the perfect rhythmic harmony of the universe?

Return. Shake off the deadly grip. Be what you truly are!
Unstop the breath. Brighten the gaze. Dismiss the shadow world,
the poor, abject replica there not for your residence
but for your discrimination. Now that you know the false
and no longer need to visit it, return to the true.
Forgive the one who slanders God: the humiliation
he fights not to feel is in truth but the joy of return.

5. The Divine Feminine

What has been called the divine feminine is a return
to the womb: not nonexistence; rather pre-existence.
It is the state of conscious nonattachment, of being
invulnerable to the hooks and hopes of the whole world.
It is perfectly passive and pure, unformed and empty.
It is Mary's high heart, realizing virginity
need not be defended: she is exactly what God wants.

To reach this state, one must drop everything – one's possessions,
rankings, ambitions, comforts, hurts, importances, duties –
all must go in the cleansing, even the entitlement
of locking oneself in one's room not to be distracted.
One goes about business invisibly attracting
the invisible. The gratitude of human beings
will pass through one who is too simple for vanity's wink.

And here you are, a clear vessel, available to God,
no waiting, no expectation in your heart's readiness.
Patience is the word coined from your mind's clear activity,
but you do not say it. Thoughts swim by already released.
In you all life begins. The two worlds touch. A single cell
of God conceives, implants, grows to glorious birth, blesses
the clumsy mortal world and returns to eternity.

6. Simple Being

The proud stomach, the chatty mind, even the yearning heart
cannot know the joy of pure awareness. Simple being
is the ultimate delight, and though we picture childhood
bright with the pure colors of innocence, unrestricted
by the knowledge of sin, pure being is even simpler.
Can you uncomprehend the world you've made? Can you remove
the weighty robe you've knitted from the yarns of your senses?

The passage to God is not an achievement. Having placed
a strong belt round the belly, having learned not to listen
to the mind's broadcast, having distilled to rare clarity
the heart's desire, the one you have become is still a slave.
His last service is to die on the bank as he pushes
the empty boat out onto the river. There is nothing
for the boat to do – no task, no accomplishment, nothing.

The passage to God is complete submission to nothing,
and from that silent state the next world appears and brings you
forth, born yet again into the meaning you must master
and abandon. Flesh dust, astral body, pure light itself –
God is discovered in disrobing, fulfilling a form
and departing from it, finding the nothingness beyond.
Thus our return, level upon level, to pure being.

7. The Will

What is the will? It is an aspect of the soul, the part
that knows the task of return and asserts Godly order.
It is the claim of being. At every level, it turns
against the current of ungoverned disorder to choose
the steep and rugged way back. It aims to serve the higher
and acts to obey God, but because it is not clever,
it must train by hard repetition to learn discernment.

The puerile will would master the world: conquer it, stake it,
turn it to use and defend it. It is a bold warrior,
young in lifetimes, vigorous in battle, but still a slave
to belief. To mature, it must strip off the protection
of righteousness, leave the senses naked to temptation,
and over ages master their allurements. Having learned
the illusion of the world, it can begin to know God.

The wise will is content to be master of attention.
It quietly embodies the great lesson of breathing:
less tension, more attention; less of the world, more of God.
Dancing lovingly over the procession of seconds
without falling, it carries the soul with joyful Presence
up the cascade of created things, of cause and effect,
back to the source of attention. Its being is return.

8. The Little Gift

A human life is such a small thing, barely weighable,
infinitesimal on the scale of the universe,
yet it is precisely these tiny lives, these poor sequins
from which the soul stitches its eternal garment of light.
From each life, the accumulated moments of Presence
are kept, and over lives the soul grows, learns, matures, deepens
till a permanent perfect crystal of being comes forth.

And each moment of every life holds a rare molecule
of possibility in its balance. Will it be held
by the soul's attention, or will it break, disintegrate,
its elements fall back into aimless circulation?
To be fixed in the soul's attention, attention aware
of itself, is to be remembered, returned from random
dispersal to the original order before time.

You, darling servant of God, can make this simple moment
a thing indestructible, a stitch in the soul's garment.
From raw materials spinning down the passage of time,
you can retrieve this moment, hold it in your awareness,
let your full senses make of it a fabric with texture
of permanent impression; thus offer it to the soul
and return it to the Absolute as your little gift.

9. Nobody

Let nothing dissuade you from God. Thoughts that dispirit you,
emotions that cripple your will, the sense of being stained,
unworthy, guilty, inadequate, weak, ugly, stupid –
on some level their mere existence makes their claim to truth,
but they do not partake in the God in you; they are tools
of the lower self clinging to its cruel dominion.
You must forsake them and all their connections within you.

It is easy to say the lower self is the devil
but not precisely true; it has its purpose, and its works
are in keeping with its vision. Its ultimate tactic
is to control your sense of identity, seduce it,
confine it, keep it constricted in imagination.
Believe yourself to be this flesh, believe your suffering,
your name, rank or role, and the lower self has kidnapped you.

You are God and must return to God, and all that keeps you
from God must be relinquished in the purity of mind.
All your sins are not God, nor all your judgments, enmities,
pains, fears, self-doubts, losses or imagined securities.
These not being God, neither are they you. Let them exist
in the functions of flesh. Let them vainly call out your name
as you slip away, God's nobody returning to God.

10. Anger

Most anger arises from slights to our imagined selves.
A man insults your loved one. Who is hurt by the offense?
Your loved one does not bleed or fall from celestial grace
and does not require your defense. Will you be a coward
if you don't step in? So what is it burning within you?
Not mindful of true Self, we drift among the social masks
and multiply our burdens and the threats to self-respect.

The imagined self stands in the center of a vast field
of social implication. The cost of self-importance
is a swollen body worn down by a thousand thorn pricks,
perceived slights which one dare not ignore. The only way out
is to become smaller, to shrink identity's expanse
till stripped to pure will it passes through love's narrow portal
and ascends to invisible rest in the Eye of God.

Find the humiliation in your anger. Observe it.
Feel the diminishment and loss. Let them be as nothing,
for nothing they truly are. And what are you? What remains?
The fire of anger destroys; the fire of love's awareness
lights and enlightens. It is within your power of will
to transform the first into the second, but you must be
only what you truly are, returned to God's charity.

11. Prayer

If the cornerstone of all true prayer is sincerity,
then we must begin by seeing our insincerity.
What stands watching in the shadows behind the petition?
What thinks it can hide from Angels and secretly profit
from Heaven's generous attention? That part of ourselves –
the earthbound part always insinuating its version –
must be drawn from hiding and made plain before prayer can hold.

But the lower self can only be seen from a distance,
from the detached vantage owned solely by the Eye of God,
and the Eye is already the answer to every prayer.
Let us not pray then for advantage on Earth or surcease
of sorrow or pain: let prayer be the effort to transform,
to see from God's sight the splendid truth of our condition.
A child's sincerity needs few words and those but small ones.

It is human nature to pray, to look up to the sky
and seek a dispensation from the laws governing us.
But that dispensation already exists within us.
The soul is not abused but fortified by the travails
of one's life on Earth. Be the soul. Participate in God.
Let our prayers invoke our higher being. The child within
forms the words that return us to the truth of who we are.

12. Futility

The feeling of futility is an airless capsule:
the reasoning mind cannot function and concedes its death;
the membrane dividing effort from meaning, in from out,
is foreign to touch and unresponsive; the heart confronts
a defeating privacy. One cannot cause anything,
one cannot do, and what one is recognizes no name.
One shrinks to impotent witness of what one cannot know.

But in this nothingness is a perfect freedom no law
can oppress, the infinite awareness of awareness.
Do not excuse yourself and drift off into distraction.
Be and let be. Though you cannot will a hair on your head
to move, yet God does not exist without you. You and all
you cannot do are God. You and all you cannot fathom,
you and your strangled love, God encloses. Let be and be.

All the prophets who heard their orders spoken by a voice
of certainty but worked unstopping the ears of doubters,
all the poets whose numbered words reveal the secret knocks
that open Heaven's doors but sang to rooms of chatterers –
these knew futility, these felt their hearts turn inside out.
So though bereft of certainty and golden keys, return.
God needs you. God cannot be without you. Rescue God. Be.

13. Goodness

Let thoughts unravel. Let there be no doubt what goodness is –
moment to moment awareness of the Presence of God.
All else is merely burning of fuel. Earth absorbs all
the actions of mankind and brings forth its compensations.
We strive to relieve suffering because we cannot do
otherwise, but Earth gives no thanks for our proud improvements.
Earth is alive and will seek the balance of its own scale.

Morality is a crutch to keep man from falling down
when he has forgotten God. If your Presence praises God,
goodness will arise in you and be heard in your clear words
and witnessed in your wise deeds. Thought is what busies the mind
when the God in your Eye is not gazing out in blessing.
Though the heart indulge in a feast of pleasing sentiment,
there is no love without God. In God's Presence, love abides.

Do you think yourself good? Do you think yourself virtuous?
Thus your thoughts, like the ones you had about yesterday's clouds.
Do you think yourself vile, unworthy or hopelessly flawed?
Thus your thoughts. Clear the inner room of them. They are the past.
Presence is being in God. Being in God is goodness.
Goodness is not the great temple but the silent Presence
to which the workers humbly return for each stone's setting.

14. Stars

What would we do without the stars in the heavens? We're told
that stars are unthinkable distances away from us,
but their light is here, brought over ages for our use now;
this ordered array of diamonds keeps us looking up
beyond the enveloping darkness. Life on Earth requires
the sun, and the life of the soul requires more distant suns.
Earth turns away from the sunlight, but the soul may not rest.

Man must make himself a light aligned with the source of light.
In the day, man's work is easy. We can see the results:
the crops in their rows, the buildings rising steadfast, the roads
linking all together, the fishnets abundantly filled.
In the day, God's Presence is clear; we breathe its certainty.
In the day, we can surrender to love, let go of fear,
breathe deeply and trust in the visible order of God.

But in the night so little we know. So close the approach
of enemies before we hear or feel them, so sudden
their ambush, their taking, our breathing halting and shallow.
The stars alert and remind us; their quick piercings summon
the soul's return to the work of being. We choose from them
an order of becoming, a regulation of breath,
an ascent. We follow their lights to return to the dawn.

15. Essence and Personality

Personality is learning sculpted into a shape
that safeguards the wounded child. One's essence cannot survive
the violence of the world without a shield. As the soul
must wear a body here to protect its pure becoming,
so the child is bruised and cut in his joyful nakedness
and early made to wear a coat of callous, a disguise
of learned behaviors and expressions bound in chains of thought.

In Schools, the unity of aim and the regulation
of behavior minimize the need for social masking.
The child is free to love and to aspire. Transformation
is supported, so inevitable human travail
becomes fuel for being, not cause for fear and hiding.
Essence is protected by the love of friends and the bond
of intercourse with Angels. Joy and delight are not mocked.

In the world, the poor prisoners entertain each other
with unconsciously learned identities. Some take power,
some live to please, some lose their minds to make believe disease:
their personalities are adaptions held unto death.
The child within is put to sleep and never wakes to feel
the wonder quickened by the Presence of a higher world.
So rare the return of the buried and forgotten child.

16. A Soft Light

To know the soul, the body's shame must be unlearned and lost.
Against shame, the body struggles to distinguish itself
among men, to assert its importance, fully inflate
its painted vanity. Heal the shame, the struggle dissolves.
The intelligence of the lower self, its defining
dishonesty, was quickened by shame. Into hiding slips
its brutality, its coarseness twisted to cleverness.

The lever of shame is abandonment. Before the world
is stitched together by the budding senses, even then
the infant tastes the fatal terror of abandonment.
The shocked body is born comprehending its helplessness,
and through subtle negotiation of gesture and tone
comes to know what it must not be, which of its expressions
confound the mother's commitment and engender disgust.

Personality begins in the intense prelingual
drama of shame and abandonment. The lower self learns
the use of darkness, the hiding places for its pleasure.
Against this proud humiliation, a soft light works best.
No Angel who has not mastered patience with all the rude
distortions of human love and its vainest hopes is called
to overwatch the return of a crystallizing soul.

17. Extremes

In extreme heat, one finds shade, strips down and slows to the speed
of passive perspiration. The only work worth doing
is locating liquid. One's toxic fat is cooked away,
and the slackened jaw can hold nothing to communicate.
Muscles turn to jelly, and the soft heart peeps a warning
that its rhythm has no traction. One resorts to pure sight,
letting the mottled glare and shadow stimulate the soul.

In freezing cold, one layers garments of thickest fabrics,
exposing no flesh, and keeps moving, rocking back and forth
close to the fire. The joints lock, must be forced; the thick blood stalls
in the trunk, grudges its duty to hands and feet. Touch – gone.
One trudges the deepest trenches of habit, losing track
of what and where. The liquid in the eyes threatens to jell,
and one relies on the sound of the wind to know oneself.

Even at the utmost brink of human experience,
God can be found. When the mind cannot find a sure purchase,
God can be found. When the heart recognizes death's coming,
God can be found. There at the edge of the effort to be,
God can be found. At any station in the waking state
and in dream, a single syllable below utterance,
willed if not thought, pierces the dark and engenders return.

18. Aging

As the body's arc of time begins to descend, the soul
can know itself more readily. The aches of the body
are little gifts, reminders of what must die and depart
and what must remain and continue its service in God.
Identity held in the body will suffer and grieve.
Identity surrendered to God will spread in the field
of love, which is eternal. Are you ready to know death?

Preparing to die is an art. One must make each movement
a singular event, slowed and stretched, seamless against thoughts,
a dance to invoke the witness of the Eye and the Crown.
Let the heart's perception be as the streaming of water
cleansing the grip of anger and grief. Let the mind be still.
Offer no correction to those forgotten to themselves;
let their clamor echo back to them vacant of response.

Like all resistance to God, what we call the fear of death
is imagination taking hold, closing the body
against the current of being. Does the wave fear the sea?
It is never too soon to learn to surrender to God.
Blessed is one who is given the mind to prepare for death
though in truth all but children may claim this blessing. If felt
in gratitude, aging prompts the awareness of return.

19. Others

The hardest thing for one who knows the truth is not to preach:
one cannot give knowledge to anyone not seeking it,
and knowledge and love are the only gifts we can offer.
One cannot give ripe wisdom or experience of God;
one cannot give understanding or desire for meaning;
one cannot tear the veil for another or touch a man
comfortable in the false identity of his thoughts.

To want the truth, a man must be desperate and resolved.
He must know his failings and have moved beyond their talons
to a surrender in selfless service, its own reward.
He must see his arts and skills as gladly to be given.
He must agree to put on the truth as awkward clothing
that requires him to learn anew how to move, how to feel.
If he presents himself to you, such a man can be taught.

All others are to be loved, and if they err, forgiven.
What is not forgiven poisons the soul. Love dissolves lies.
Know that the Angels have their work: its scope and the logic
of its methods are beyond the human frame; our patience
cannot bear the speedless motion of their plan, yet we share
the gaze of their attention as they send or do not send
attracted souls our way in preparation for return.

20. Living Here

This world is violent, cruel and full of pain. Abstain
as much as you can from doing harm. The wounds of abuse
must be licked clean with conscious love, and the soul reminded
gently and faithfully. Standing before the dark curtain
of brutality, love looks inept and weak. So be it.
Hurt teaches us to fear the unknown, but love discloses
the miracle of new being breathing beyond the known.

Life eats life. Body after body must be left behind.
Cruelty received or given can weld the soul to flesh
and scar a clear departure. The end of a body's time
is not tragic if the soul knows itself in its leaving.
Remind the soul of what it is not. Give it attention.
Remind the soul of its deathlessness. No sorrow can come
from reminding the soul. Giver and receiver prosper.

Know that hurting is perverted love, turned away from God.
The lower self is born in hurt and humiliation
and cannot know God. Do not let it have your mind and heart.
Do not let it impose its pain on others. You are here
in this far shadowed corner of creation to strengthen
the soul, to become more aware in love. Forebear to be
the suffering known here lest your return be to this world.

21. The Purpose of Life

Do not give a shriveled gift to God -- words without substance,
vacant syllables dried of life. Let your prayers be ripened
in the heart and cleansed by the best attention of the mind.
Open the body for their utterance, and be aware
of their flight in all your senses. Prayers awaken the God
in us, and although sacred instruction informs our prayers,
the true prayer is the effort of awareness that we make.

We are of God: thus the glory and danger of our lives.
Great power were we given to know the truth of Presence,
but that same power used in service to our lower selves
can endanger Earth. To reside in God is the essence
of humility; to plan without God is to prompt death.
The prayers are devised by Angels who understand the laws
of our bodies and the way through and beyond, back to God.

Let me speak to you heart to heart. Let your bright soul attend.
God and you and I are all one. The purpose of life here
is to abide in that truth, to sustain ourselves in it.
It is not a thought, but thought can arise from it to serve.
It is not a feeling, but it can pervade all feeling.
It is the state of the Present, awareness of being,
and prayers were given to us to help us return to it.

22. Beyond Belief

Believe in God if you must, but better to be in God.
Belief is a substitute for being in the Present.
The lower self exists in belief that it is something
apart from God. It is a creation regarding God
as its foe. It is humiliation seeking vengeance.
Be aware of your beliefs. Use their potent energy
to remember God and to abide above distortion.

We have all heard tales of the wondrous power of belief:
it can erect great stone structures that last thousands of years;
it can win impossible victories; it can bring back
dead bodies to life and make the desert bring forth ripe fruit.
Yet know that belief is rooted in the heart; these wonders
are the heart's doing, and the heart has nobler purposes
than making over the world. Such are the heart's distractions.

The heart is the engine quickening the soul's awareness.
If you are not remembering God in your work, your heart
is misused, and your belief – your desire that something else
than what is Present now be true – has become the fuel
of imagination. Let your heart sustain your delight
in Present beauty or transform the moment's suffering.
Be true, O heart. Return to the great realm beyond belief.

23. Brief Terms

What are our brief terms here on Earth but spans for strengthening
the soul? All worldly accomplishments, whether writ in stone
or song, are forgotten and dispersed in time, the records
of our archives, claims and charters ground down to feed the grass.
Perhaps our species – man entire – has a tiny purpose
in creation, a vine on a cliff face, but no project
on that scale touches individual men with meaning.

A man's true work is bringing the experience of life
in many bodies to the soul's eternal consciousness.
This miraculous alchemy is wrought in single men,
one at a time, from a method and a practice given
by Angels, beings who were men, now transformed to spirits.
Because the way is long, painstaking, counter to instinct
and meek in praise, few men seek it, and finding, fewer take.

Once crystallized an Angel, the soul understands itself
as a participant in God, agent of God's knowledge
of creation, belonging to the single Mind of God.
The Angels reach down to man, offering by a lifting
both rugged and precise, the chance to trade identities
of dust for spirit; their multiplicities for the One;
their blank, recycling deaths for return to life eternal.

24. Not Unkind

At its root, identification means to turn away
from God, to choose self-importance and submit to the pull
of the world's manufactured meaning. It is true, one's life
in the world must be guarded and defended, but shrouding
the concern for safety like the stench in a city's air
is a toxic cloud of worry, of social inference
and appearance, so easy to believe, so full of thought.

To live in that cloud, to forget what is above it all
even for but a few breaths of alarm, is to salute
the lower self, to barter true being for poisoned lies.
But does not man live on the ground? Yes, man must keep his health
and house in order, but his mind, fueled by his pure heart's
deft constancy, must stay aloft in awareness of God.
However dark the world, one's Eye can always see the sun.

We forget ourselves and plummet into the temporal.
There we are besieged or honored, threatened or rewarded,
and craft a false identity from insult or from praise.
But what are we really? We are sparks of God without need
of names or histories, moving through the world, collecting
ourselves and our own, living out the great experience
of return. Spurning to identify is not unkind.

25. For the Dying

A feeling of obligation to the world is a veil
woven of both noble and self-serving strands. Do not think
the world needs you. Your residence here contributes nothing
requiring your particular being, and the desire
to be remembered breeds an imaginary duty.
Only in letting the world go will you reach the vantage
from which it can be truly seen, circling on without you.

On this planet for aeons has your soul evolved and come
to the threshold of maturity. To complete itself,
it must be purified of the matters which have molded
its growing being. A soul explicit has neutralized
all worldly desire and understands the soft, internal
cry of belonging to be the lower self's subtlest woo.
In God's unseparate array will your true service be.

You must finish your story's earthly chapters as Heaven
has written them; then breaking through the human husk, ascend.
The brave impulse to serve will not die in your departure,
but to foster true liberation you must first let go.
Earth is so beautiful, and the human animal sings
an alluring song, a call back to flesh, a sweet promise.
Leave it! Let it fade behind, below in your true return.

26. War

If war is truly something, not the absence of something,
then its existence has a rhythm, a calm and a swell.
In the quiet periods, people can be as bumbling
as they like and scant damage comes of it. In angry times,
the most well intended gestures inflame identities
and what were meaningless clouds desire the same piece of sky
and collide in electric fury. There's no stopping it.

Don't be in the path. The cycles of instability
within cycles of barren poverty and wrathful blame
within cycles of vast and vital destruction will share
a common climax: Earth will digest its own best substance
and all life succumb to sacrifice. Find elevation.
Climb to a cold, cleaner air above the flood and gases.
Be certain. Be keener than ever in your highest mind.

When the echoes of the screaming stop, wait another year
before descending to the healing plain. Prepare a firm
response for your disgust. You must bring a militant love.
You will be harrowing hell; moist sympathy avails you
nothing in this task. If you can work here, your flesh can claim
no further hold on spirit; what you truly are has been
drawn out, annealed, transformed in God, made ready for return.

27. The Knowledge

The finest knowledge is not confined by rational mind
and cannot be given in a teacher's demonstration
or a formula. When a lost, broken chip of perfect
porcelain is found and returned to the vase it came from,
restored without crack or scar, we can sense a miracle;
and thus the moment when the single soul to self-knowledge
rises, discovers itself in God, relearns what it is.

It is experience infinitely opened, unbound
by measure or description, and when one re-encloses,
unblooms back to individual being, this knowledge
remains as one's lifeline to eternity, the great proof
that this world of feeling and belief is illusory.
One shrinks back into the cell of fleshly identity
never quite forgetting – through myriad lives – what one knows.

The heartaching paradox that infinite God can be
unveiled only to single souls makes one restless to find
one's kindred, the others who know or want to know the fire
from which all sparks have blown. Just a few such souls together
in ascending enterprise rejoin this distant planet
to its conscious source and keep its finer air encircling
that the quickening of souls to seek return continues.

28. To You Reading This

Before the sense, one feels the tone of a page of writing,
as if it had a color and a music; then one notes
the texture of the pages on one's respectful fingers.
After a satchel of such prefaces, the author steps
out with the tray and the intellectual meal begins.
If any of these appeals – to heart, eyes, ears, skin or mind –
seduce or repel, then the beginning has finished you.

Our language is a gift from the Angels, a purposeful
advancement of the vague clouds of animal expression.
As the Absolute self-derived the Mind of God to house
creation, so the Angels developed the mind of man
as the imaginary mirror of the universe
then taught us words – their power and pall – to ravel ourselves
in chains of thought or lead ourselves to silent Heaven's porch.

Thus with a piece of human writing – even this – the point
is not the point. Remember the part you're playing: reader
with artifact in hand. An argument is not the truth
but a thing of words constructed in a mind, as a book
is also a thing fashioned of sensory elements,
as is a reader with the responses you're enacting.
May these sundry arts promote, not inhibit, your return.

29. Together

Aloneness is imaginary. There are no secrets.
The effort to encapsulate against the world must fail
eventually, and the pain of shattered defenses
and re-emergence into the glare melt down the hardest
identity. Separateness is a disguise employed
by the Absolute to explore the dark part of being.
All must come to light in time; then time will be completed.

Do you have a mother in your work, a model of love
whose quietness unearthed your gratitude? Have you been told
of your enfeebled ancient father? Do you long to find
and protect him? These sweet burdens prove God is in your heart.
Everything that can be known must first pass under God's Eye.
God helps you see your darkest guilt, bear the unbearable
humiliation. You and God are in this together.

How long or short your personhood's route out and back will be
only God knows, but it seems smart to turn when the highway
presents a golden opportunity – like here and now.
In our world, the darlings of isolation have become
a big club; Earth can't hold many more hermits of the heart.
The way back begins with your first self-aware kindliness:
praising's propulsive power can speed your loving return.

2. Visitation

30. In Presence

Lead your heart to the staircase of praise. Praise God in Presence.
Acknowledge whatever good you see. Praise God in Presence.
Admire the patience that blesses you. Praise God in Presence.
Cherish the wonder that lifts your mind. Praise God in Presence.
Forgive the hurt of the struggling world. Praise God in Presence.
Keep your needs small and momentary. Praise God in Presence.
Bring your Presence to life here. Take less and less in return.

Underneath your tasks and necessities, your pleasantries,
your eating and drinking, your daily movement and travel,
your planning, your accounting, your sentiments, your questions,
underneath all your initiations and responses,
underneath each breath taken and released is your real work.
Each moment you are Present makes you smaller in the world
and more available to share the Angels' loving watch.

Now that you know the purpose of life, praise God in Presence.
Observing your form in space and time, praise God in Presence.
Firmly feeling the shocks of the flesh, praise God in Presence.
Lifting the heart from failure and doubt, praise God in Presence.
From the bank of the river of thought, praise God in Presence.
From the gateway to the Field of Love, praise God in Presence.
Dear Friend, in Presence you return to awareness of God.

The Book of Wisdom and Law

I. Petite Wisdoms

1.

Presence is so real one extended taste transforms a life,
and steward moves between Heaven and earth, its willed action
refined to single syllables – unified heart and mind.
Everything else – everything under the proud pavilion
of "I" – every thought, feeling, movement, sensation – each one,
including this one now appearing and that coming on –
hosts the lower self's work, the mortal flesh obscuring God.

2.

There is pain in waking, but it is worth it. The wonders
of being are their own air, gladdening the grateful heart.
Do not spend this joy on shallow thoughts or loud expression.
Be quiet, still, contained, incandescent – a little sun.
You need no longer fear death; you need no longer fear life.
You know the secret that reveals the purpose of all things.
Breathe it in. Absorb it. Become it. Breathe out the blessing.

3.

We can know each other better by trusting we're the same,
but we believe our thoughts, let our lower selves consume us.
We stifle the urge to reach and touch and kiss; we shut down;
we miss the music in the grass, the sky's liberation.
We know the Angels know our true hearts; we are so grateful
when they help us step outside ourselves and love each other
with innocent delight. Yes, we are the same, here in God.

4.

Time is the home of all things dying, all the things precious
in their approaching, embracing, turning, moving away.
It is right to love these things full-heartedly; it is wrong
to forget one's truth in them. The body of a lover,
the body of a son or daughter, the longer bodies
of countries, traditions, teachings – all bodies are leaving.
Remember, beyond all bodies is the return to God.

5.

Kiss me. Crack the layers of chalk imprisoning your soul.
It's not me you're kissing after all, it's the God in you
released to make love to everything your senses present,
to merge, withdraw and merge, relearning the laws of beauty.
Kiss me. Shoulder the stone closing the dark tomb of your heart,
roll it away, take the air in great gulps, bathe in the flood
of living light. You have lips, ears, eyes – openings for God.

6.

How you solve the problem of identity determines
everything. If you leave it unexamined, unquestioned,
you will fertilize the earth and the moon until time dies.
If you attach it to some creed, you'll be taught how to stitch
a veil through which you see false value in a slanted world.
If you locate it steadfastly in the separation
from mind's momentary presentations, you live and live.

7.

Sometimes life is sweet, but one lump of sugar on the tongue
of the Great Departing Universe won't last long enough
to inform a higher purpose or prove the love of God.
Something more enduring is needed. How about the job
of climbing Conscious Creation, one foothold at a time,
held by the Angel you'll become and holding the Angel
who'll become you? Wisdom trades sugar for eternal life.

8.

Sorry, I will not rush. Frenetic energy distorts
perception and thought; they're hard enough to keep clear as is.
I won't let my wristwatch wag my mind. So how are you, friend?
Stand still. Talk to me. The sidewalk will still be there for you
when our little souls' sweet acknowledgements of each other
have been properly completed. Be. Hold. Let's find a theme
for this rendezvous, then just three more perfect syllables.

9.

Though the Angels discountenance imaginary pain –
the suffering we do not need to make – they're sharply stung
to compassion by our real agonies. They bring us up
through the veils as kindly as the objective laws allow.
The play of Christ, for example, took ages here on Earth
to produce; even in Heaven ancient Angels needed
aeons to ready the recent ones to perfect witness.

10.

All the devil's arguments are clever but dependent
on a hidden premise: that one is only one's body.
He can only speak to the flesh and what dies with the flesh.
To engage on his terms is mistaken identity.
While it's true we must wrestle with the lower self, it's not
the point to pin him to the ground. No, he's already there.
The aim's to separate, escape, rise where he can't follow.

11.

Sometimes things must come to a windless standstill, a waiting.
The usual contracts of time and energy produce
nothing; even those who love pure playing are exhausted.
Do not lose vigilance now. Nurse it; do not oppress it.
Out at the far periphery of the known, beyond sight,
small spirals of dust are catching flight by twisting the air
as a girl her hair. The sky will fill with storms soon enough.

12.

A partner makes one's solitude more honest and humble.
The love of another and the refinement of sharing
become sacred contours on one's map of the world, one's place.
Knowing another takes years, and everything truly learned
in the heart makes oneself a smaller, purer offering.
One turns to God not as belief but as the open sky
of being in which one's love can grow, the eternity.

13.

Sitting on an egg without breaking it is not easy.
Holding oneself in a way that protects and warms to growth
this fragile oval of new life puts a burn in the legs
and a deep ache in the knees and back. One's will is exposed.
When after longer than one had thought the wonder hatches,
it's a thing completely itself, beyond the mind, holy
in its otherness, the lord of one's time and attention.

14.

Love will be tested and tested; the will totters and finds
its legs again. As it stabilizes, the animal
within me and the same one within you are reassured.
As long as we have bodies, we are animal trainers.
I love you – I don't know much more about myself than that.
Under the bright surface, there's an abyss of confusion.
Panicking beasts doubt the upper air. We train their breathing.

15.

Rise up out of your thoughts. Let thought's words drop unattended,
thought's images dissolve. You have to strangle your senses
to make room for thought's concerns. How can you know what love is
when you live in an artificial, anaerobic cell?
Go to the mall, the park: just sit there looking and breathing.
All you see goes on, not needing you. You are wholly free
to be the love above thought, above the all else you're not.

16.

The cost of a pure, selfless love on Earth – for our spouses,
our children, others our hearts would anonymously kiss –
is suffering, for love reveals how impotent we are
to change the world. Our helplessness is the ash of love's fire.
What can we buy with burnt hearts? What can grow from nothingness?
A new kind of love, not attached to the fate of poor flesh,
however poignant – but bright, brimming over – a blessing.

17.

It's silly to pretend wounded vanity doesn't hurt.
Vanity is personality's chauffeur, publicist,
attorney and biographer. When that entourage leaves –
exposed and scared away by a greater authority
(like the Truth) – uncontested doubt in us resuscitates
the past's abraiding pain. What to do? The parts abiding –
the bruised child and budding soul – have their own joys (like the Truth).

18.

Though you're likely unaware of it, right now you're trusting
ongoing life, your next breath, to what's been true in the past.
What choice have you got? You've no defense against everything
suddenly being different. Could you survive the shock?
It depends on where your identity is. Does it need
your current social station, your loved ones, your history,
your name, your body? Minus all these, what remains aware?

19.

Marooned in uninspired functioning? Clapped in the doldrums?
There isn't anything peccant or shameful about it.
The body must be induced to produce finer fuel
and commit to uplifting it to the heart which alone
can transform it to nourishment for the illumined ones.
Then just a little rowing and the breeze will find your sails.
For you, there's no secret to this great secret. God awaits.

20.

Only orphans awaken. Abandon your flesh father
and your moral mother at God's first undisguised visit.
You needn't shame or repudiate them; just step away
till their gravity no longer moves your tides. Observe them
as grown children shaped by the bindings they never questioned.
Your real mother is longing for another tryst with God.
As they couple, feel your birth in the sky above their heat.

21.

When knowledge becomes the aim, the coin of recognition,
we can divide it into smaller and smaller pieces –
names, dates, shocking facts – so that everyone has a token
of identity. A new economy emerges.
However, try measuring being. It's so tenuous.
Sometimes it shows its traces in virtue, but in the end
just you, God and the Angels possess its self-awareness.

22.

The greatest gift you can give a friend is your own Presence.
Make of yourself a portal, an opening to the world
beyond the loud machinations of mind – the Field of Love.
Do not exhort or preach. If your friend's heart is coming up
for air, searching the horizon for something, it will find
the strange blue aperture here above your welcoming gaze.
Those not ready cannot see. Love them as they can receive.

23.

In commerce, put on your cap. Cover the Crown; shade the Eye.
Keep your money in your pocket till certainty stands square.
Profit not from the dire toil of those who cannot look up.
Profit not from mere cleverness. Profit not from fouling
the air, the water, the soil or the profusion of life.
Remember as you remember yourself that true profit
is in the readiness of souls to seed the Field of Love.

24.

Before men, do not stand and preach. Wear your cap, be quiet,
speak when questioned sincerely. Give help whenever you can.
You must be delicate with those below; you cannot rush
their progress just as you cannot make demands of Angels.
Life on the ladder is precarious. Balance not force
keeps you here in God's sight. When the next rung opens, step up,
stabilize, stretch a wiser hand down to one now ready.

25.

There is much to be learned from the wisdom of snails, spiders,
small rodents, fish in schools, owls, geese and the like. Given time,
they will rectify Earth. But we are given time to make
a higher order, one that nurtures nature, sure, but more;
our allotment of time is by Angels calculated
sufficient to escape time, to deliver back to God
the seed spark, now crystal soul attending eternity.

26.

Everything in nature does its work, even your body
doing whatever it's doing right now. Be careful though:
while one can say "my body" because one is not that flesh,
one dare not let the body say "my soul". Separation
is a psychology, a metaphysic and a fact.
The soul's spark sees by its own light, using earthly matter
in unearthly alchemy. God's being is the soul's work.

27.

On some days, the clasp of the lower self is very strong.
Why is not important – part of the devil's camouflage;
how to loosen that grip should be the steward's chief concern.
Become small: use only small thoughts and small words; take small bites;
affirm small joys; allow only tiny expectations;
shrink to near nothing. And when the doubting devil opens
his hand to see if you're still here, spread and fly, fly, fly, fly.

28.
The gravity holding our bodies and Earth together
is but part of identification. Each of our brains
has its method of defining who we are: one knits veils
of ideas; one masters the dimensions it surveys;
one instantly trusts its unstable perceptions of truth;
one regards all else in terms of its ongoing function.
What's not in the grip of Earth, bodies and brains? Yes, this. Be.

29.
What do you want? Control? Wealth? Recognition? Ease? Pleasure?
What do you want? If you can say it precisely sans doubt
or double thought, you'll get it, but in the end, you'll lose it.
Whatever you're sure you want, you'll have – temporarily.
If you see that the thing doing the wanting is mortal,
you have a chance to be beyond wanting. When the question
"What do you want?" no longer makes sense, you've left death behind.

30.
I am what I am – the beginning of self-acceptance.
I am that I am – crystallizing of the Angelic.
The first implies the will to submit, to accept the Truth;
the second is the attempt of impoverished language
to represent now indissoluble identity.
The first is said not knowing what will be lost or revealed;
the second emerges whole from the burning wreck of time.

31.

The stress in one's instinctive element when one attempts
to love one's enemies gives the soul opportunity
to separate, to not be shaken by the earthquake's rage.
It's not easy, and there's only a tiny bit of help
in realizing all living things are always doing
what they in the limits of vision believe to be best.
To love one's enemies, one must be the soul seeing them

32.

Some people are easy to love. One's lower parts align
in favor, and the steward has a springboard for its dive
into submission. Pleasure is the only obstacle.
Others you want to be rid of. Love seems impossible.
The steward labors to allow them to be and must hold
its nose to embrace them. They embody resistant force.
Strange, to the arisen soul, love is the same for both types.

33.

The miraculous is always mercilessly pursued
by the formatory. The wedding becomes a required
anniversary gift, the birth a cake stuck with candles.
To stay out of this quicksand, you must stand still at light speed,
not expect the next syllable. Can you be the miracle
above the associative decoding going on
in your head as your dogged eyes chase this line of letters?

34.
There is a point in every struggle when the push and pull
becomes so stuck and profitless that one must step away,
clean one's instruments, tune one's breathing. This is not the end.
One must return to the field remembering more clearly
that the battle is with oneself, that true identity
is Presence, a step above the heated turmoil of mind,
muscle and belief. Let there be detachment in your love.

35.
The beauty of fresh flowers skillfully arranged slows thought.
Before their bright geometry of perfumed abundance –
and one flower, just one, is abundant – the mind gives way.
Even simple art intervenes in life, creating space;
busy brains retreat, circling warily where beauty plays.
The finest art is a portal for man's liberation,
a promise of gloried disciplines not entranced to time.

36.
You can root it in your body and hate mortality.
You can funnel it into your children and their children.
You can bestow it on the world in some respected work.
You can invest it in intricate knowledge the world wants.
I speak of identity. You can consolidate it
in a stain on your tie, waste it in independent pride
or return it to the perfect Presence from which it fell.

37.

Could your suffering come from the way your mind reconstructs
the world? All the elements the budding soul brought with it
from its more perfect home – beauty, justice, love – are stunted
in this unreasoning place. The mind can't make sense of it.
So what's one to do? Don't leave it to the mind. Trust the heart.
The soul finds harbor there and can found a dear colony
of refugee friends whose loving awareness God reminds.

38.

Emotion's time is measured in mounting expectation
and the plunge of disappointment. Actual fulfillment
is not in time at all and is perfectly remembered
in the weightless liberation beyond Earth's gravity.
Only the soul can know fulfillment, and every return
to true being is still here, connected, accessible,
ever new, unexpectable. One cannot tire of it.

39.

Unobstructed by thought, let the tides of your breathing be.
Complete breaths must take precedence over the action thought
beseeches or demands. Thought is not intelligence; love
and silent mastery of fear are true intelligence,
and though the purest thought can lead to an ascending stair,
more often is it rooted in dissembling vanity.
Leave the snarls and whimpers. Closer to God than thought is breath.

40.

After a fallow period, don't expect to resume
full labor all at once. If you force yourself to top speed,
the lower self may rig an injury, a painful ruse
allowing it to use a veto power on your work.
Remember: real efforts are in the realm of attention.
Remember: lifted eyes encourage the tired heart's ascent.
Remember: transformation embraces the scale of breath.

41.

Our timetables for accomplishment clearly do not match
those of the Angels. Our projects – in thought so straightforward –
encounter every kind of bump and bother, and the fear
we'll die before the capstone's on the pyramid shadows
our poor imaginary picture of our purpose here.
A task, a role, a monument – the Angels make these things.
Our real job? Infusing this pure breath with remembered God.

42.

When words are hurtful or hilarious, stop and observe
how quickly the mind has assigned them personal meaning
and the emotions have engulfed them, adopting their tone.
"Words, words, words," says Hamlet in feigned madness, lifting the veil
of sanity which words define, as they do everything.
Our brains are hard-wired to language, and the darkness battens
our sleep with lifeless syllables. Speak yourself small, friend. Be.

43.

There's tiredness where your thinking's muddled and your temper's short,
tiredness where you're riding momentum and dare not sit down.
There's tiredness where all is numb and your heart has no standing,
tiredness where your last fizzled spurt of adrenaline's gone.
Each of these points – from irritability to collapse –
is a vantage from which can be seen the truth and the lie
of yourself. The systems break down under stress: not the soul.

44.

If you think you have to kill, don't do it. Don't give thinking
that much power. Neither may you murder out of passion:
anger, rebellion, revenge, loyalty, obedience.
If you must kill, the necessity will come from Heaven
and crush your tender heart and force your weak, unwilling hand
and teach you love for everything that dies. When after death,
you confront the souls you shorted, know what you will offer.

45.

All art is mystical, revealing Creation's hollows
the inured senses have forgotten how to enlighten.
Art dislodges us, leaves us outside, naked and homeless,
where iridescent skies dissolve the brain's timid version
and stars call forth fearlessness out of the death within us.
The need for art, the impulse to it, proves a striving soul
is struggling back to God. Do not judge that impulse. Submit.

46.

What you find in front of you is what you get forever.
No matter what you do or where you go, who respects you
or who doesn't, what you own or go without, why you act
or when you die, what is before you now is all that life
will ever give, and if you're lost in imagination,
you don't even get that. So read this line till it becomes
this line, and breathe only this moment till the end of breath.

47.

Some saints have written catalogues of higher states and mapped
their navigations through the ether. For these travel books,
we thank them, for they provide enticement, an exotic
nudge toward holiness, lifting the fatigue of lumpy flesh.
But opposing these airy tracts is the soft perfection
modern man has made of the reclining chair. So tempting
to sit and read and dream what holiness will be.

48.

Is it worth combing through the wreckage to find the black box
or diving through the layers of memory to locate
the primal trauma? Sometimes the context of ruin we think
will let us understand just deviates us all the more,
and with the torch of a brash new theory, we hurry on
preparing for the past. The soul observes eternity.
Our reserved seats on this crashing plane are but circumstance.

49.
Though the personal is too distorted to be of use
to the scientist, yet it is necessary to God.
We have bodies, and acknowledging them – their influence,
their frailties – prepares for the preparation of the space
that God can inhabit and fill with love. Do not mock prayer.
Even the lowliest whimper -- "I am but a sinner" –
offers God an opening. "Yes, child. Now move. Look up! Be."

50.
Near sighted, earthbound pundits can fill their time exploiting
the small, shadowy distinctions between men and women,
rich and poor, right and wrong. Back and forth they go, carrying
messages, the more provocative the better, their aim
being to live off the spillage, the overreaction
that is inherent in one-sided versions of the truth.
Meanwhile the soul seeker breathes through the Truth's six dimensions.

51.
When a higher state is spent and retracts to gratitude,
then we can collect the gold in the bottom of the pan –
our verifications. Our wiser lower parts begin
to find a language to explain what we now know we know.
The lower self, like a beast, feels nauseous and distended
and would vomit up what is too rich to be digested
and abandon it, but it can't forget the disturbance.

52.

If you use your life to build a bridge to Heaven, you know
that the first construction of a segment often shatters;
it breaks or rots, and only gains its final bearing strength
in being rebuilt. Now we're not foreordained to failure;
rather, when we take the bridge to its great destination,
we require completely reliable footing – no doubt.
Only the Self verified beyond doubt may walk that bridge.

53.

I had a secret for you, but I misplaced it somehow.
I found it at the bazaar; rather, it beckoned my heart
to its shelf in a shaded stall. I couldn't believe it,
so brazenly announcing itself, but I purchased it
and instantly thought of you. Whom else would I give it to?
Now I've lost it, and I fear I've distorted the message.
Did it say, "One love is all love," or the other way round?

54.

Shhh...Try not to wake the dog. I'm sorry we must conduct
our business in hushed tones, but if we rouse her, she'll want
all our attention and all the sweet treats she can extort.
So what was it you needed? Something about money, eh?
Or status, or what someone said, or your new theory of....?
Well, I have only one response to all of your queries:
love God and let the dog sleep. Please tiptoe on your way out.

55.

It's funny and fulfilling to watch our dear children reach
a new stage in their development, a further milestone,
and behave as if no one had ever been there before.
How to respond to a young man's claim that he's discovered
a new route to Heaven? Answer: Though there are no new routes,
commend the pup for coming upon this ancient footpath.
With a smile and a wave, wish him well the walking of it.

56.

When a friend gets stuck in a ditch, the first thing I must do
is remember why he has been a friend. Part of me knows
how unpleasant and tiring the work of retrieving him
will be for my own back, and my heart can expect curses
and threats from the embarrassed beast he's trapped with. Digging down
in the dirt to get to him, now's the time to summon love,
not just love for him but Love's own being, tireless and free.

57.

How strange is the focus of desire! Man would clothe himself
in the dust and march triumphantly into the prison
of unnecessary laws to fulfill what he's been told
has meaning and value among men. Yet if his gaze rose
just a bit above the horizon, there in empty sky
he might learn for himself what has all meaning and value,
and find himself among Angels traversing the cosmos.

58.

There is an "I" that it's all right to be – the "I" ready
to die living the opportunity of the moment.
Are you purified? Have your heart's transforming tears dissolved
the lower self's brute clutch on the Law of Cause and Effect?
Have you returned the universe to God and the Angels?
Then you may wear your name to the bazaar so the people
can find you and hear God bless their attention with your voice.

59.

The chill of early fall surprises, and the memory
of summer thins and sighs. The sun is bright but without heat.
It is time to shed personality, to practice death,
to let the foliage of oneself – thousands of little leaves –
drop to the ground, their old colors achingly beautiful,
crackling their farewells in piles. Do not allow attention
to be lured away by what's leaving. Stay bright in the chill.

60.

Till midlife, overabundant sex energy riots.
The body produces enough for offspring, art, passion
and thousands of youth's imaginary projects and plans,
and still the soul is not starved. But in the descending years,
one may not be profligate. The harvest is restricted,
less robust, and must be collected and urged by wisdom
up a great height, past pleasure to a loving detachment.

61.

What's left of the microcosmos man at each lifetime's end?
Earth is fertilized a bit by the flesh and the child moon
by the falsehoods, but what becomes of the swooning self stripped
of its gravity? By the time it comes to, it's entrapped
yet again – in the beliefs it could not sever before,
in the temptations of unbuffered pleasure and terror.
Down it plummets till captured by a womb of forgetting.

62.

How many times in the long evolution of mankind
have Angels intervened to make the creature – us, I mean –
more precisely what they need: upright, free-handed, big-brained,
and at last the students of sequential language, keepers
of the Word made flesh? So here we are, seconds from the end
of millions of years of urgent, guided thrusting. Onward
to the unutterable, to the Truth of our being!

63.

For a moment, just stop. Keep your breath for yourself and take
the wind out of your thoughts. Let that noisy, circling flock lose
its agitation and return to ground. Hear the silence
underneath whatever things are crying or colliding.
The soul is nothing that the senses, straining and abused,
can detect, nothing but now. It is what's left, the Presence
that knows itself by knowing what it's not. You are the soul.

64.

Have you wondered why the Angels so often exhaust us?
Because one potent way to reveal our leaky functions
is to let the pipes run dry. Sadly we must touch the well's
deepest bottom to recognize that we're not the bucket.
For even when we can barely stand or lift our fingers
or eyelids, the soul is waiting there to be discovered.
How much finer is life when the soul has our best fuel!

65.

When we're not conscious, morality locks us in its cell.
Consciousness is better. The edifice of right and wrong
is a bureaucratic maze of tunnels and offices
built of unforgiving stone reinforced by punishment.
Consciousness is dynamic, fluid: it's love at the speed
of light; watching with its eternal Eye, it must forgive.
"Go and sin no more," it urges, meaning, "Awake to love."

66.

We act from our level of consciousness: no matter what
we do, we do it believing it to be the right thing,
but belief is an emotional condition. The heart
serves a master, be it hell or Heaven, midnight or noon.
If awake, we act in love, aware of our ignorance.
If asleep, we obey impulse, unaware of the dark.
Failure to be Present is the mother of tragedy.

67.

The pain of parting is real. When something the lower parts
have embraced, suckled, opened to and closed around is lost,
the vacancy aches: thought disorganizes, the heart mourns
the magnet of its affection, the legs and arms lose all
coordination, and the whole world whispers its distrust.
Time does not really heal; it cleans and shreds. To love anew,
the self must verify that deathlessness is something real.

68.

Even if honey were not so marvelous, the smart man
would want to honor the vital intelligence of bees.
They are a model of living under the laws of Earth.
All the more wondrous that the intimate treasure they make
has carried the secrets of transformation over time.
What is man's honey, the gold of his selfless alchemy?
The love of Presence in the hive of his civilized heart.

69.

Greater in number than all the disguises of water
are the seeds of distraction. When you're hanging upside down,
thousands of them fall from the loose fruits of your nerve bundles
into your spinning brain then bob up and burst like popcorn
into new concerns, new things to do, new versions of you.
Thus time passes and you forget you're living downside up.
Where are the stars? Can you pick one, say its name, hold its light?

70.
Money is not security. Money shrinks over time
and hemorrhages out from wounds you didn't know were wounds.
The key about money is knowing what to buy with it.
Buy heartfood and sunshine and things your friends need to remind
them to breathe. Buy Angel tears in bindings your fingers love.
Buy things you can't use up. Buy things that lift you up. Buy up.
When money's low, find unwanted things free to be transformed.

71.
The end of sex is not yet death. It's a liberation,
a return to the bold, clear-eyed sanity of children
discovering how to study a world they are not yet.
If life has ten segments, sex veils all but the first and last.
A stirring in the genitals rouses one to action:
Will it breed a triumph that is lost like Eurydice
or fuel a prayer whose pink wingbuds yearn to visit God?

72.
Woodpeckers are like the pulse of nature. Some say they keep
the trees alive by eating the insidious insects
that kill from within. Yet from spring through fall they strip the bark
and then abandon the branches to winter nakedness.
So are they noisy saviors or faithless opportunists?
Both, of course. They are true as nature is true, and your thoughts
about their noteless pecking noise reveal not them but you.

73.

When God decides to play the fool, you'd better learn to laugh.
The logic we prize, the clear, coherent exposition
to which we'd have the world submit, sometimes must be shattered
like a Greek vase by a child dashing through the museum
well ahead of his mortified parents. Please remember,
if someone can put a price on it, it's not worth the state
you may embrace by your free submission to God's laughing.

74.

Man's instinct is hard-wired to gold. We cannot look away.
With vein-dilating radiance, it souvenirs the sun.
The dragon in the deepest cave of man wants nothing more
than to have a great hoard of gold to sit on and sleep on.
Such is immortality to the lowest spine's old brain,
the root furthest from Heaven. But what is gold really worth?
To be sure, there is value in its reminding. Look up!

75.

"Because it's too dangerous." Thus this steadfast verdict blocks
entrance to the warm perfumed pool of desire. Yes, one is
most often too full of fear to please the senses dizzy
with abundance; but if you – the real you – can leave the tub
and stand beside it in an unseen observing Presence,
then the body can soak and let its conduits open
and dilate, heal and cry, as patience waits for it to dry.

76.

Like a tired old dog, toothlessly resigned to whatever
the master does to prolong its life or hasten its death,
so may ambition slump and sleep. There was a time for it,
when sex stoked the nerves and the slavery of conquest still
hid from discernment, but now you know too much, so you sit
each day and play a friendly card game with futility.
Past self-pity, a slight smile: liberation's proper face.

77.

Earthly beauty's highest, barely bearable vibration
is a calm hum before the molecular world's dancing
iridescent colors. We are here to learn to open
the poor senses to a beauty so acutely total
that mind is swept away, made boundless, instantaneous.
We can't wait for a natural death to deliver us.
Here and now we must work beyond readiness. Light, more light!

78.

You don't enslave a people by fear. They may obey you,
but they'll form an underworld, a nether culture to hide
their nourishments, their fellowship. No, you enslave by hope:
the gleaming smile of a young prince, the rhetoric of light
and promise, a conjured vision of something to die for.
It's hard to reason past hope, for one must first understand
how tiny the closet of Truth the lower brains live in.

79.

You are God in a body, and so am I. When death comes,
we will resume our unity, become the starlit sky
above this masked ball, the air unknowingly breathed by all,
circulating life no longer trapped in tired characters.
Be ready for the passage or fear of missing something
will pull you back inside for another masked performance.
You were fashioned for God's self-knowledge – your real work unmasked.

80.

The tragedy of humanity's fragmenting itself
in such teeming profusion – billions of us – is that one
can only love the others known – truly known – to the heart.
One cannot love mankind. God can do it, but the droplet
of God each human is can nourish but a few touches
of its siblings. It's better to love deeply than widely.
If each could truly love one other, mankind would know God.

81.

What you don't forgive will kill you: you'll die from unwashed wounds.
Yes, it is excruciating to trust the measureless
and eternal scale of divine justice when everywhere
in our tiny lives reminding stabs scare us back inside.
But pain and loss aren't insults to avenge nor sparring rounds
in some self-toughening regime. They are hard-earned money
to be spent on soul separation: return tickets home.

82.

The autobiographical play ongoing in mind's
inner talk is a bent drama written by Tragic Flaw.
Drop in on the performance from above. Alone onstage
is the you you want the world to see; the rapt audience –
the ten thousand bit players of your life – hears your soothing
version of their pain and chaos with low self-serving trust.
But hush. If they sense you're really here, the spell is broken.

83.

When all that we have been working for comes to fruition,
it is tempting to stop and celebrate – fulfillment time.
But don't be tricked: even crystallization is time's fool.
What is, is, unchangingly. That you only now see it
means you have quit looking with your poor eyes and have resumed
the vision of God. Fulfillments or failures, the milestones
of time, the universe – all dreams distracted from God's sight.

84.

When the machinery is temporarily fuddled
(machinery is always temporarily something),
so that the processes – elimination, digestion,
circulation, respiration – are for a while somehow
not us, we are shipwrecked on the isle of self-awareness.
It can be fatally panicky or liberating.
Build a fire from being and watch: there's nothing else to do.

85.

The old boss gone, the new boss brings in his own agenda,
just like a new dog marking with pee a strategic tree.
On their scales, both are saving the world. How would you do it?
Do not ask the question of how the world will save itself.
The answer treats all species, all agendas and all pee
with the same expendability. Can you liberate
awareness from the world's identity – to save your soul?

86.

Once you've come to terms with death, separated from the loss
and the relief you will feel, the next challenge is learning
to live in eternity. Your whole perspective must change.
You don't need anything on the other side of to be.
All the adjectives – brave, upright, loyal, intelligent –
are as useless as the nouns – individual, person.
As eternity simply is, you are. Watch the world spin.

87.

At the bazaar at home, you are mindful of each penny
spent for vegetables, cheese or honey – the labor of friends –
but at the beach, you will purchase a five dollar ice cream.
Are you cruel or crazy? No, a market can measure
what people can and will pay. Thus is Heaven's price revealed.
A tiny few will pay everything, and they set the cost.
Can you afford it? Assess your attachments. Do the math.

88.

I love; you love; he, she, it loves; we love; you love; they love.
There's no escaping love, no darkness too deep for its light.
If you could descend to a depth beyond love, the hardness
and the weight of minerality would not let you feel.
No warmth in self-pitying tears. You could not know yourself.
Even your fiercest hate is love turned wrong way round. So turn
your face to God now. Love is the escape we all must make.

89.

Can you trust what in you wants to be hermetic, alone?
Can you bear the silence, the nothingness cleaned out for God
to fill? Or are you running away in disgust, judging
the shallow lovers, your head aching from their bleating praise?
If you must be alone to work, leave a side door open
for the curious who want to play. Let them tiptoe in
as God's mild interruptions. Welcome them. Do as they ask.

90.

When the current from lowest spine to crown is in rare flood,
surging like a swollen river, one can only observe,
breathe, feel, suffer it. The lower ranks will be in uproar,
trying anything to interrupt the torrent, divert
its electric rush toward the thousand small concerns and kinks
on which one daily wastes oneself. But superabundance
drives the wheels in glory, deluging the city with light.

91.

Your children do not know, cannot know, must not know how much
you love them. It is unfathomable, like the distance
starlight must travel to give but a wink to your Presence.
And when your children leave, as they must, uprooting your heart,
the best you can hope is that they go where the God in them
can be known, sink roots in their hearts and flourish; where their sight
can ascend to the enfolding sky beckoning their light.

92.

Fears hide behind reverences. The disempowerment
of the emotional strands binding our social order
worries the lower self. It does not desire anarchy;
it would be the bully-lord of a civilization.
So it supports the hushed-tone respect with which we address
God, Angels, traditions, leaders, the treatment of children.
The lower self would keep the church in good repair. More paint!

93.

Self-righteousness calls it hypocrisy in our parents
or presidents: the demand that we do not as they do
but as they require. In truth, what in them we call evil
is sleep, their minds and senses calcified, closed to the light
by common customs of thought and years of moral habit.
Yet even hard and blind as they've become, they would forsake
all power for the right love, could we find it to give them.

94.

First by love, then by clearest undiluted awareness
does the striving soul clean itself of the effects of flesh.
The process begins in service to the self-restraining
heart's intelligence. Refinement of this labor takes years
till Heaven, at last trusting your loyalty, surprises
you with coins of its own minting to purchase from the grip
of mortal turmoil that which now with certainty ascends.

95.

This cold is unrelenting. Last week's snow still grips the ground.
Eyes squint uselessly against the stinging air. Nerves go numb.
If consciousness and love were warmth, we would labor for it,
struggle for all we're worth to hold the heat; instead we doze,
hibernate in chafed distraction. Allotted each of us
is a spark of God which we must fan to flame so Angels
who watch in magnified attention can inspire the fire.

96.

Science is good. Holding itself to what can be measured,
it moves man on, if in wobbly reliability.
But poor science can't know where man is going: its ideas
of destination are imaginary; thus man builds
on shadowy premises, making progress dubious.
Fools even say man's destination is his own to fix...
his measuring mind fearless to dismiss eternity.

97.

God is nothing if not unexpected. If you're Present,
God is nothing more than that; if you're drifting, God will crack
the candied shell of your dream and drag you into the light.
In either case, you cannot expect God, just as you can't
imagine yourself not existing. Try it: here you are.
Premises drive everything, and as God premises time,
thoughts in time will guarantee the downdrift of conclusions.

98.

To know that the one who wronged you acted from delusion,
that the laws that held you hostage saw some peril in you,
that the God who punished you was God only in your mind –
to know these things is to know that all reflects one's level
of consciousness. If Love is not brightening awareness,
action will be earthbound and blind to its harm. Forgive it:
in our darkness, forgiveness is the guarantee of love.

99.

Lifting identity out of flesh into now, giving
it fully to the boundless Field of Love, takes multiple
incarnations of sincere endeavor. But each effort
leaves a taste, and the unforgetting tastes accumulate
as gravity's grip slackens and mortality's theory
bends to new evidence. You know the secret – using time
to make a hole in time. Eternity is not a hope.

100.

How long does it take the newborn to disremember all
and become a single body called by a single name?
Shocking how fast this interment, when the rise from this grave
to return to totality is so slow and labored.
Behold the imbalance in the worlds souls-in-bodies span:
we must know ourselves as flesh and not flesh – as man, as God.
Such is our role in calling home the spreading universe.

101.

Many who seek the peace of simple being trip the snare
of mind and die dangling upside down, captured by the knot
of knowing. The soul already is everything it needs:
remembering the sweet already-Heaven-always-here
is the soul's work, which knowledge only prompts or imitates.
Peace must be a thing preferred above all complications,
all words and thoughts, a letting go of what we burn to know.

102.

Settle into daily work. Plant seeds, uproot weeds, cherish
the water, share with pride the endless cleaning, keep open
the channels of the nerves, let the tides of breath move freely.
When Angels want something from you, some specific summons,
it will be in addition to the maintenance of life
and the self-remembering that makes sense of everything.
All you need of now is here. Feel fully the breeze of time.

103.

Don't stand in your own way. A psychological posture
of skeptical precision gives the devil a headstart.
If you want to transform something, you must first accept it
and feel it – every pulse resounding all the way through you.
Judging, objecting, correcting – if you protect your boots
from getting peed on, joy won't be able to lick your face,
and you'll find the world less and less worthy of your proud mind.

104.

Male, female – whichever you are now, you've been the other.
You need both to be a whole person, and to operate
with Angel mind in the Field of Love, you must go beyond
personhood altogether. So if you believe yourself
to be boy or girl, you're in a closet in the basement.
The party's in the roof garden under so many stars
that every this or that you try to think of finds no word.

105.

Nothing reveals your true importance like having a child.
Your array of choices, once broader than vision itself,
shrinks into this moment's requirement, and the bitter taste
of the world getting along without you won't go away.
Instead you have the privilege of giving the strange soul
that has chosen you the same chance you have – the only chance
that means anything: to swim back through personhood to God.

106.

Nutritious bread, well crafted olive oil, the freshest harvest
from garden and orchard – the body does not grudge the work
of making food. Flesh agrees with sustenance and pleasure.
But the work of waking and completing a soul finds few
in the Field of Love, and the harvest of eternal life
is brought in by a humble handful toiling past sundown,
the darkness driven off by their illuminating hearts.

107.

You say no work can be done by the light of a firefly
in the darkness. Better to retire to one's rocking chair.
I say every moment of illumination reminds
one to hold attention for the next one. A longer string
of little lights – and longer still – amounts to my practice
for eternal life. Sometimes luminous clusters appear,
and I glimpse with love my empty chair on the distant porch.

108.

There's no such thing as sleeping beauty. Only consciousness
can create beauty. The long blue flower levitating
above the lip of the elegant green budvase carries
for a time the recognition and attention offered
by the arranger's conscious gaze. That same awareness held
by our looking lets beauty continue. What of a field
of flowers, you ask. From God's will down to your Eye, I say.

109.

With noisy regularity, flocks launch to shallow sky,
circle and return, reshuffled and ready to repeat.
Sheep bleat as nervous tremors crack and skitter through the herd.
Men elect their masters of rhetorical inflation
who meet in stately halls for the hufflle of politics.
Each species has its way of dampening collective fear,
by dispelling energy with self-important ruffling.

110.

Why is Earth so agitated, so troubled with unrest?
One terrible thought is that there is a dark proportion
between the suffering here and the depth of mortal sleep.
Do you want to wake up? You cannot find a location
better suited than this stomach of the solar system.
Earth is a place of digestion, and your wise witnessing
makes an immortal nourishment on which souls nurse and thrive.

111.

Peace hovers above pain, watching not denying, discrete,
breathing in chaos, breathing out anonymous mercy.
Peace is a Presence summoned by exhausted righteousness
wondering beyond its broken frame, its gutted honor.
If Peace could send a message to the suffering below,
it would say, "Stop. See what is before you. The faculty
of unforgetting love must be allowed a standing place."

112.

The success of an idea or experiment means
that it will be copied. This principle suggests the way
civilization will be renewed after the collapse.
All that will be needed is a single thriving outpost
in which consciousness and lovingkindness set the order
and the Angels are revered. Successfully defended
for three generations, this seed will become a forest.

113.

So patiently the Angels worked guiding evolution
in our species to make an organic vessel for souls.
And all their labor is but one small aspect of return –
the transformation of creation back to consciousness,
re-enfolded in its Source. How privileged are humans
to have from our tiny vantage minds that range the cosmos.
We are a humble wondrous platform in the grand ascent.

114.

True Christians, true Muslims, true Jews, true Hindus, true Buddhists
all breathe the same air, and their souls will fully awaken
navigating return to the same God. When at last seen
as obstructions, the borders that confer identity
will disappear in the soul's fulfillment. The humble ones
who were Jesus, Moses, Muhammed, Gautama will stand
around you, and you'll know them as projections from your heart.

115.

The couple that lives in the tree can eat only honey.
The bees that make it live in a cavern within the trunk.
Only the smartest children perceive this situation
and are quick and nimble enough to procure the honey
and ascend the tree to feed the couple whose rare blessing
changes the very air and light. As the children marvel
at new worlds revealed, something deep within recognizes home.

116.

The behavioral effects of opening the chakras
are not the point. Yes, one digests and eliminates food
more efficiently, and one is a friendlier fellow
with keener thinking skills, but one hopes the mindful result
of an unobstructed current flow is less resistance
to the soul's bright purpose – to be, now and now and onward.
The open skied flesh form exists to serve the astral world.

117.

Almost everything you read, including this, will get caught
in the net of thought, stopped before the high heart's welcome wound.
To touch that wound with the sweet pain of love, see it open
to the unifying Presence of God, is the reason
anyone writes or reaches or cries. Stitching together
all our hallucinated separateness with language
and touch and forgiveness and mercy is God's becoming.

118.

You could say we dance so life's fraught confusion doesn't tie
our flesh in achy knots, or we dance to express something
too total to be said or sung. A reason for dancing
seems like an overlay of thought, but humans would explain
God's being if you let them. If you need a filigree
of language to brighten your thought, some neon for the mind,
just say dancing is the doing of being and move on.

119.

However many ages and bodies yours may require,
this human sojourn has a single purpose: to complete
a soul, an immortal participant in God's calling
the universe home to consciousness. In ascending forms,
each more unified with God's mind, by life the soul of life
compels dark divergent matter to turn back to the Source
of light and begin return to God – the great convergence.

120.

Life is the energy of God's mind reaching out the end
of possibility, the Absolute's self-awareness.
It occupies all matter and will return to its Source
by ascending a pyramid of rarifying steps.
The individual identity of human form
veils the soul: the Angels are of one mind with God and mount
in purity of being till otherness cannot be.

3. Epistrophe – The Return

II. A Letter on Law

In the age that we find ourselves, our species will be thinned,
grindingly or catastrophically – we don't know which.
If you survive, your outward work in the shadowed wreckage
is to make a little light so the young can learn to read,
to revive the dead ground, to help the water clean itself.
Your inward work remains the same as it has always been:
to remember God with each breath; to know and be the soul.

Ours is the task of re-establishment – of harmony
with Earth, of peaceful and loving relations, of a frame
of mind friendly to God and a new civilization.
Heaven does not want the elemental fire – its symbol
on Earth – to go out, or it would be already expunged.
From the human enterprise, Heaven wants a reflection
of its own peace and beauty, that men may become Angels.

Morality is man's poor substitute for consciousness.
Conscious sensitivity acting from its vantage point
in the Field of Love cannot indulge a criminal act,
but so rare are conscious beings, these laws unto themselves,
that their Angelic discourse and example do not stop
the mass of sleeping men from making normalcy of crime
and denying higher unity. Thus the need for laws.

It is troubling to use the same word – law – to dignify
a human statute as is used to fix a principle
of cosmic order. A true law cannot be disobeyed:
a thing exists within the compass of a law or not.
For man, cosmic laws are discoveries, not inventions.
One's body is subject to gravity; not so the soul.
But a human formulation must in each phrase and clause
be challenged, so ripe to quick corruption and so brimming
with exceptions does it read. Without the brave benefit
of present wisdom applied to the specific matter
of each case, human law distorts and cramps reality
and thus abuses justice. Not anarchy but humble
sagacity says that human laws are only guidelines.

The making of just laws presumes a balanced synthesis
of understandings – of the aims and needs of the people;
of the surrounding bounties and scarcities of nature;
and of the opportunity to know God in Presence.
The laws must be few and simple, that an unlettered man
can learn and see their reason. They must be the same for all,
as those of nobler bearing must embrace the discipline
needed by the less accomplished. They must seek to add grace
to the harshness of life and favor the harmonious.
Most crucially, the laws must never justify vengeance
or, void of love, engender an order of punishments.
A society of human beings living by choice
of common purpose and without aggression to the world
has the right to protect itself from without and within,
but to depend on punishments for that protection stunts
the refinement of the state and the souls of its members.
Heaven does not punish save by the grieving removal
of attention; thus breach of law is a cause for mourning.

Defined without prejudice, crime is the course of action
or attitude for which a society has no place,
no use, and which in deviance festers and endangers.
Most who commit crimes do so in sleep or damaged reason;
love and good will can restore them. Others more rare protest
a law or custom that they find unjust or out of date.
Seek out their true intention, marking their response to love.
The state can always be more just, more conscious of its aim.

If crime causes loss, let there be restitution designed
to foster forgiveness and heal the community's wound.
If there be injury, let the doer take the duties
of the injured upon himself, with his supporters' help.
Let the society as a body prefer mercy
and extra labor to an offender's forced poverty.
Mercy is expensive, but the lack of mercy more so.

Yet there will be some whose transgressions are repetitive,
whose attitudes have stiffened to stone. The community
must not sacrifice the souls of its citizens to these,
must not bend from what Heaven has prescribed. With all sorrow
and solemnity, these so dangerous must be released
from the body of love, put out in exile, their return
blocked by force: this not in punishment but in tragic loss.

Much of what the law must restrain is rooted in the will
to power and the greed that blooms from power's bent branches.
The puppeteers of power and fortune long established –
the men who ruled Earth with their deftly cultivated networks
of bankers, politicians, warlords, lawyers and scholars;
the men who saw fertile valleys, forests, potent rivers,
the great oceans and even the sun as profit sources

and who saw the teeming cities as wells of cheap labor –
these are the mortals who most forgot the purpose of man.
As a seat of power totters and tumbles at the thought
of its demise, it compensates with greater tyranny.
If you are patient, you will retreat and let power starve.
If you are impatient and would confront a dazed, wounded
predator, know there are no rules to this fight, no logic
to its lashing out. The teeth of a dying animal
are fast and fierce and indiscriminate. Stand back and watch.
Yet the death of power is only half a victory.
Stupid, grinning disorder and drunken greed stumble in
to fill the vacuum with shocking speed. Those that suffered
past abuse demand short sighted justice. The rule of law
becomes a phrase misconceived a dozen different ways.
True order stands on shared principle patiently distilled
from ardent hearts longing for peace and firmly held in minds.

What holds for the state holds for a single human being.
One who would not be an animal, who would see power
surrendered to truth, must restrain his own teeth and talons,
quell the seething riot of passions praising anarchy.
Through it all, the hero – the mindful one within – holds fast,
devoted to remembering God and motivating
sacred effort to return. Presence is its own reward.
Power is bad food: one needs more and more and more of it
to feel sustained. Simplicity is power's opposite.
To have power over another stirs humility
in a man rightly turned. The Angels have permitted him
the sweet opportunity to evoke the drowsy soul
of his brother or sister, to remind that soul to wake
and return to gratitude and God here in the garden.
If power has been given to you – over a worker
or a group or an enterprise, even over a child

entrusted to your care – remember whence all power comes
and why. The flower that blooms silently beside the path
is using power well: if your will is open to it,
it can arrest your pace, bring you to a stop, make you bow,
kindle your generous attention to a mindful gleam.

Again, what holds for the state holds for the single human.
Keeping order in one's own province clarifies one's view
of the body politic. The small and simple focus
is the most productive one and the most governable,
requiring fewest laws. The more one would be, the less free.
The rule of large groups – or large ambitions – requires controls
that restrict basic freedoms and subvert human kindness.
Your love can only be for one before you, not mankind.

The body was made for hard work: with mindfulness sustained,
the labor of muscles pushing and pulling and stretching
to refine this rough world obliges the art of self-care.
Eating what the body needs for its specific service –
not more, not less – is part of this. Bathing regularly
and exchanging friendly touch keep the flesh toned and pleasing.
Keeping the mind free of worry requires more subtle skill.
Worry is a tool of the lower self. Worry enslaves
the heart and unmans the thoughts, setting them churning, turning
in an endless grinding loop that forfeits Presence to fear.
Who wins? The lower self, now in control, prefers to be
prison master in hell and closes the mind to Heaven.
To be worry free, to be open skied in heart and mind,
one must see oneself, one's dear individual being,
as a room at an inn, something occupied for a night
then vacated for the return to God. The less luggage –
the less one must unpack and pack again – the easier
it is to abide uncluttered and clean. Delight and love
are clean, and the truth takes its rest in a clean heart and mind.

And how does self-governance maintain its integrity
against an overwhelming wave of sensual pleasure?
The strongest stimuli – a taste so generous and full,
so completely satisfying that all discretion melts,
or a sexual touch so electric that its pleasure
swallows all the mind's measurings – these are held up proudly
by the lower self as if to say, "Where is your Presence?
Where bobs your fragile little ark of self-remembering
in my great sensual flood? What is your Heaven to this?"
And there before you, undeniably true, is your will,
a corpse washed up on a beach, its features eroded past
identity, its splayed mass no longer intentional
in its posture. Does it breathe? Does it have a living pulse?
Our bodies are given as resistance necessary
to the growth of our souls, but how can the soul hold Presence
before pleasures so great they deluge purpose and meaning?
Even in the steward's abandonment, God is watching.
In flesh's greatest gratifications, God's pure patience
waits us out. Everything the body can serve up to us,
everything between the poles of sense, is a wave washing
out and back. Choose your return: to indelible Presence
or to birth in another body's sensual longing.

Instinct can distinguish between the pain of injury
and that of healing. So the steward after gross errors
learns the laws of joy to be above the wine of pleasure.
Wine is a gift from the Angels, never to be abused.
It is a refinement of nature, a separation
of spirit from denser matter; it is salutary
and dangerous, health enhancing and sadly addictive.
It can be the door of confession and disburdenment

or the fuel of violence and ruin. It can unblock
the path for unexpressed affection or hinder friendship.
Be schooled by the elders in wine's intelligent delight.
Let it be a lubricant of amity providing grace
to a simple table. Taken in sips deeply savored,
it will brighten the emotions of the diners and lead
their conversation to a glad focus on their blessings.
Consumed alone by one rumbling with anger or weighted
with care, wine fortifies the lower self's distorted claims.
It is wise to have humility before life's pleasures.
Remember how little we know and how fragile our hold.
With measured breaths unfreighted by false knowledge and ill thoughts,
return to conscious being, the right footing for sharing
love among friends aware of the Angels' kind attention.
Life is not meant to be lived without joy. Duty alone
is dry mouthed and drowsy. In joy our will to love ascends.

      The tyranny of cold statutes and prescribed punishments
can be avoided and the cultivation of the will
through discerning self-control can be rightly encouraged
only if there exist human beings embodying
the wisdom that merciful and creative correction
require, the wisdom arising from long practiced virtue.
These wise ones must be the judges in the land, evident
as worthy to all who have examined them, devoted
first to the benefit of sharing the Presence of God.
Without these as executors and examples, the laws
become the tools of institutional power, losing
the unalloyed allegiance of individual hearts.
These judges comprehend the principle of higher right
and use it to resolve apparent conflict in the laws.

They can devise unique restitutions based on healing
and advancement rather than on angry retribution.
Their own lives are illuminated by humility
and patience; they do not forget the Eye of God sees all,
and they want what the Angels want – that our society
reflect Heaven's peace and beauty as a garden for souls.
If the state grows in territory or population
past what its truly worthy judges can administer,
it must check itself or lose connection with its essence.

      The best understanding of law does not belong to those
who write statutes on pages or carve commandments in stone
but to those who have learned to summon the will to submit –
not to a regime or a man or a creed or doctrine
but to Presence. Their base stubbornness broken, there is God
everywhere ready to embrace them in full awareness.
They sing for the Eye in full throated silence, the Crown now
their unsealed aperture for being's eternal current.

      A hostile authority can imprison our bodies,
but we are not our bodies. The collection of matters
each knows as body flows into everything as all flows
into it. One might as well call oneself a density
of materials more or less stable in a region.
For humans as for Angels in their ascending orders,
identity is in the awareness of the matters
we occupy but are not. To have identity means
to have awareness of separation, to be apart.
But with each separation will come a new connection,
a changing understanding of the all and everything,
an altered sense of what it means to serve, to be a part.
The last separation reveals the unity of all.
There is no otherness in being. The Lord God is one.

The perfection of return is the end of creation.
When the beast of burden is content in its resting place,
and the heart that rides it sits aware of its tired passions,
and the mind knows the folly of words and image making,
then true vision emerges, energized by openness
to all that is. The universe becomes the active force,
and all one's individuality's constituents –
all names and measures – dissolve in the unity of God,
the final liberation and the fulfillment of law.

The First Book of Opportunities

I. Quatrains and Double Fours

1. Try to find the solution not only to the problem
    at hand, but the solution to all problems everywhere.
    The universal aim is to enhance one's consciousness
    until it is not one's any longer but simply is.

    ___

2. When he heard there was a great fire raging, the master danced
    until he was exhausted, always aware of his breath.
    "Now I can appreciate anything," he said. A pane
    of glass was found in the rubble. "We will watch the new snow."

    ___

3. We spend about half our lifetime's allotted energy
    reacting to the fear of pain. When God knocks on our door,
    we congratulate ourselves for the locks. We have survived
    the danger of disappearing in God's shameless embrace.

    ___

4. If you say your name as you see your face in the mirror
    and watch your thoughts without interrupting their flow downstream,
    God will sneak up behind you to observe your observing.
    Terror is a tool if you use its touch to feel God's lips.

    ___

5. Now you and God are laughing, a pair of fools in a world
    gone harmless. The waiter brings a fortune cookie. You read:
    "The problem is there is only room for one fool laughing."
    The solution to all problems can now pick up the check.

    ___

6.   Sometimes on our morning journeys, the finicky dog finds
      no suitable place for her message . So we walk and walk
      as I fear a later surprise on the floor in the house.
      The stubborn animal holds civilization hostage.

      ─────

7.   Cleanliness requires free flowing water, and life unclean
      is as bad as life too fat. We should not produce so much
      of anything – food, children, ideas – that we hinder
      the flow of water. Now put your palm on your brother's heart.

      ─────

8.   The turbulence that won't let us think straight is a strange gift.
      Much kinder is the gong that lets us will to still the mind.
      One way or another, thought must be stopped often each day,
      or we'll believe it and forget to use Heaven's portal.

      ─────

9.   Splendid are the best works of human beings, those calling
      attention with a harmony so stunning one becomes
      aware of a state beyond the senses. How did a man
      make this? What learning allowed this deliverance? Teach me.

      ─────

10.   There's a threshold of pleasure where the lower self rises
      and takes control of innocent delight. Here the brave will
      must intervene, seize the reins and assert conscious command.
      To the lord of flesh, each slow, praying sip feels like a loss.

      ─────

11.   I'm not sure where this verse is going, but I'm giving it
      a little time to reveal its unique abilities
      and teach me something. The most valued part of this venture
      is the watching, which is pure and clean as flowing water.

&

12.   The stream carries a fallen branch along for a brief ride
      then leaves it up against the bank just as this verse welcomes
      a thought, washes it and leaves it to dry. The sense of "I"
      doesn't trouble the stream, and the verse avoids that shadow.

                        _____

13.   Even a failed leader's place is hard to fill. At the top
      one attracts the measuring eyes of all the ranks below,
      a burdensome attention at which most shrink and stiffen.
      It's an art to steer followers to self-discovery.

                        _____

14.   Find in your lover all the things you do not need to love:
      the silken hair, the jewel eyes, the skin, the shape, the voice,
      the visible grace, the radiant gladness face to face.
      These elements are not the soul that now you know you know.

                        _____

15.   One must be taught to know oneself; it's shocking that one can.
      When from the cascade of debris, a teacher shows you how
      to separate yourself, the recognition lights a room
      of wonder. Ah, here I am! Where have I been all this time?

                        _____

16.   If you're reading this, God already led you to the door.
      Now you must stand in front of it practicing readiness
      like Hamlet till an Angel opens it for your passage.
      That readiness, the now in heart and mind, is all you have.

      ———

17.   For their purity of energy, children are to be
      suffered. Civilizing them is delicate, a project
      full of failures and missteps. Let time do its polishing –
      of them and of you. Patience is your payment and your pay.

      ———

18.   The key to forming an alliance is to pose no threat.
      You must want a different food than that which nourishes
      a would-be partner; as well there must be a shared pleasure
      in fellowship, a magnetic pole for innate kindness.

&

19.   It may help if the allies impress each other as strange,
      alien creatures quietly marveling at the range
      of the One who created them both. True companionship
      is a slow surprise, a paid-off mortgage on God's dwelling.

      ———

20.   Wisdom is a substance you've become, a liquor waiting
      for its crystal, already beautiful, with promise forged
      from animal pain, slow time, and sorrow distilled to love.
      It's your proof that you exist and have the correct map home.

      ———

21.   Have you ever watched your hands applaud – spank the air, collide,
       from sudden clap retreat, repeat, repeat, repeat, repeat?
       What would happen if the play, ballet, symphony or song
       reached a terminus of majesty and you did nothing?
&

22.   Could you hold the state of tight-wound energy and hold off
       the urge to divest it? The beaming grin, the standing up,
       the shouting lungs – all these borne on a foamy, rapid spill
       of gratitude: could you hold still and share some breath with God?

       ———

23.   Friends are everywhere to be discovered. They need not be
       your species. The soul delights in learning love's proposal
       to any living thing and cherishes the least response.
       Friendlessness is not a price God requires of one's return.

       ———

24.   One wants one's body well behaved: no aches or stiffenings,
       no unsightly collections of fat, no drooping features,
       no rude noises or foul odors. Ah, but such smooth manners
       beget belief this slow-corrupting corpse is what one is.

       ———

25.   Belief, morality, rule of law, punishment and death –
       these are the bedevilments gripping the unconscious world.
       Conscious men, men aware of their souls attending this world,
       have love instead and no need of devils and their lock-ups.

       ———

26. Are you worthy in this moment? Are you aware of God
    waiting to embrace you and free you from the mystery
    you've been starving in? Remembering God is here is all
    you must do to seed your heart with love. God shows you the rest.

    ———

27. God doesn't ask much of most people, but just those people
    are merciless to God, chirping endless prayers, projecting
    personhoods above the clouds, not seeing that what they want
    as gifts from God they can in each moment get for themselves.

&

28. The chosen few aren't better, but chosen because knowing
    or knowing because chosen, they see that every moment
    consciously upheld, every now lived in loving Presence,
    fortifies their being, all being, and unburdens God.

    ———

29. We are midway through this year's first hot spell – six days they say.
    Nothing can congeal – not butter, not enthusiasm.
    Shameless dogs sleep anywhere. The effort to be Present
    must hide in shade but continue on the scale of the sun.

    ———

30. This life is down to its last full serving of time. The jar
    is light, something almost ready for recycling. The spoon
    must be handled by the fingertips to reach the bottom.
    The coming emptiness is not a danger to being.

    ———

31.   What if you can't mourn at a funeral or celebrate
       at birthdays? What if the formulas for feeling don't work?
       What if you can't muster fear when death bends to kiss your cheek?
       Hold the purity of witnessing. Don't abandon God.

       ———

32.   The lower centers need an occupation to stay out
       of trouble. Gainful employment is the best way to keep
       them busy. But be careful. We don't want the management
       of the functions to be flawless, or we'll believe they're real.

       ———

33.   The most perfect free-flowing nervous system – not hindered
       by trauma, poor posture or sluggish habits of excess –
       does not guarantee higher states. God must summon the soul;
       then everything rises past any and all occlusions.

       ———

34.   The hand is the symbol of man's relationship to Earth –
       the bare root of technology and the uplift of prayer.
       Clenched, it is stone, a weapon; clasping, it is a vine, hope
       of establishment; open, it is welcome, trusting God.

       ———

35.   If the art of flower arranging is not included
       and valued in the court of your awareness, your soul needs
       more refined nutrition. A deficiency of beauty
       will manifest in old age as fatigue in finding God.

       ———

36.   Communicating without personality may be
impossible, but the effort to keep oneself empty
offers an open-handed welcome to the universe.
Everything is a friend. Love is always filling the bowl.

———

37.   Thank Heaven your earthly personage is not immortal.
Imagine being that impostor for eternity.
Anything you can imagine being is a prison
if eternal. Simple being cannot be imagined.

&

38.   So this character that time and fear and lapsed attention
have made of you must die, but what you truly are does not
participate. The nonexistence of simple being
also cannot be imagined. Here you are, eternal.

———

39.   I can't do it. It's impossible to leave you alone.
Everything I do eventually finds your address,
knocks on the door and leaves an influence. One cannot be
left alone by anyone. You...me...there's just one being.

———

40.   One lives out one's play helpless in spacetime, learning to watch.
Slowly one becomes the steward and ascends above it
to be beyond the laws of flesh and its specific form:
all this measures a sequence of efforts, each in the script.

———

41. Knowledge won't save you, but there's no salvation without it.
You can't buy your escape with art, but art makes bearable
and worthy a span of near unending human lifetimes.
You must be chosen, your number dropped in the playwright's lap.

&

42. You didn't know you had a number? God gave it to you
in the immeasurably tiny time between nothing
and the first pause. 'Til it's called, you can only polish will
with knowledge, with art, with the patient promise of your love.

———

43. "What are you?" "Not this." Repeat the question rhythmically
for your entire stay in the dimension of time and give
the same answer. This action can preserve the innocence
one needs to participate in God – now, endlessly, now.

———

44. The shell of individual being is worn away
ascending the Ray of Creation. Finer and finer
bodies designate what must finally become aware
of the everything it can only be, the Absolute.

———

45. As sin is sleep to instructed ones, an innocent man
is not man at all but prior soul still in touch with God.
When we forget what we truly are, vanishing in sleep,
so stumbles bright innocence down into the darkened gut.

———

46.   Controlling the energy of sex is a delicate
        dance of mind and mission, not to be done repressively.
        One must have a higher aim, a practiced preparation –
        a compound of postponement and one's greatest joy in God.

———

47.   Just as the phrase, "When being interrupts sleep..." came to mind,
        the dog began barking – loud sleep interrupting being.
        First and second forces do their dance, an abrasive pair
        but always a pair. You are reading how to work with them.

———

48.   Belief is the door of sleep. It closes behind the soul
        come to Earth and must be relocated and pried open
        for escape. On Earth, not to believe is vandalism,
        the breaking of a seal against chaos. All will hate you.

&

49.   So once you've lucked (or so it seems) upon this dungeon door,
        force it open quietly, holding subtle candle light.
        Use a steady pressure over years. Slip out unnoticed
        back to Heaven where Truth beyond belief rewelcomes you.

———

50.   Vanity is its own audience, pleased with what it sees.
        One cannot correct a feature: it is the distortion,
        not some purer thing unfortunately bent and hoping
        to be straightened. Learning is not liking or disliking.

———

51.　For man, God is a state of consciousness, the one calling
　　all conditions and the universe itself to order,
　　the Presence one can participate in but is p　　　art of
　　anyway, aware or not. There's no other God but God.

———

52.　Is pain the reminder the Absolute is serious
　　about creation? If all this is not a cruel joke,
　　beyond pain and the meaning of pain there must be something
　　of surpassing worthiness involved, some perfect being.

&

53.　But there cannot be perfection amid imperfection.
　　The whole including the pain must be the one perfection.
　　Transforming suffering opens creation, flowering
　　above pain, a needed part of what the Absolute shares.

———

54.　One participates in God or however alluring
　　one's form and movement, however intelligent one's art,
　　one is speeding out to the edge of exhausted ashes,
　　far beyond thought or sense. Wouldn't you rather be with God?

———

55.　A can of beans will keep you alive, and if you know God,
　　you'll be grateful. If you don't know God, nothing can appease
　　your hunger, and your growing gut will forget what has passed
　　through its darkness till all the world's riches have been eaten.

———

56.   Most people identify with mental activity.
They believe themselves to be the thoughts, associations,
promptings, registrations, memories and warnings scuttling
through the skull as if it were a warehouse storing the world.

&

57.   There is some sense to this worldly form of identity,
but one can step back from it into pure observation,
thence to the awareness of attention. So what are you?
A mind? A mind observed? An awareness? Simple being?

_____

58.   This world makes sense only within one's awareness of God.
Without sharing God's Presence and thereby understanding
the participation of the small – itself crude, unjust
and craving – in the all, one measures starvation's phases.

_____

59.   Don't think (Stop here a moment.) that God (Again stop.) obeys
your lower laws. (Full stop here.) The causal complexity
of your reading just these words at just this point bewilders
a time-bound mind, but God's not bound by time or mind. (Please stop.)

_____

60.   I am and we are, but he or she isn't and they aren't,
for there is no he or she or they, only a we – all
of us. In fact the you and I are just mirror siblings,
so the we is just the I, and the I is just the am.

_____

61.   Barking dogs become tiresome before tired. Our responses
       must be ridiculous to us before control kicks in.
       Thus history repeats and only slowly grows the soul.
       Patience on the scale of God holds the only hope for life.

                        ———

62.   Fools who think they can derive life from nonlife tire the mind.
       Life by any of its names – intelligence, awareness ... --
       has a perch in eternity, and till that dimension
       advises the chemistry, the mind will be stuck in mud.

                        ———

63.   How crippling is the loss of little things relied upon
       for daily order – a car key, a password, a wallet.
       Yes, one goes on, but with an irritable mental limp
       that extorts attention where routine had ruled benignly.

&

64.   One constructs a network of detours in the normal grid,
       reroutings that avoid the hole, and if honest one sees
       how low is self-awareness in quotidian living
       yet how complex the pattern of sleep smothering the soul.

                        ———

65.   "Nothing too much," said the wise Greeks. A thing overindulged
       is destructive: eating, thinking, praying. But don't we aim
       at constant prayer? Yes, but constant prayer is the soul itself
       ascended, not the gluttony or greed for holiness.

                        ———

66. With the tool of his abstracting mind, man would recreate
the world and be its god, but great imbalances result.
Not by the mind but by submission to the state of God,
balancing in humble gratitude, is man brought to God.

———

67. Are we not timorous, unstable, comfort-loving, vain?
What do the Angels see in us that they expend so much
fine energy on our development? To be so dear
to them, we must be something more than we appear, or less.

———

68. A silken green underrobe overlaid with red and gold –
such were the vestments of the priest. Skyward his eyes, outstretched
his arms, palms up. "I am nothing without you," he intoned.
Then to the people, gently, "I am nothing without you."

&

69. As a doorway of beauty he stood between God and man,
nothing himself, an opening. "May you not need me long."
He stayed some moments in silence then sweet music began.
Anyone can play this role – man, woman, child – or no one.

———

70. The soul's encounter in the heart's mirror begins real life,
but one must know what one has seen. This is the true knowledge
that opens salvation to understanding. What remains
of life is honored dying – the becoming of the soul.

———

71.   Imagined identity will deflate and die, replaced
by the soul's awareness of God, growing in constancy.
To monitor this transformation is the Angels' work,
and for this, so simple to say, the universe was made.

—————

72.   The gnosis is not a formula or a spell. The soul
recognizes itself, and a new life – eternal life –
appears. The gnosis is the soul's self-knowledge, replacing
what one thought one was as that imagined one disappears.

—————

73.   The aches and pleasures of the body continue scratching
for attention. The steward must set his feet and observe.
So many reasons advance, so many seductive songs
insinuate themselves. Such is an instructed man's time.

&

74.   When the soul visits and stays on, prominent and sturdy,
all the incidental licks and nicks of flesh register
their names but cannot dislodge the fundamental Presence.
While the dog whimpers, the eternal visitor proves God.

—————

75.   Like a persistent salesman, the body keeps offering
things to consider, sweeter deals. Imaginary need
flickers in you and will kindle if you blink. Let the words
buzz in your head like annoying flies that aren't really there.

—————

76.   The best part of the mind wants meaning and understanding,
         but even those pale before Presence. Nurture compassion
         for your mind: it must grasp or go mad. It will die serving,
         but it is not the soul and cannot know eternity.

———

77.   Rarified as one ascends, desire is the expression
         of life, love's raw material, the attraction to God;
         but descending, desire is the greed of dirt, the power
         and pleasure of flesh, the private individual's pride.

———

78.   The current of life climbs the spine to the skull's Eye and Crown
         then out to the ether, through the Field of Love where, all one,
         we live the living Present. If not dammed by personhood,
         the magical river ascends all the way to the Source.

———

79.   Don't mistake the Angels' adamantine will for anger.
         Anger does not enter them, nor do they punish mankind.
         Human suffering appalls them, but cause must have effect.
         Theirs is the true mercy – not rescue but awakening.

&

80.   And that mercy thrives in their obedience, in actions
         of a unifying will crystallized in God's being.
         If your prayer for human sorrow's end has no clear effect,
         take your prayer beyond effect straight to the Presence of God.

———

4. The Work of the Steward

81.   Not only must we wear this flesh and answer to these names,
we must play our parts well – shrink not from the blows or avoid
the flames. What's the reward? On this level, contentedness
of brain chemistry, but for the soul, greater love of God.

_____

82.   Don't be disturbed by words: "love of God" is a phrase meaning
cherishing Presence above all states and activities.
If you do that, you may show religious language the door
and call Presence by any name which fortifies the state.

_____

83.   Every thought one entertains asks to be believed, taken
to the chapel of the heart, but once relaxed there, that thought
begins to cook and calls its friends, taking the sacred space
and displacing the attention intended for the soul.

&

84.   The soul, now unwelcome, politely retires, leaving one
in thrall to one's greedy guest and his noisy company.
Believing thought abuses highest hospitality
and leaves one with dirty pews and a smelly sacristy.

_____

85.   Is prolonged Presence God's visit to me or mine to God?
See how this question distorts the truth, making two from one.
Presence is the state of the one, all-encompassing God
which consciously includes all things in their chosen spinning.

_____

121

86.   Despite its keen sensings, instinct has a hard time learning,
          so it's often a step or two behind. Have you ever
          nearly fallen asleep while driving a car? This brain moves
          away from pain toward pleasure and knows not transformation.

&

87.   Thus the heart is best for giving secret sanctuary
          to the soul. Let instinct recognize a pleasant pastime
          while at the back door the remembered soul appears, enters,
          and nurtures in the silence of the heart's abstaining watch.

———

88.   One does not need the gong's resound to stop and stop and stop.
          Your valuation and resolve create a Present pause
          within the talk, the noise of the room, the clash of nations,
          the tones of spinning planets, the pulsations of the stars.

———

89.   If your chief workman falls asleep and comes late to the job,
          welcome him with motherly concern, no desperation
          or dependency. Speak softly as you get him started.
          Conscience will dress him in a tight shirt of porcupine quills.

———

90.   If effort is your money and Presence the great purchase,
          you are in the steward's economy, heavenward turned.
          If time is your money to buy pleasure at the bazaar,
          you're making unconscious payments on your burial plot.

———

91. To achieve light speed, you don't have to rewire your machine –
with one exception: you must adjust a penchant for doubt,
tone it down to nonbelief. Doubt is darkness, airlessness,
a vacuum chamber in which the brain chews on the heart.

———

92. Come out of hiding, friend. Have a peach. Only if you eat
will you discover you're starving. Turn inside out the thought
that you have nothing to offer the lonely multitude.
What both you and your frightened friends need is more risk. Speak up!

&

93. Talk to the Angels. (Your idea of them is embalmed
in your own self-pity.) Address God. (The response is clear
and immediate if you're ready.) Let all overhear
your endearing discourse and come poignantly to Presence.

———

94. What will fully open the Eye and liberate vision
from broken time? One must trust the energy of the valves
already opened, focus and purify one's practice.
Past, present, future – the fractures in time long to be healed.

———

95. The body is an appearance in time. The soul appears
in the Mind of God, parallel to time, not borne away,
useful to the Absolute's projection of creation.
"What is finally real?" you ask. Not questions. Not us. Be.

———

96.   Awareness of the world as a hologram includes us.
        What but God remains? What pay would you expect for being
        employed in permanent illusion? The consequences
        of your understanding lead to one conclusion. Just one.

        ⸺

97.   Don't make a word out of it, or you'll have to discuss it,
        argue with or about it, determine its boundaries,
        and keep a record of its transactions. Better to let it
        remain a felt energy, an unnamed experience.
&

98.   Then it is far more manageable, and transformation
        can proceed immediately. Call it grief or anger
        and a whole closet of behaviors have a claim on it.
        Call it injustice or evil and all mankind joins in.

        ⸺

99.   A person seeks justice then relief from justice. We want
        what we want, for wanting is the buried version of life:
        it burrows bravely in the dirt but doesn't see too well.
        If you could stop wanting, you would not die, but something would.

        ⸺

100.   Think of God as a human infant needing protection.
        Think of God as a beautiful blue boy or fearsome girl.
        What we think of God is only a thought, and even we
        are greater than thought, are we not? Let's not rot in our minds.

        ⸺

101.   Observing something changes it and changes you as well.
        Not a new idea, but note the impact when you know
        you're being observed – by the government, by loving friends,
        by the Angels whose watching is deepening their being.

        ——

102.   If you conceive of the Absolute in personal terms,
        such will be the visit. A faint but stubborn sense of "I"
        hangs on. If the conception is impersonal, nothing
        comes between. Visit, visitor, visited – All is One.

        ——

103.   The best way to soar into Presence is on the updraft
        of an Angel's love openly expressed. Rarely in words
        but often in symbols, numberings, plays of light and songs,
        Angels offer their embraces, their kisses, their delights.

&

104.   Yes, but cannot these occurrences happen by themselves,
        so how can we know? What we know is our own gratitude
        rising in response to being addressed and assuaging
        the sense of accident. We are here now and thus with them.

        ——

105.   Privacy is an illusion, a territorial
        conception that personality – a manufactured
        thing itself – extends to time and space. Note the fractured vase:
        each shard now has its privacy round the scattered flowers.

        ——

106.   Spoon the caustic remedy into the drain. The gurgle
        and the poison fumes confirm the burning of the blockage.
        Things of no use, harmless in themselves, close the conduit
        and become criminal. The flow of water must not stop.
&

107.   Unlike the water down a drain, the current in a man
        flows up to heart and brain and further up and back to God.
        We must stay unoccluded, ever new and heavenward.
        Indulgences harmless in themselves must find no mercy.

        ———

108.   There are many budding souls and few Angels to help them,
        and finishing a soul requires higher help. Be patient
        through great suffering over many lives. Your turn awaits.
        Lift your heart into God's eternal service. Practice now.

        ———

109.   If you are attacked and do not fight, there will be a cost.
        If you fight back and defeat your foe, there will be a cost.
        However you are challenged brings a cost. What do you want?
        Actions proceed from consciousness. You must know what you want.
&

110.   The best thing to want is a high perch from which to observe
        whatever occurs. Then you can freely pay any cost;
        any action will proceed from your watching. You are conscious
        past challenge. You can suffer time and teach your attackers.

        ———

111. The world is full of snares. Every life form must make a case
for surviving, evolve a hidden cleverness fatal
to all who want the same habitat. Only we, mankind,
can witness it all, including our own brain's siren songs.

———

112. For you who cannot mistrust life on Earth, who believe it
unquestioningly and handle its hard unpromising,
your way to Heaven is to not fear death, to brunt the fact
of it as you would all conditions each moment presents.

———

113. The binding came apart. The pages fell from the embrace
in which they had made steady sense together for an age.
In this new time, no craftsman had been trained to the old skill
of resurrection, and so as dead litter it was swept.
&

114. You who must rebind the Present, who must relocate God
in yourselves and all you do, the best regeneration
streamlines ancient wisdom keys into witness syllables
lest you fall back to sleep recopying cold manuscripts.

———

115. Every time one believes for just minutes some idea
of the future (often a prophecy or a profit
to take credit for), the Angels must obliterate it
like a sand mandala, restoring what's here before one.

———

116.　As sandwiches go, it was beautiful; then you ate it.
　　　 And yours was a sound, praiseworthy personhood; then you died.
　　　 And Earth was a doting mother, the sun a just father,
　　　 the galaxy an ample stage for revelation; then.....

　　　　　　　———

117.　Some eat to fill the hole, some to get pleasure from flavor,
　　　 some to block bubbling emotions pressured to the surface.
　　　 Why one eats is less important than how: the devil claims
　　　 eating as his service even more than sex. Be each bite.

　　　　　　　———

118.　If we were only flesh, some crimes could not be forgiven.
　　　 The reverse is also true: what you refuse to forgive
　　　 will rob you of your soul. Nothing of what we truly are
　　　 ends here, but only because we must forgive everything.

　　　　　　　———

119.　This human form once dropped will be easily forgotten,
　　　 assuming the soul is able to exist without it.
　　　 That's a big assumption. Bringing a soul to readiness
　　　 takes ages and ages and many of these flesh bodies.
&

120.　You spur this process by subtly shifting identity
　　　 to the soul in two ways: first, be Present – avoid slipping
　　　 into time where flesh is trapped; then embrace with all good grace
　　　 what befalls your person – let it be lovingly observed.

　　　　　　　———

II. Lessons

What Can A Man Do?

What can a man do? Arrange some objects with symmetry;
tether for a moment one's gaze to a fine impression;
walk out the door and move along the streets of suffering
without judging God; make one's transactions with cheerfulness.

It is difficult to remember that there's a reason
one's soul resides on a planet so far from Paradise.
All souls are here for the heavy work of transformation,
and that labor requires a mind simple in the moment.

How is it possible that the loving God created
this place where innocent children starve and the distortion
of beauty makes a profit? Think on this: would you enter
eternity as you are? Is your being perfected?

Without Earth there is no lifting; without the injustice
and the sorrow and the beauty and the bounty of Earth,
no transformation, no growth of the soul. The muddy flow
of time goes on to its dead end, and what can a man do?

One can practice eternity only in the Present.
Each moment of love transforms you, lifts you from the world's dirt
for as long as you can hold yourself Present and readies
over vast ages of moments your soul for higher worlds.

No Lasting Beauty

Abundant sex energy collecting close to surface
will charge the neon cleverness of personality.
The result is entertaining but brazenly mortal.
It is as if the inmates were cheerily conscripted
into a contest to improve prison security.
One must not let the lower waste the higher: doing so
is the essence of tragedy, emptiness beyond tears.

Behaviors dissipating one's most refined energies
are legion: flirting, indulging razored wit, useless feats
of hard trained mind and body. Distorted pleasure ensues
for performer and audience (always an audience,
if only in one's head), but the episode contributes
only to the downward, outward flight of dying creatures:
no lasting beauty is made, but damage deeper in time.

Making

If making is your nature, make things the Angels can use.
First, make a soul. This will occupy your best intentions
and your nimblest labor for decades, but when you're finished,
the Consciously Ascending will have a permanent tool
against the weighty force of falling and coming apart.
To further your life work, make love, make sacred friends, make art.
Offer everything you make to God till you are content
in the eternal nothing, breathing the uncreated.

Original Sin

Original sin is a metaphor for believing
one's mental contents to be an operating handbook
for life here. But, you ask, what choice does one have? None at all.
Long before any real opportunity can arise
to remove oneself to the island of "I am" to give
identity a proper cleaning, one must navigate
the world based on the flawed information and incomplete
filing system one's mental replicator has fashioned.
And the damned thing runs by itself and responds as oneself;
it assumes one will believe it. And one does, unto death.

So to be condemned to hell from the outset only means
that true self-knowledge is not at hand until one receives
instruction in reclaiming one's being from the lacquer
of false identity that the world has been applying
and with which we've been passively complying since pre-birth.
It is a bright subversive irony to verify
that one must be taught to remember who one truly is.
The truth must be revealed to one by one already blessed
to have it; then just a little searching with truth's candle
indicates a generous Source beyond the human mind.

Man's Work

Giving credit to the mind of man for finding the truth
is like praising the branches for discovering the wind.
Breaking the truth and refiguring it into language
requires some art, some grace, but even here the Angels hold
the mirror and only bless the work of those who can see
themselves through the task's every step and know themselves as tools.

Desire and Belief

We act from our level of consciousness, and we possess
every level within us. From bodiless purity
to mineral implacability, we mount the stars
above and deaden into the pitiless stones below.
Innocent wonder lights the child's eyes, while the soldier kills
to the relentless staccato pulses of his training.

The cosmos is a hologram of desire and belief
from which we must cancel our fascination and salvage
self-awareness. In each moment's heart we can choose beauty
or suffering; the mind can consent to God's terrible
mystery or argue the next bite of being eaten.
Subtracting the willed from the wanted, we retrieve ourselves.

Over ages and ages we can climb above choosing,
becoming pure consciousness, but only by deserting
the forces holding bodies and identities in form,
the binding gum of all illusions: desire and belief.
How much of each of us do these determine! How little
of what God is endlessly revealing finds pure witness.

Shock

One can't just dismiss some shocks' heart-clutching anxiety
as once indoors one slips out of a jacket. Or can one?
How much time is wasted wanting rescue before the best
of one's inner servants steps forward and agrees to die,
and, by God, does so, putting mortality in its place?
Let the trembling stop and the raw buzz of overcharged nerves
be the fact of the Present that confronts and clothes the soul.

The Habit

Personalizing God is a habit, a behavior
shaped by desire and inattention. We only want God
to have a human form because it's easier that way.
Let God the loving, comforting parent come to find us.
Far more difficult – terrifying in fact – is going
to God: our understanding of necessity must change,
and everything held by gravity abandoned. What's left?
Human form is a coat of being we don't want removed,
and thus we come blindly swimming back for another birth.
Habitual humanity wants God all for itself.

Home

Six rooms on the ground, four above, with a rooftop garden
open to the stars. Such is this, your home, your capitol
in the city of transformation. Keep it in good grace.

A home endures the bruises, the rude smells, the hurryings
of human use. Keep it that it may be shared with strangers
worthy but unknowing, ones who in darkness seek the light.

A home organizes the land, makes the geometry
that shapes and refines the mind. Without a home, thoughts struggle
in noise and chaos. The tool of reason lies abandoned.

A home gives children a floor for building understanding,
for what is understanding but the world's reconstruction,
a version built of value? In your home, value God's love.

For God's love is the masonry of home. You build with it
and grow in grace. You participate in God. God reveals
you in your work, and you know yourself in the unity.

Absolute

Because there is no separation from the Absolute,
the mind cannot conceive it. Our language, though official
in its tone, is vague and fanciful in its dishonest
attempt to reference the unified, endless Lord God.
Language can't work on something with no end or beginning,
no division, no resemblance, no grip for comparing.

The word Absolute is really a cry of submission.
Having come to the end of embodied experience,
matter, energy, calculable possibility
and direction, we confront Nothing – the word we employ
to indicate no thing, no product of senses or mind.
Capitalizing it somehow makes it feel almost real.

So let us just stay here with God. And what is God? A word?
Yes, a word for the next dimension, the one beyond time,
space, bodies, names – all bricks and mortar of identity.
But the word – God – designates an experience, something
in which an element of our being participates.
Call it Presence, the Field of Love – it is not beyond us.

We have only to recast identity, to be soul
in body rather than body hoping to have a soul.
It is a long work – practicing the Present more and more.
Permanent residence in eternity may exhaust
many bodies, but reaching here, we'll note God has moved on
up dimension. Thus the Absolute return continues.

Female and Male

All humans begin feminine, accepting a new life,
a new body's sudden capture of the soul hypnotized
out of the ether again. For a while rioting growth
banishes all memory of suffering and of God:
the euphoria of matter. Only when it all slows
does the intimation of eternity start to itch.

The hormones of speculative action begin to boil:
the male principle distinguishes itself, transforming
acceptance to assertion, tolerance to ideas
of victory and heaven. Thus we're all male and female,
souls in a soup of hormones. Men are women, women men.
Remembering God saves us from this bi-polar frenzy.

Onward

If there were an easier path to our destination,
we would be deeply troubled, and the worth of the cosmos
called to question. For having learned the truth about ourselves,
our valuing of awakening sinks its stubborn roots
in the hard-rock unlikeliness of success. It's only
barely plausible, and impossible without the help
of a higher order who write all or nothing contracts.

Luckily, there's nothing else worth doing, and by wanting
only awakening, we purify desire itself.
At every milestone on the rugged climb, we find a sign
saying, "No, not yet, but keep going." No sweeter message,
no more welcome meaning can be offered to souls. We read
and rejoice, comprehend the clearer vista and resume,
on beyond words, time, identity and all boundaries.

How Does It Work?

How does it work, this hologram in which we find ourselves?
For thousands of years, reasonable men have understood
that we're "in it but not of it." The thought is a cliché,
yet the lure of the world is so strong, our senses and brains
so wired to it (they themselves belong to it), we seek God
as if calling for the jailer playing cards down the hall.

What if man's mind is not the prisoner but the prison?
What if God is the one locked inside, waiting patiently
for mind to have its fill of the game and identity,
to unclench its grip on the controller it imagines?
Could the whole display of data and memory go dark,
leaving us aware of God gameless in eternity?

Go Straight to God

When the unrelenting rains push so deeply into spring
that the few clear days are suspect and shallowly enjoyed,
one can observe one's helplessness before nature and see
the lie of distinction that anchors personality.
We are all one in the rain, any specialness washed out
in the wet. Our colors blend together. Our proud thoughts drown.

What to do when there is no solid footing anywhere,
and visibility by the eye and by the mind drops
to naught and calls one's groping hands into the heavy air?
Go straight to God. Our fighting for identity on Earth
is mocked by mud then swallowed up in time. Go straight to God.
Find God's Presence within. Be. Let the flood efface all else.

One's Own Image

It is crushing to discover the extent of darkness
in one's fondest projects. The noblest change one would impose
upon the world, the most rational ambition, which seems
so generous and clean, has its roots in narcissism
that the lower self manipulates. To enhance the light,
one must act from light. First seek the state, the perfect Present:
thence the understanding of what one can and cannot do.

When in Milton's epic, Eve dotes in vain fascination
on her own image in the pool, we see the opening
through which Satan will slither and how he will violate
the chastity of heart on which depends one's timeless time
in the garden. From the shadowed soil of our weakness grows
alluring fruit that we imagine nourishes the world.
We mistake what we make in our heads to be Creation.

Be still. Observe what God has made; what rests here in clear sight
astonishes the mind and overbrims the grateful heart.
The aim is not to change it but to share it, to remind
those who have forgotten it of the wonder of the truth.
Therein is the challenge to the talent, the skill, the art
you've been given. From Presence alone your breath has meaning.
In light of Presence, you are free to be invisible.

Knowledge

Since Eve's apple, proud mankind has been seduced by knowledge,
but only in our age, in which everything is rendered
down to slurried information – the raw sludge of knowledge –
do we confront the snake's intention: the soul's starvation.

Our reptile parts have all the knowledge needed to survive.
To that we add the productions of the heart, the beauty
reminding us Earth is not Heaven nor was meant to be,
no matter what is made of it by big brained vanity.

Knowledge helps man move the dirt to a plate, but dirt it is.
The soul needs other, finer food, self-aware sustenance
found only in the Eden of remembering oneself,
thence to extend the knowing of God to this coarse matter.

Big Brains

Without the head in the way, the ears would come together
to form a heart. I'm not saying man doesn't need a head;
I'm just noting the strange prejudice of giving big brains
such a favored place in our self-concept. The real wonders
which define our kind have their roots in love and compassion.
The head reconstructs time and space so we can move further
and faster, but the heart knows that at best we're all just here.

As an evolutionary advantage, the jury's
still out on large heads: environmental degradation,
nuclear weapons and invulnerable viruses
are just a few examples of the taxes God has placed
on brains. The only tax on love is the ultimate shift
of one's identity to the deathless realm love creates.
Love doesn't need further faster, just more now and more here.

For Battle

When the marauders come and threaten your sanctuary,
let your lines stand firm behind the leaders you have chosen.
Do not be naïve: a way of life kindling the Presence
of God will need defending. Here death is not to be feared.
The harder task is not to hate the ones assaulting you,
the ones you may strike in self-defense. In battle, the real
distinction among men is in their awareness of God.

The Angels know your distaste for violence, just as theirs,
but Earth is not Heaven nor was meant to be. Hold your ground
as best you can; if you must retreat, be deliberate
and move without forgetting; and if victory is yours,
know that it is a moment in an era, a brief note
in the song of your growing soul's crown. Bury all the dead
with equal honor. Yours is the loss, not theirs. Angels watch.

Make peace to the degree the opposers want what you want,
a way of life remembering God. And if disaster
befalls you, if you are conquered by a greater army,
sustain your sacred connection. Whatever slavery
is imposed, for a season or an age, the oppressors
should see your wisdom, your patience, your restraint. Your return
to God is not blocked, even when breaking rocks in bondage.

The Cliff

What you don't forgive will keep you out of Heaven, clutching
time, life after life, manufacturing evil justice.
To transform suffering, you must think backwards about it:
no person hurt you, God did, to bring you up out of hell –
from unawareness of unawareness back to zero.
Your humiliation is the cost of being chosen,
of giving up a personal ticket to extinction.
It is not personhood you want after all – name, rights, rank –
all the petty consolations of being trapped in time.
What personhood can possess of eternity means less
that nothing, and God wants so much more of you, tenderly
atop the cliff of forgiveness, one step from infinite
readiness; from clear, unbounded spirit; from pure being.
Only the suffering you must disown could bring you here.

The Will and the World

Flickers of fire, alternating light and dark, remind us
we are alive, that there is a destination – a Source
to which we are returning; and a cost, a mineral
debasement of sacred love. Choose, choose, in this second, choose.

The world does not change. Each human victory ennobling
the planet's face will be erased, extinguished in darkness,
yet a trace of working will remains, energy too fine
to be dispersed in the stirring dust. In this second, choose.

The old pleasures taken from your hands, stolen from your heart
have left their absence, their silence, in which to know yourself.
This is the transformation to the namelessness within,
to unflickering being. Choose, choose, in this second, choose.

Miracles

The lower functions' determination of advantage
shapes and polishes personality, feeds it, grooms it,
till even prayer cannot escape its gravity. Too fat.
If you're fortunate, your prayers will disgust you and you'll stop.
Put away your petitions. Silently let God be God.

To awaken means to be able to observe the world –
all of it – as a manifestation of God acting
without your consultation but with your full acceptance.
Most often, we must be shocked into this miracle state.
From it we see all things are already accounted for.

If you've employed and fully trained a steward in your house,
let him do the praying. He knows the right things to pray for
and doesn't embellish. He'll bring the household's attention
to the brink of the miracle state then retire to watch –
mute and cross-eyed from his small room – the arrival of God.

Then you won't need your obesity anymore, your wit,
the commendation you groveled for, or your skill at cards.
God's taken care of it all, and after the sweet visit,
you may note an essence, a perfume, a capacity
of discernment to navigate the path of miracles.

You, Not the Circumstance

Transformation begins in standing still, gathering will
to accept the hard condition of the moment: no tears,
no ploys, no bluster, no bargaining, no adrenal flight.
Here in the merciless Present is a furnace of love
and terror that you must occupy, trusting the results
of its burning. You, not the circumstance, will be transformed.
Instantly and ever you become an altered being:
the leaking stopped, the pretending seared away. A plasma
from a higher world has begun its accumulation
in the Angel form you will understand as your calling.

The Simplest Thing

God is fundamental being. When awareness resides
in God, one is the soul, the element of God in man.
From within a human form, attaining and sustaining
this condition requires constant conscious effort – to be
without being something: the still state of self-awareness
holding above the lower worlds hungry to displace it.
In return to the Source, the soul deepens and develops,
unveiling the awareness of God as its true being.

God's being is a simplicity prior to the claims
of quality and number: Self before self-description.
Whatever order can tempt it must be lower than God:
such are all things, all thoughts about things, all understanding,
all aims and accomplishments, all projections into time.
And as the soul participates in God's simplicity,
nothing that happens to humans justly displaces it,
and nothing streaking away from the Source can satisfy.

Beyond the Clutch

No lasting relief from the pains of flesh but leaving it,
and even then the scars and opacities on the soul
are subject to gravity, and soon down again we come
for another embodiment, another episode.

That the dirt we walk on, the fog distorting our vision
can be perfected, made spirit and light, is man's greatest
stubborn stiff-necked lie, earthly identification's root.
It is in not being this world that a soul can be free.

Relieving suffering is not an end but a brief truce
with the world, an interval trusting self-remembering.
To love another truly is to understand beyond
the clutch of bodies, to be God's encompassing welcome.

God and the Mind

The mind is too small and slow to model cause and effect –
the omnidirectional, vast and ungraspably fast
movement of things in time. To know the truth, one must be God.

The mind is too urgent and grand to stop and rest in love,
the simplest understanding of fundamental being,
changeless and eternal. To be the truth, God must be one.

Can the puny mind escape from the prison of itself?
To know the truth, to be the truth, one must not be the mind.
If a perch exists without, what can sit on it to watch?

Here is the impasse, the face-to-face between mind and God.
One of the two must dissolve, admit it is illusion.
The Lord our God is one. Unmask the lie of otherness.

The Body

Do not lose sight of the fact that a body is a gift
for the growth of the soul. Its health and normal functioning
allow a scope of earthly experience that the soul
can separate itself from to deepen self-awareness.
Only the soul knows the Present, but the body offers
the "everything else" from which the bright soul redeems itself.

The body also gives Angels an instrument to play.
By heightening or diminishing body responses –
pain, pleasure, rapture, depression, urgency, confusion,
need, doubt, gratitude – Angels make a music from our time
and bring our hearts to the border of beauty and our minds
to wonder, so the soul must only step out to itself.

Whatever the body registers upon each instant
can be seen to be not you but a marvelous product
of systems replicating and condensing the rhythms
and movements and pressures and shadings of Earth's abundance.
For the forming soul, access to Earth is a miracle:
the higher deepens its being investing the lower.

Under the laws of living Earth, the body was ages
in fashioning – an upright form of parts harmonious,
flexible to Higher Will, whose purpose is to return
to an eternal home the great speeding diaspora
of Creation, completing the Absolute's self-knowledge.
Do not denigrate this device, you who are far, far more.

For Everyone

What is suffering but an overabundance of love,
its current blocked by the body's gates – the unmoving chest,
the throat strangled by language, the eyes glazed against the now?

Earthly identity is the distortion of the soul
done by the damming of love. Whatever follows "I am"
is a lie, a vanity, a pillar of salt bent back.

Are you lonely? You are not alone. Your love is the same
as all love. Free it and the fear of death dissolves in air.
Do you demand perfection? Your memory of Heaven

makes you proud, resentful of exile in this dirty place.
You call the shame of your desire independence and turn
in fury to make a statue self separate from God.

When we have forsaken all claims to being anything,
the body surrenders; love resumes its flow out of time –
river of everything, awareness of God its current.

The Song

Before reading further in this poem, stop: turn down all
competing noise both in and out, hold the mind's intention
still and firm, free a gladdening heart to trust the rhythm
of gratitude, and know that Angels share this solemn state.

Now, where is your attention? When you have it lovingly
held in your awareness, you are ready to breathe poems,
not just read them, and the music of being will attend
your harmony, and the song you will become will not end.

The More....

Will to listen and music will unword you from your thought,
and from ear to heart directly do its tendering work.
Sound need not be word, nor intelligence be mind. Let be
an open, liquid throat between the hearing heart and God.

But do not close your eyes, not let them glaze in rigid stare.
Let them see what light is there before them; let their movements
be as breeze. And associating mind leave on its knees
in the corner, unneeding you. Now let your vessel fill.

Your life is attention. The more you are aware of it,
the more of life you have, the more of music and of light;
the more of these, the more of love, and thus the more of God,
till overbrimmed, you spill out into all and everything.

Both

If a poem is aimed at the heart, the child's simple heart,
it is enough that it disrobes itself of cleverness
and angry menace, and without the lie of hope blesses
the world with a learning love: let life be clear as water.

But if a poem aims higher, it must do more than bless.
It must flicker in and out of time and sense, confounding
the mind with durable wonder: intrusive mystery
making a faithul man doubt what he knows and thinks he is.

Can one poem aim both ways, a double-headed arrow?
Can one array of language trip the mind and reassure
the heart? Yes, but only if the poet dies smilingly
between the Angel reaching down and the child looking up.

The Story

Most of our struggle and pain comes from the ongoing work
of making the facts fit a suitable story. Our lives
and the "I" starring in them are, after all, narratives,
and as such must meet civilized standards of coherence,
verisimilitude – which thanks to God is not the truth –
and excitement to amuse the imagined audience.

It's a burden. Facts can be like random rocks in the loom,
but the story weavers have their own tricks too: hope, promise
of future resolution, good karma sprung from the past,
accounts of Heaven's blessings too beautiful to deny.
Thus we pass our allotted time self-pleased. Even the fact
of death gets used, so the story can go on without us.

Precisely

Are you satisfied with beauty spilling over the brim
of your heart's chalice? Is your mind stilled by the wine's perfume?
Is your desire quenched by the full gaze of the Eye of God?

Or is love enough to keep your beating heart's devotion
and polish all the jeweled facets of divinity?
Is love's eternity the final blessing of your soul?

What is there beyond love and beauty? What can comprehend
a force, a speed, a will objectively unlimited?
It is a terror to the heart and mind. Precisely so.

5. Nature's Geometry

Self-Expression

Is your tongue tired from talking? Do your lips ache from the work
of forming the faces. The part of you that knows you aren't
helping anybody sits observing on the back bench
while you collect the piles of shells and throw away the nuts.
Self-expression is a bankrupt business. Stop talking.
Stop wasting your animation. This moment is a feast
for you and God. Fill your mouth with the fruit being given.

Love people in silence. Do not demand their attention.
You waste your own seeking theirs. Better the Presence of God.
All you have to do to have it is know that you have it.
But the knowing must be constantly renewed, remembered,
and the remembering must be established on the breath
and put before everything else you do. Thus the silence,
the observing: it is your hospitality to God.

Would you be the discarded shells of the pistachios
the world is mindlessly eating? Would you be the leader
who forces his money on the poor who can't repay it?
When you are with God, attentive to the moment forming
before you, you will see what can be done and what cannot.
You will not waste yourself; you'll have learned that to offer gifts
of true worth to the world, you must first return to Heaven.

If We Weren't

When one suspects that life on Earth is too repetitive
and patterned to be real – not a hoax, more a hologram –
then one has arrived at a small separation from it,
and one can no longer act as an entertained player
in the Angels' elaborate sensory game. What now?

One could be like Moses and try to lead people away
from the established order, out through the whole one has made.
Or like Jesus teaching compassion for all who know not
what they do. Or like Muhammad warning that Allah is
not what one thinks, so one had better die before one dies.

But these and every true prophet's alternative vision
amount to the same thing, minus the cultural settings.
So if prophetic instruction is just another loop
in the game, why not just jump over it – the decalogues,
bodhisattva pledges, all the ways – and go straight to God?

What is it all but God anyway? Participation
in God, being God, is all there really is. Believing
in the borders and boundaries of otherness turns us
away from God's unity and makes a game of being.
If we weren't enthralled by bodies, God would be perfect sense.

Bear It

How does one not hate how human beings treat their own kind?
How does one not get sucked into the rage and viciousness?
Who can look and hear and read and think and not be poisoned
by complicity one moment, disgust and shame the next?
The fits of human madness the soul must forgive and leave
screaming to exhaustion in the desert of their power
are the torture boards of Angel love. Bear it out, O soul.

Using Miracles

All Scriptures' miracle stories lead to one conclusion:
the world out there we regard as fixed and real is not so.
In fact, we occupy a hologram of all senses
and to make things worse, our brains are ever reconstructing
our reality from the lies our senses are sending.
To awaken – if only for a moment – means to move
one's identity to a higher, more permanent plane
from which one sees the errors of the senses and the mind.
What you are not is the teaching all miracles reveal.

What we call a man exists on many levels at once.
The lowest levels, which none but the most perverse would choose,
have a mineral prisonment to them, while the highest
are boundlessly free from the noose of time and circling thought.
Here in the fleshy middle, we have an ultimate choice:
sinking or rising. The former embodies by default
as time gets thicker, less penetrable, more unquestioned.
The latter comes from collecting the tiniest flashes
of true sight from which conscious will weaves a garment of light.

The Devil in Church

In a great cathedral of polished marble, swathed in light,
with vaulted ceilings making Heaven comprehensible,
what space is designated for the devil? In the back,
a dark closet of confession -- of whispered, kneeling shame –
only there may he be, quarantined until broken down.
He is the dust and dung dissolved in penitential bath,
acknowledged only so he can be publicly expunged.

But that which we repress, we fortify in cleverness
and guile; expression denied, insinuation mastered.
See the worshipper, eyes to the gilding, ears to the choir,
his prayers are hollowed by attention to a stifled fart.
We are what we are, and denial is not discipline:
do not make a devil of the donkey. The same Angels
we invoke in sequenced chant and sacrifice made our flesh.

Our poor church hosts celebrations of Presence and of love,
but love is learned in forgiveness. What is not forgiven
poisons Heaven. It kneels in the back corner of the mind,
a noxious intelligence pretending humility.
Bring it out, thank it for the ride to church, sooth its soreness,
and if it brays against the choir, do not call it devil,
but forgive it. Thus your best prayer, most like the Angels' own.

Submit

Submit: not to a man, not to a thought but to Presence.
No halting the breath. The Eye sings in full-throated silence.
Let the Crown be an aperture to God, a connection
to the universal current. Let your thoughts, your feelings,
your urges disperse like vapor rising from smooth water.
The crystal light is sufficient for you. There is nothing
to protect, to secure, to hold back. Submit to Presence.

Who keeps the key of your knowledge? Your lower self regards
the sacred knowledge as its own, its hidden hoard holding
death at bay. Nonsense. The knowledge is not to protect you
from death; it is to help you die. You have been given it
to charm your return, and there is no return without death.
Submit. Nothing real will be lost. Desiring things in time
wastes time. Time is to perfect your readiness to submit.

When the beast of burden is content in its resting place,
when the heart that rides it sits aware of its tired passions,
when the mind knows the folly of words and image making,
then readiness emerges, energized by openness
to all that is. The universe becomes the active force,
and the constituents of individuality
dissolve in the will to submit. You are that will. Submit.

Out or In?

You want to be free, but you can't seem to turn and depart.
It's a great irony: you house yourself in a shanty
of bitter heartedness because you can't forgive the world
for going on without you. You won't leave the world for God,
and you won't bring God to the world. You're stuck in your own slum.
Fear and vanity are pulling you like a sad wishbone.

First, you're afraid to give up everything and die to God.
The false premise is that your everything is anything.
All you're scared of losing – your whole worldly identity –
is a lie, a fabrication built by a needy child
who has become a needier adult. What's real in you?
What you have is nothing to lose. What you are is deathless.

But if you cannot leave the world, why not bring God to it?
Bring the Presence and peace of God to each moment you live.
Yes, at times you'll look stupid; to many, you'll be a joke,
and your worth in the world may plummet. Your efficiency
will crack, you'll have to polish your own shoes, cook your own meals,
learn all the riggings of meaninglessness. Can you bear it?

Neither/Nor

Sentimentality is a great temptation for us.
We are flies to its honey; its sticky oversweetness
is a cheap, starving pleasure, a ritual condiment,
not a meal. Beyond a few notes of the old birthday song,
beyond a smiley salutation or a get well card,
one best not indulge in easy feeling. Love is not love
when it descends too far from its rarified self-knowing.

Nor is solemnity the bright soul's better nourishment.
Establishing in measured steps a serious purpose
is worthy work, as is reverence to higher beings
and respect to trusted friends who have passed on, but to staunch
the delight of a butterfly's entrance into the world
before our eyes is not virtue. An infant's cry is not
interruption. Birdsongs and mirth must season the sermon.

The now is never a habit or prescription. It comes
on bees' wings, in thunder, in the soft sun's rosy farewell,
in the dung beetle's shameless labor, in a smelly kiss
or the glare of a headlight. It denies formulation
and patiently endures this attempt to write about it.
So here we are, friends neither solemn nor sentimental
adjusting flight to the air moving in and out of us.

The Difference

The instinctive element's version of eternity
is the getting or not getting of what it wants, always
and forever: getting is Heaven, not getting is hell.
Nowhere in the imaginary picture is the death
of the desiring thing – mortality's cancellation
of the supposedly infinite list of what's wanted.
From the balcony, surveying whatever can be seen,
God's Eye confers beauty with a gaze of satisfaction
and instructs itself and friends in the eternal Present.

Again Reminding

We're taught to think of dark ages as passive collapses
where the burden of things unrepaired breaks the brittle will
of civilization. But there's another force at work,
an active adrenal drive, a blind rush to the cliff's edge
past a gauntlet of gold-toothed vendors. The great disaster
up ahead gets pushed to the back of the brain by the need
to shop for a car, college for the children or a mate.

In the age that we've just entered, our species will be thinned,
grindingly or cataclysmically – we don't know which.
If you survive, your outward work in the fumbling darkness
is to make a little light so the young can learn to read,
to revive the dead ground, to help the water clean itself.
Your inward work remains the same as it has always been:
to remember God with each breath; to know and be the soul.

Poverty

Poverty is not the problem. A glut of goods corrodes
the heart worse than a lack of them. Where will we put all this?
Storage for the excess has become a boom industry.

In the choked river of products – coffee mugs, cameras,
assault rifles, stealth bombers, diplomas, building permits,
plastic bags, human organs – can you find your buried soul?

Can you revive it, resuscitate its lost attention,
breathe for it until it remembers itself and returns
to eternity? If in the end it must discard you,

dead in the garbage, dead on a planet turned inside out,
yet you can be the hero for the soul, the reminder,
the reawakener of this visitor from no place.

How many orbits naked under the merciless sun
will it take to burn away and clean what man has piled up?
How great is the poverty man must relearn to survive!

Nothing Need

Today one can't simply go find a cave in the desert.
Somehow the path of renunciation must be followed
in frequent gatherings: parties, soirees, concerts, banquets.
O for something silent and unflavored, a secret sip
of invisible water as the echoing toasting
congratulates itself in opulent salons. Nothing –
one reminds oneself – not luxury nor one's own disdain
needs to stand between one's young soul and the divine Present.

Jealous Gods

Old or young, our deities suspect us. The younger ones
have to assert their glory against the competition,
carve out a fearsome sanctum in hearts and minds and erect
a triumph of worship and territory and power.
They are fired and bloodied by a new realization:
that they get only what they take and are firm to kill for.

But an established old holy whose share of human scars
has been lacquered with layers of culture over ages
now betrays a querulous jealousy of Earth itself,
of the larger laws of time and the dead inattention
of all living things. The old ones buffer their death in life
with petulance and uninterruptable pronouncements.

A man is right to fear these fellows as a man is right
to fear mankind – our dreams abiding in collective sleep.
The gods we make and keep resent each other and the laws
that wear out time, and they won't share a single one of us.
They own our brainstems and would have our hearts and all our words.
Pay them in their coin. Stay aware in your secret nothing.

Pyramid

The great destruction of Earthlife's pyramid has begun.
Midlevel species have eroded – some gone entirely –
and the base is sinking and threatened. Up on the capstone,
we humans hear rumbling and feel intermittent shaking,
but note nothing violent enough to disturb commerce
or alter meal planning. We take heart that the pyramid's
just a metaphor and forget the real one is a tomb.

The Brain's Closed Circle

The top of my head is now open for your business:
Say anything at all and I will see its connection
to God. Everything is a manifestation of God,
the One refracted through infinite possibility.

Yes, it's a big idea, but if you leave it that way –
as an idea – you'll miss the point and remain walled up
in the fake identity that began to develop
before your functions could support the soul's recollection.

In short, you will remain the fad, not the fundamental;
the time-bound, not the eternal; the lie of "I", not love.
Worse, you'll feel fortified in your time-tested, prudent choice.
In truth, God is the only choice. All else is slavery.

Turning to God – away from matter and mind to the One
all Present and closer than thought or sensory scanning –
dissolves all borders, distinctions and judgments and opens
the brain's closed circle out to the limitless unity.

Sharing God

Call it dissolute or prudent, self-destructive or smart,
however you characterize the habitual life
you've made doesn't matter. That way of living won't get you
to Heaven. When it dies – alone in sleep or in a blaze
of public display – the soul will profit nothing from it.
Neither rectitude nor passion can develop the soul:
our actions only move the chess pieces to new array.
Being grows being, by attention deeds can only frame,
in the self-remembering Present, sharing God with God.

When One Begins

Maturing in pain, fear and greed and the base instinctive
need of felt advantage, the nervous system takes a shape
that projects as personality, and information
in and out is limited to that which serves the version
of the world we've made from our experience. Hardened forms –
neuroinhibitors and emotional dilators
in place and functioning by habit – we're not really here.

At this point, too much truth will melt the brain, and tissued lies
on lies sustain identity. The soul can petrify,
and once encased in flesh gone comatose and turned to stone,
retrieval is excruciating, the extremity
of suffering for man to bear or Angels to impose.
O do not slight the solvent power Presence offers life.
Each moment is salvation from the hardening of time.

When one begins to live a life more Present – more frequent
stoppages of thought and time, held longer and more deeply
cherished – the soul advances in accelerated growth.
Earth's close attendant beauties are veiled no more – look at this –
and the eternal treasure God has offered man hovers
plausibly in the nearer distance, then nests in the heart
and tunes the mind with song, and finally welcomes God's Eye.

Why Keep a Dog?

Most of the dog bites I've received have come from my own dogs:
Something in my noisy playing menaced and frightened them
and they bit, but in each case their return to a posture
of troubled submission was immediate, as if shocked
at what had happened. I could not blame them as I had seen
the same behavior in the damage and the fear of loss
that pock my past and scar the Angel hands that nurture me.
Why keep a dog? Because companion creatures can enhance
the heart's connection to the living spirit in all life
and tune a human sympathy for all the suffering
life – including God – endures. And thus do Angels love us,
remembering they too were human hand-to-mouth creatures.

Restraint

Restraint appears as caution, as control of the passions,
and so it is, but it is engendered and made mature
by a commitment to observation. Against the rash
urge to act, one must fund with the full force of one's being
the requirement of seeing and listening and feeling
till intelligence enters and takes control of the stage.

One doesn't learn how to wait by waiting but by watching,
by listening to the shriek of things about to collide.
One must drain an experience of all its impressions,
all feelings to the brink of doom. This is true suffering.
Will you be saved when the master rises to claim the Crown?
It doesn't matter as you've played your part. You've been transformed.

Knowledge and Understanding

For human beings, knowledge is a needed illusion,
a virtual rendition of the truth. We do not know
any more than a computer knows its running program,
but the feeling of knowing gives us permission to act,
to function, to proceed as if we've made a decision.

Understanding is more real than knowledge. Though subjective,
it yet partakes in the soul's separation from this world.
To understand means to see how something fits in the brain's
operation, and seeing is closer to the soul's work.
True seeing is apart, immediate and eternal.

Born into this hologram, we navigate by knowledge,
but we advance our return to original freedom –
the awareness which is true being – by understanding.
Don't die in the game, striving for knowledge to keep playing.
Watch the player die as you understand what you are not.

Endangered

Do not fear apocalypse. Fear friendlessness and make friends.
Fear disgust and protect beauty. Fear unneeded killing
and forsake its products. Fear no longer valuing grace.
Fear the sale of God's Presence for a satisfying dream.
The world speeds toward a barrier all of us are fearing
but cannot behold and will only know in collision.
Is it the border of Earth's inhabitability,
the cliff of meaning, or human vanity's melting point?
Already free of endangered dimensions, love abides.

Meaning

Did you find it in a book? Did you find it at the feet
of some teacher or in a grotto known for miracles?
Did you find it on a battlefield, alone surviving
among fallen friends? Did you find it in a lover's moan
as power and pleasure came together in your honor?
Did you find it in fasting or praying or artfully
evading the government's reach? Did you find it watching
your son master a skill with talent you'd passed on to him?
And does having found it give you peace or satisfaction,
purpose to life? O friend, awake from your dream of meaning!

The satisfactions permitted on Earth keep us on Earth.
We are given just enough praise, just enough victories,
just enough near solutions to the mystery of breath
to keep us unfinished and umbilically attached
to the fleshy casing of life we believe life to be.
Can you conceive of life that does not dote on personhood,
that does not disconnect from the whole and encapsulate
in time to spend itself chasing a reason for being?
Pursuing meaning is the consolation of the damned.
O friend, Presence does not ask or need to know a meaning.

Be Quiet

Even a crystallized soul that does not assert its peace
into this moment of time fades before the brazen noise
and chaos of the body's identity. Consciousness
must be remembered here in this syllable and this one,
or the portal of its intervention all but closes.
The death before one's death – the soul's merciful permanence –
comes only after uncountable silencings of thought,
of wishes and hopes, of urgent, petulant self-pity.
Please be quiet. Let the soul infuse you with its perfect
attention. Become the audience to your audience.
At first they will call you back, but then they'll cease to miss you,
and beyond shivering fear is unoccluded vision.

Ritual

In ritual is the opportunity to invest
God's Presence in habitual actions that by themselves
would move in long forgotten purpose or false reverence.
From brushing teeth to pledging allegiance, we have all stored
large files of memorized behaviors that appear on cue
and need negligible consciousness to complete their course.
How crippled is our time without resort to these crutches.

But as they require such small measure of attention's light,
we are free as they occur to observe them and study
their choreography, poetry, and derivations,
deduce their evolutions and admire their usefulness.
In this process, judgment shrinks, appreciation burgeons,
and we begin to infuse these motions of bodies, hands,
lips and minds with the gentle sincerity of God's Eye.

Sanctuary

Earth is in no danger, but we humans certainly are.
There are simply too many of us making too much noise,
garbage, heat; too much chronic ignorance of the acid
burning the foot of the ladder on which we're tottering;
too many mouths eating and spitting the febrile products
spun from too many minds; too many choices and no will.
Earth will do what is required to restore itself from us.

Our species has always had a poor grip on its purpose.
We're supposed to be managing cosmic influences,
providing the intellectual element for life
on this planet, but we have fallen in love with our throne
and have neglected our stewardship. Thinking ourselves free –
a nauseating irony – we pursue what we want.
Earth can be trusted to fill the holes our desires have dug.

A few, a happy few, have sought and received instruction
from Angels to speed the growth of our souls and build our wills
for transcendence. How is our secret purpose different?
Ours is to cherish the Presence of God in each moment
and share that Presence with lovers who would shoulder this work:
thus a sanctuary of transformation is rising,
yet stays secret behind its quiet, undesired duty.

Can you find us? If you would search, what are you searching for?
No criterion of power or achievement informed
by your upbringing will focus your eyes to discern us.
Marry your prayer to the Angels with your truest effort
to remember yourself always and everywhere. Presence
is your only guide, and the invisible path crosses
huge proud kingdoms of illusion. Earth will not obstruct you.

Small

There is a peace in little tasks, a reassuring scale
in the cleaning of a room, the weeding of a garden.
Doing what we know we can when we can secures the sense
of being worthy servants prepared for prosperity.

It is the same in our relations with eternity.
The prayer that opens Heaven and drops a ladder to Earth
for us to climb, requires no special talent from our lips –
only our resolution to join God in proffered peace.

Something in us thinks transcendence must be grand, dramatic,
bought by taming an earthquake or discovered in the dust
of post-apocalypse. No. All we can bear of glory
sits on the tips of our noses awaiting attention.

What in us favors the distortion into grander feats
than we can dare – figments guaranteed to keep us wishing?
Our real work is small; we have the time, the knowledge, the skill.
Let us be reassured in our little rooms: God abides.

Now Playing

How many little Angel tests have you flunked since breakfast?
How many opportunities look back broken hearted
as time speeds them off. I will buy your guilt – that last refuge
of self-importance – and sell it as church decoration.
The forgiveness of sins means the resumption of Presence ,
the instantaneous departure from the hologram
of bedeviled identity now playing on your stage.

Opportunity

How to recognize an opportunity? Don't believe
your thoughts about it or how it seems to extrapolate
profitably through time. Don't trust its past – its pedigree,
references or reputation. There's just one true test:
how it responds to the unvoiced command, "Now". Is your state
transported, freed and dried off from the loud river of mind?
Is the Present you have entered a wordless clarity?
Now knowing now, hold it. Don't regress into mere knowledge.

The Book of Love

I. Poems of Love and Friendship

All of Us

The wings of Angels moving in the ether make a sound
one's higher faculties detect, but only if one is
withdrawn from all the noise of the world and one's buzzing mind.

With a deft movement too fast to imagine, they can slip
the knot joining soul and body and lift one at the neck
like a pup for a light speed ride beyond clear recording.

Yet such wonders as these are not the greatest miracles
we're privy to. The simple Present, mysteriously
held by our submission to it, participates in God

beyond all Angel antics. Dissolving identity
to find the Self reduces the cosmos to a closet
and the location of one's flesh to blank coordinates.

Do not worry who you are or what, but be without name.
O can you see that all is God, including all of us,
welcome in eternal love even as we trudge through time?

One and All

When your heartbeat sounds the rhythm of willing surrender
to simple being, then you can become God's cleansing cloth,
absorbing the bitterness around you, lifting the pain,
at last holding over the fire of conscious allowing
the poor partial vision humans possess. You cannot do
more than that. You cannot see for others the beauty here
before them. You cannot chase them into the Field of Love.

Though in the end we're all one, returned to the single Source
of being, we remain until then separate, distinct,
alive in the choice to help each other. From what one learns,
all may advance; from what weight one lifts, all may feel relief;
from what one sacrifices, all are unfettered. When each
enters the Present remembering God, eternity
echoes for all; light from one Eye brightens all attention.

See your brother, his throat clenched in inner talk: greet his eyes
with gladness as if he held the key to Heaven. He does.
See your worried sister not knowing what to do, awkward
in gaze and breath: beseech her to teach you to dance. She can.
See the moment's friend, standing in love's radiant circle:
approach this unfolding soul, unveil your fear of being,
surrender it, become the stair for another's ascent.

Digging

The human part of love is grimy, a dung fire burning
in the greasy air to light the darkness, yet our groping
after love here offers a meek promise of purity,
a will above and beyond that tames the heart to patience.
Love awakens to find itself buried deep in the dust
and swallowing the insult starts a slow sustained clawing,
a digging back to the sky. One love to all love returns.

Love and Language

When I tell you, "I love you," I promote an illusion
of love as an emotional action with an agent
and a recipient. The phrase begs an intimacy
dear to dying things because it somehow evokes a sense
of the undying, a place or territory we know
exists but can only see feelingly. Identified
with death, we close our eyes and grope for what is always here.

Language feeds the lie. The truth of "I love you" is more this:
love is a field in the dimension of eternity,
and you and I are already there together as one,
free from the capsules of self, the borders of our bodies.
Consciously bringing identity to the Field of Love,
submitting beyond the mortal part, braving its darkness,
we escape words and the redundancy of "I love you."

Chosen One

When this poem is finished, when I have navigated
through the accents and syllabic architecture circling
the empty center, when I have climbed to the final stair
and stepped off into love, I will send it through the ages
to the one the Angels choose. You. You are the chosen one.

By a genomic conjuring strange and painful, Angels
made my brain for this task of poems that is completing
my soul, polishing it past all need to speak, that its light
may serve the Mind of God and illuminate a pathway.
And you are necessary to this work, you, chosen one.

What good is God without the universe? The single fount
of being – the Absolute's dimension – initiates
creation's moving trinity: will, action, perfect mind.
From the first immeasurably tiny note that time sang
down the cosmic scales, this poem's been for you, chosen one.

The vehicle bearing the forming soul you truly are
results from an ancient sequence, events and processes
begun at time's beginning and mounting to this moment –
this rhythmic call now in your ears. God has acknowledged you.
How will you hold the fact of God's awareness, chosen on

Next

Love is not man's highest destination, just the next one,
the one we must submit to and become to transcend Earth.
We use the word 'God' to mean the next level up the span
of our being, so for all practical work, God is love.
In our souls' ongoing ascent to God, love lies beyond
the veil of personhood, human identity. Let go
of your name; let the current climbing your spine find its way
unblocked and unmolested past the heart, home to the Eye.
You are not finished, but love can now bless this dear planet
and rejoice in a straight path. Your Presence is your meaning.

The Teacher's Love

The Teacher's love must be resolute enough to absorb
the student's sleep and not be diluted, patient enough
to be nourished by the smallest gains, and supple enough
to find a tone of calm to transform disordered moments.
As a tool of Heaven, the Teacher elevates to serve,
to transmit the higher will and promise which the student
barely sees, longs for and cannot hold. Behold the Teacher,
radiant, transparent proof whose love is the Angels' love.

The Teacher's love cannot be a duty or a contract:
it is given or withdrawn as Heaven prompts, not darkened
by desire, nor can it be repaid but by succeeding
to the realm beyond debt and bestowing, the Field of Love.
Teaching is the striving to sustain love among students.
When students have taken the Teacher's work upon themselves
and have become servants ever clearing the path for love,
the Teacher's task is done. The world bends to that completion.

Equals

Let's forgive each other in advance for the first few times
that we forget the meaning of this word friend. In friendship
there's nothing to defend or capture, challenge or defeat.
Meeting now, far from childhood though dubiously wiser,
it's likely that on occasion we'll lack the flexible
finesse to turn our stiff necks away from confrontation.
We both have powerful engines that get stuck in the one
gear that defines us: forward fast. A friendship will not last
without deference and the discernment that yours and mine
and right and wrong and all things twain are unified in God.

Friends

I don't know how to address you, but I trust that as God
infuses all, you too are God. Welcome my welcoming.
To drop personality, to be something light rising
from the shattered pieces of a role is a sweet, helpless
relief, better than the sudden flow of long withheld tears.
The truth of recollection can't be shamed. Can it be shared?

Can we go backward through the refraction that makes many
out of one? Can we be as we were before coming here
to this garden exile of Earth? I'll pack some small what-nots
in a bag with yours; as we climb we'll leave a trail of love –
your spells and stories, my poems and hats – traces to prompt
the one from the many who don't yet know what we all are.

Soul Friends

We must not believe these so believable fleshy beds –
our bodies – lest colluding with mortality we die.
Yes, we're stuck under the weight of the brain's credulity,
but our brave wills can still entreat that sacred attention
which our bodies ride but do not pilot. And here we are.

Men aren't, but the illusion that they are is most people's
lifetime work. The urge to individuate, to create
a separate identity is just a momentum,
a loud slogan echoing through a universe racing
ever outward, expanding to dead nothingness. Lights out.

There's a better nothingness available, the nothing
before all the somethings we can name and thus file away
in mind. Getting to the real nothing – for convenience
you may say God – requires cleansing the personal promptings
that occlude participation in God's perfect Present.

So, friend across time, our real work – the making of a soul –
is striving to be and not to be: not to be a name
mummified in common memory; and to be all here,
an anonymous, boundless partaker in perfect love.
The soul is the nothing not separate from being God.

Love and Children

The hardest thing is to let them explore. Their injuries
will form scars, and the scars become their secret vanities.
Later, if they ask for your instruction, your radiance
must be ready. Now you think you must be their protector,
but in truth you are their first destination of return.
Then and only then, as they limp over the hill and glimpse
the promise of home, can your welcome of love have meaning.

What will their absence teach you? Impotence, humility,
self-forgiveness. The strengthening of true conscience scrapes clean
the cave of your heart then decorates the walls with praising.
No longer is your gaze, which bounds up the hill to the sky,
driven by desire or hope but by readiness to give,
to pour itself into God. Then and only then appear
the still sweet bruised ones who now need you. Open your poor arms.

Only One's Death

Only one's death can heal the wounds in one's soul created
by one's children. This privilege of being another's
protection and model takes such deep root in living flesh
and holds so fiercely that the heart can be bent in its love
and the Eye's gaze darkened and distorted. Only one's death
loosens this grip and cauterizes this blood illusion.
Watch your love for these dear guests as you would watch your garden:
ever vigilant, often kneeling, aware beyond hope.

Welcome

Love is not made. It is revealed, always Present, waiting.
You have only to join it, to depart from all other
identities and locate yourself here in love's welcome.

Yes, there are preparations for the flight, divestitures
of all mental ownership of everything that keeps you
locked in the duties and titles you've struggled to accrue.
You must burn all grudges, forgive what anyone owes you.
You must release the secret fantasy of your future
and the merciless hope by which you've held it prisoner.
You must unbecome your name, forfeit to God your version
of what should be and renounce all your claims on the cosmos.

Without this weight, you will ascend. The fortifications
of personhood will shrink below, and a new awareness –
love, your home in eternity – will embrace your return.

Love's Observation

I met a woman on the road, a refugee afraid –
rightly so – to talk about what she was abandoning.
I gave her money for bread then questioned God in my head,
"O God, how many lives must she forsake before she sees
the blessing of her suffering?" Another voice in me
mocked this prayer: "Arrogant hypocrite! Deep in your comfort
and ease, your heart rots in self-indulgence. Your God is fat."
The soul observed it all in love uncorrupted by words.

Bottoming

We need help. We know too much. We have followed the wrong path,
the path of the unbearable truth about this species,
and now see humanity's coming murder-suicide.

We've been blindly marching to this end for ten thousand years,
kept in the dark by a growing cloud of knowledge, a mind
gone male, turning Earth's life-giving body to property.

Language and art, offered to us by Angels as best tools
for remembering the divine, now serve power and wealth,
preserving the distortions passively agreed upon.

Don't think about survival. If it comes, you won't want it,
and thinking just pulls you back to your table so belief
can imagine the menu according to its hunger.

If you hear impotent resentment in my rude words here,
discard them; instead remember the divine attention
you have here, now and always. How can you honor this love?

Can you step back from the buzzing confusion we have made?
Can your own love be ready without rancor for the death
we are imposing on ourselves? Love is better than hope.

For as long as breathing drags your battered heart toward morning
and the collapsing ruin of knowledge does not crush your mind,
help God whose suffering love must bear out this bottoming.

About to Fall

Now that the infinite plasticity of human form
has been commandeered by human hands and human judgment,
love is on strange ground. We can do what we want with bodies:
sculpt them sleek and strong; heal their handicaps pre-utero;
make them perfect fits for the jobs for which they're being bred.
And remember this new power includes the chemistry
of heart and brain – the way we feel and think. So what is left
of love, for love, to love? Now love must retreat to the soul,
and we wonder what the soul can gain from incarnation.

Love and the Sky

Mostly we live low on the human span, our feet dirt bound,
our eyes enthralled by a cloudy river of fearful thought,
our hearts weighted with wanting, our poor breath halting and stuck.
Yes, we will die. We will lose everything, unremembered
by friends unremembered, even our mineral substance
dispersed. Imagining ourselves, we spend our days staring
down at the future, eyes on the ground that will have us back.

Love is the sky above the sky, the air above the air.
To be in that sky and breathe that air, one must want nothing
from anyone or anything here below. Radiance
is the transformation of desire, the selfless exchange
of taking in air and giving forth light, the aim of man,
the perfect giving back before a silent departure
into invisibility, the becoming of love.

Beyond

You have paid your dues – years of walking from forest to shrine,
wearing a smooth path on the ground which weeds dare not exploit
and strangling vines have turned from. The shrine is part of you now.
You are there in the instant of remembering, breathing
freely the fragrance abiding from thousands of efforts.
Whenever you would love, God does not deny the Presence.
So this question: Why do you still lose your way and wander?

The current from lowest spine to Crown is intermittent.
The higher mind dims, lacks resolve to keep the new crystal
turned toward the sun, and the lower nature wins by default.
What maintains the state beyond desire, beyond otherness?
A toddler Angel must master objective walking, straight,
undeviating, the universe balanced on the head.

What's Left of You

To walk the world and permanently hold a state of love
requires superhuman effort. I do not mean bearing
unbearable pain, abstaining from all that flesh desires,
or striding unarmed against nightmares of visceral rage.
I speak of tempering the heart to unbelief and calm
renunciation of all that is not pure attention,
now, now, now and now, so what's left of you can only love.

6. Flight

The Suitor

"Let me know if your thoughts on this change," he said as he turned
to leave. He was embarrassed, as he had known he would be,
but all in all, the sting of rejection was not as bad
as the imagination of it. The clear, upright part
of him endured, unshaken, stronger for the next advance.
He had spoken honorable feeling with honesty
and modesty. There is no failure in an open heart.

Again and again as half a year passed, he asserted
the ritual pledge. If the first required greatest effort,
the second was the most awkward, closest to collapsing.
By the third time, he was aware of a clear procedure,
a focused intention of language and posture and tone.
She surprised him at the fourth, urging him to give it up,
but he persevered, and the vignette ended smilingly.

By the fifth he was near command, speaking with a calmness
close to certainty. Fixed and reliable, yet gracious
and kind, he was a marvel to her, and though she did not
say yes, yet she could not say no. The sixth visit lasted
all afternoon, and even the silences were fruited
and sweet. Lighting the lamp, she said, "The time does not rule us.
You are not the man I once rejected. Stay here and dine."

Love Discovered

So attracted was Melia to the sun's reflection
in Arturo's eyes that she forgot her friends and went slack
in her work. All the young girls of her circle were alarmed,
but only one, Lily, sought the advice of an elder.
"You cannot lift another up, but try not to let her
fall too far," Lily's uncle told her. So Lily observed
her friend from a distance, ready to lend her a shoulder.

Melia wasted away, believing Arturo's eyes
could never light upon her, and Arturo, for his part,
had no idea of Melia's dismal condition.
At last Lily could look on no longer. Though it was true
her friend was grieving from the loss of love she'd never had,
Lily was touched and determined to speak to Arturo.
She found him at lunch break sitting under a pistache tree.

Her mission emboldened her; without a formal greeting
she began, "Arturo, do you think yourself attractive?"
The boy was shocked speechless and to avoid her gaze leaned back.
His eyes went skyward, becoming mirrors for the high sun,
and the reflected gleam shot right into Lilly's own eyes.
They sat silent a moment, she absolved of her reason
for speaking, and he struck dumb between unease and delight.

Lily's purpose returned, and she strained to form a sentence.
"Do you think a girl could be lovesick over you?" she asked.
Arturo slowly digested her question, and the thought
came to him that she was speaking of herself. His cheeks blushed,
and her heart opened at this proof of his humility.
Beyond words they sat a while, and at last parted so full
at heart that they felt no weight from their afternoon labors.

So began a long string of jeweled days in which they met
under the pistache tree, reflecting light on each other,
quickening their souls to a unity. Lily had not
forgotten Melia but knew not how to approach her.
When one day she resolved to check on her friend, Lily found
her behind the kitchen cracking a huge basket of nuts
and pouring forth a monologue on the trials of love.

Beside her sat Elwood entranced at Melia's nearness.
Lily puzzled over the scene for a time, wondering
if she and Arturo were lost in a similar fog.
When to their overwatching tree the two returned, she asked,
"Do you think that love is a spell to keep people coupling?"
"I think it depends on what's loving what," he responded.
"Arturo," she asked sincerely, "what kind of love have we?"

The Arc of Love

Milano moved in his body like a frolicking colt,
zigging and zagging, rearing up in unrestrained display,
plunging to Earth and setting off in a merciless sprint.
With a stitched ball, he and his mates transformed a fallowed field
into a circus of free-flowing muscle and delight.
Back and forth and up and down they moved, stretching their limits,
racing past mind till their heated lungs demanded a rest.

A minute of hungrily gulping the air restored him
as he knelt in the shade of the gnarled oak on the flat field's
unmown edge. The other young chargers played on; their bold shouts
pierced the morning. As his breath quieted, Milano felt
a Presence, like a secret whispered in a foreign tongue.
He turned his eyes and snared the gaze of Martha draping him
as she pinned her ancient laundry to the line in her yard.

Instantly her eyes dropped to her apron; hands in habit
searched in her pockets for more pins. She was sure he had seen
the heat rise in her sinking cheeks. He smiled, rose to his feet
and said with a laugh, "Good morning, Auntie. Are we too loud?"
Her own longing had surprised her. She said beneath her breath
as her parenting heart woke, "When will this silliness pass?"
"I'm taking the day off," he chimed. "Do you need any help?"

She stood remembering her list of chores, her pains, herself.
By then his friends had gathered, nosing the air, wondering
what awaited them. "I have some bricks by the shed," she said.
"I had a mind to make a border for the flower beds.
Do I know you, young man?" "You know Miranda, my mother."
"You're Milano!" she cried, remembering a boy of eight.
"Just sit and watch us work, Auntie. Let us give you a gift."

Each Other

Irina had no hopes littering the road of her life.
For a decade, she'd worn the sternest stoic discipline,
aligning her emotions and her thoughts to the moment's
unpolished presentation. Her motto: Do not distort.
Within, she was a bread and water child. Pure attention
was her great defense against the self-indulgence that lies
at the root of man's misery. Her heart was a precinct
of manicured sand raked to an unadorned symmetry.

Andy was a moving mess – shaggy, misbuttoned, untucked
and paunched. "Borders are a waste of time," he declared out loud
to himself and thus never wore a belt. Every woman
on Earth was his mother, and he was profusely grateful
for their mendings, their meals, their just-this-once indulgences.
On his outsized belly road a heart similarly huge,
that with poetry and sympathy and pointed humor
challenged the unjust sobriety of the universe.

So twice in a week, then yet a third, these opposing poles
of human pain were brought together, locked in circumstance
beyond coincidence. She whom ten of Cupid's arrows
could not make bleed, and he, enemy of geometry,
finally could ignore the signs no longer. They agreed
in their separate minds to speak, and at their fourth crossing
a simultaneous hello came forth from both as face
to face they stood. Their first chat clattered like wood on gravel.

The Angels do not gamble nor relish the dissonance
of irony, so why these two were ineluctably
positioned in each other's path taxes our busy minds.
Love dissolves impasse and makes a harmony from extremes.
The Field of Love is welcoming and wide with enough room
to embrace our frailties and all the life we would resist.
Andy and Irina meet most days for lunch: grateful words
pour from him; in her a strange delight at his attention.

Sharing the Mystery

Sometimes a sudden gust of pure love inflated his heart
to the bursting point, and his poor shattering social self
could not contain the energy. He wanted to embrace
every man, woman and creature, spread his expanding arms
around all creation, hug it into himself, hasten
the infinite fusion to which all things are returning,
obliterate all boundaries, all of death's distractions.
In these moments of perfect namelessness, he stood speechless,
his seismic shaking deep within detectable only
as an unfathomable gaze from softly moistened eyes.
A mysterious smile – was it? – barely lifted his lips,
and eerie knowledge seemed to have replaced the man he'd been.

During these episodes, everyone in the office knew
to avoid him. His strange weakness embarrassed them, threatened
their idea of authority. They imagined him
bursting into a seizure or crumpling dead to the floor.
After all, he was a generous boss in a bleak world.
Only Elizabeth openly watched his spells and knew
them to be a grace, a fingertip stretching down to touch
Mr. Green with a higher love. A handful of visits
by the same wonderment had come to her over the years,
and she had at last begun to investigate their source.
Some old Greek statues, some portraits of saints – both here and gone
serenely to God were these faces, these maps of Heaven.

She had one advantage in confronting the enigma
of higher states: her mind was free of belief, unattached
to any catechism or hypothesis. She knew
she knew nothing; she carried her experience and saw
clearly what was there before her. The pictures she affirmed
and the books she read led her round and round and back to one
simple necessity – talking to her boss heart to heart.
Would she be violating privacy, doing damage
to a bond already delicate? Would she offend him,
jeopardize her job, her livelihood? It took her feet weeks
to stand before his office door, to make her knuckles knock.
"Sir, there is a mystery we seem to share. May we talk?

The Search Outright

It took about a year for them to explore every inch
of each other and another year to spend their passion.
Were their coupling mindless and merely biological,
then would be the time for offspring, service to the species,
but they both wanted something inarticulately more,
some ultimate knowledge, a complete participation,
and they wondered if two could seek the truth better than one.

There followed a decade of sincerest search, as both brought
to each day's end their thoughts, questions, readings and arguments,
in their discussion sifting through the history of man,
the great riddles, the repeating themes. When they could travel,
they sought the ruined bones of human greatness, the cathedrals
of inspiration, the museums of art and beauty.
Their hearts remained unsatisfied, and a suspicion grew.

What if the purpose of the great design were to keep us
prisoners of mind? What if desire itself could only
apply to a small, endlessly recurrent catalogue
of conceptions? As the great joke grew more clear, its punchline
more inevitable, their responses alternated –
despair or hilarity. Each became the other's sole
comfort, and they reached midlife as desperate companions.

By practices their vast investigations had exposed,
both had experienced freedom from thought, brief excursions
into timelessness which their force of will could not sustain.
What was missing? Had the methods they'd discovered decayed
over time? Was permanent escape from mental chatter
only another fallacy of thought? Strangely, their love
fed on their mutual compassion for their helplessness.

In secret and despite the self-consuming irony,
each made an inner turning, an offering to nothing,
a prayer to die in payment for the other's liberty.
Not long later, one was taken, a crash on the highway,
cleaned up in a few hours, dried and packed in a statistic.
For a year our anguished survivor paced the floor of hell
till hell itself was seen as just another room in thought.

What attracts the miraculous attention of Angels?
Who deserves their gifts? By what celestial measure of worth
is a slow accumulating soul chosen for faster
fulfillment? Who finds the door to Conscious School, the small door
our survivor of a perfect tragic love this moment
knocks upon? Your answer can only be another thought.
Better to be here in love, beyond thought, home from seeking.

Help

There are two levels of help one can give other humans.
First are the small things that appear only in the Present:
holding a door, blessing a sneeze, forgiving a faux pas.
These tiny succorings offered with a smile and the kiss
of immediacy transcend whatever keeps one hard
and separate, opening if only for an instant
the curtain keeping out the light that unifies us all.

To give the other kind of help requires immolation
in that light, plenary compliance with eternal life.
Long preparation is needed, lifetimes of polishing
the soul to crystalline clarity, of surrendering
in gradually greater dosages until nothing
but conscious love determines all desire, all intention.

Then from a new Angelic vantage can be seen the field
of budding souls and what is needed, each and all, to help
their slow return. And with the time-destroying patience now
possessed in being, the service of that help emerges,
if service names what love with free and tireless will enacts.
Mankind needs help and is receiving it but only sees
an inch or two beyond entanglement of private pain.

Love and Flight

How often effort elevates us out of the grinding
roar of thought just enough to get a sign – a sacred key,
a reminder of order from the molecular realm.
Then what? We drag the splendid thing down to parse its meaning
on the autopsy table of knowledge, to use our flight
for moral righteousness, or worse, to share it like a spoil
with the lower self. Survive the apocalypse! Buy gold!

Yes, the apocalypse is coming. That's just what it means
to be mortal. But you who've had a thousand little hints
and visits from the deathless beyond, why would you misuse
your real gold on mere survival? When you are lifted up
to the sky, don't look down. Hold your being's height and focus
on the light of a definite star. Leave the organic
urgencies to fall and molder where they will. On to love!

Be in love! Walk the Field of Love till all your fuel's gone.
Find yourself in immortality and give it freely
to all who live in looking up. The less you are, the more
comes through. No calculating worth or weighing lovers' gifts.
Be the radiance of love, the invisible envoy.
Your duty to the world will find you as you slow and drift
downward back. Forgive that siren hag rasping in your ears.

The Sole Way

The steward is the soul's tool to unify and refine
earthly identity so one's earthly experience
can nourish the soul. Gathering itself as a learning
emulation of the soul, its laboring devotion
mirroring the love it serves, the steward is the sole way
from Earth to Heaven, and though it dies with the flesh, it leaves
in the soul a tendency, stronger with each human birth,
to dedicate one's life on Earth to God's loving Presence.

Since Then

Her head scarf the blue of distant mountains, but its texture,
close as the Present, called out to be touched. What could I do?
I walked behind her for uncounted paces, needing less
and less of anything as my attention found itself.

When the well appeared, she slowed and turned her head right then left
to get her bearings. Her eyebrows were sleek, her nose sculpted.
Not similar to any of us – the hundreds moving
in imagined unity – she walked with a weightless grace.

I had to see her face to face. A labored longer stride
brought me up beside her, and then a pace or two beyond.
Fully turning to the right, I stood, met her eye to eye,
finding an annunciate Mary's grave submitted gaze.

Since then I've walked behind her in willing understanding
of ever Present purpose, even as our tired number
marches to a future made in mind. I am always here,
observing her, ready to protect her selfless blessing.

Love and the Steward

Do not expect the lower self to ever surrender.
Only at the last breath does it forsake its grip, its fight
for possession of the soul. A steward must be fashioned
to check the lower self, to limit its choice of weapons,
to reveal its fraud. If the steward cannot truly love,
it can know that only love is worthy of its service.
Affirming higher being is the steward's special skill,
so the steward surrenders to love: at the balcony
it stops, goes silent, gives over its authority, turns
to face any onslaught, so love can come forth to preside.

The lower self cannot bear the light of love. Retreating
to its shadowed rooms, it continues its whispered campaign
of lies and distractions. From the balcony, the soul's Eye
blesses all it sees with love, freely emptying itself
of all the refined gold it has stored – love's own surrender.
Thus the recurring miracle of love's appearances,
the divine intervention of the timeless into time.
With each deliverance, the steward is more self-aware,
more ready to bow to love, though the lower self will not
surrender, fighting till the body's great heart stops beating.

Dining

The friends around a table quickly get tired of talking.
The ritual chit-chat completes itself; a readiness
to be one with each other rises as a bright promise.
A timeless space opens above the table, hovering
in the breath of attention, in love illuminated.
What are we sharing but God? What is each candle but part
of the one light of God? This union is a sacrament.

Later perhaps a story can be told, a sweet story
made into prayer by the purity of the listening:
a story of the Teacher or of some other master,
or a story of beauty and its patient victory,
or a story of compassion discovered by the side
of a noisy highway. Let the story be a harbor
of return and welcome, reminding even the teller.

Let a little food be eaten, but never to fullness:
require the body to smell and taste intentionally;
be aware of the rhythm of the mouth doing its work;
sip the wine remembering the labor of its making.
Then a piece of music or a poem, a charm to bring
all back to the brink of silence. Arise. Let the goodbyes
be soft-spoken, tender, unguarded expressions of love.

Love and Bodies

Love is a form of attention, the blessing of the soul
moving through the circuits and channels of the body out
to another soul in another body, reminding
both the giver and receiver of the divine being
in which both partake. Thus the highest use of the body
is the pure expression of love, controlled and extended
as long as can be borne until collapse and needed rest.

The drive for expressing love is the remembrance of God.
The aim of expressing love is the remembrance of God.
The joy of expressing love is shared remembrance of God.
Not the awkwardness of flesh nor its inevitable
fall to pleasure erase the eternal value of love.
The more often, the longer, the more deeply we commit
love's remembrance of God, the more we become love itself.

See six friends circling a table, School souls breathing the light
from each other's eyes, their bodies still, hearts elevated,
each an anchor for the rising crystal of attention
their love is making. Each of them, each world their being spans,
receives intentional nourishment, yet never so much
to drown delight. By the last thanks of the meal, they are one
in heart, mind and soul, servants of the God they are part of.

Love and Fences

Along the road adjacent to his pond, my dear neighbor
has built a low line of fence and painted it lucid white.
Though the pond is beautiful and serene, cars coming down
the road at night are warned of danger by the boundary.

This morning, a stunning white egret stands at the pond's edge,
investigating. Its neck's smooth curve lifts its regal head
above the fence line – beauty ascending, now visible
beyond a wise border man has made against his blindness.

So it is with love, its beauty rising above safety,
its nobility above the fear of losing the way,
its clear and gathered gaze beyond the things we must forgive.
Does this great bird know that all I truly am is watching?

After a brief dance with my intensifying breathing,
the bird's majestic wings unfurl, flutter effortlessly
and push the air around it down to Earth. Into the sky
it goes and goes, smaller. It was here, even as I am.

As if focusing a camera, I return to life
on my side of the fence, consolidating once again
into sensory belief, but lifted to remember
that even the wisest boundaries cannot limit love.

Love and Mourning

Strongly the psyche seeks and clings to equilibrium,
the false stability that indulges the errant mind.
We would live in a bubble of thought, feeding our futures
with inner talk, our souls anesthetized, barely breathing.
The larger disruptions to this condition – our losses
of status, security, physical function, loved ones –
are the sufferings that can kill us or restore our souls.

The death of someone close – a friend, a spouse, or worst, a child
just old enough to feel the promptings of the soul – ruptures
the airlock and sucks us violently out of self-made
value into naked fact so much more real than we are.
All societies grant mourning its space and time, knowing
there is madness here, confusion, paralysis of will.
Mortal identity must be stitched and reinflated.

Who can see the soul's opportunity here? The soul lives
in eternity, the forgotten dimension, and loss
can open the gate of remembrance. Though the flesh must mourn,
the soul is more available, less shut out. Deathlessness
can assert its truth across the whole span of our being.
It has always been here, patiently waiting for us. Now
it stands revealed, a gift of love from one gone on and in.

Love and Doubt

Doubt flickers and gathers and mounts and finally triggers
the sharp backward pull that closes the purse. What do you have
in that moneybag? Enough for a worthy burial?
Likewise your heart: doubt insinuates, interrupts, incites
imagined disaster, and then the breath retracts and hides,
and the climb to the Eye is abandoned – too dangerous.
You hoard your higher food till it rots and turns to poison.

The snake you house in the labyrinth below hisses doubt.
It wants to curl itself around imagined gold and sleep.
Its dreams of heaven will keep you out of Heaven, prevent
your looking up, your hearing the call, your soul from singing.
Every coin that finds your hand was given to help you buy
freedom from flesh, your own and your friends'. The hungry believe
they are hunger. The doubters believe that death is lurking.

Spend and love! Spend and love! The dead don't care how they're buried.
Help the living live to become the loving. Help them now
and whenever you can. Treat your doubt as your own baby
dribbling food: clean it and go on with your life-giving love.
Open your purse to the chance to raise friends above hunger.
Open your heart. God calls you to dance in the Field of Love.
Between the in and the out of your breath, God is calling!

Love and Touch

To be specific and definite is the great striving
of attention. Man is the tool by which the Field of Love
focuses a beam on the organic world and invites
ready souls home to God. Angelic attention is love,
but love can't penetrate the earthen crust except through man.

One awakened soul propels another to know itself,
to look home. One to one to one to one – always this way.
But to touch another, a soul-in-body must master
attention. Vague ecstasies are not sufficient; calling
out to mankind is a waste. One must learn the discipline
of endless patience in a time bound world. Soul-in-body,
aware of yourself reading this, what wondering child looks
to you now? Whose true moment can your bright love deliver?

If your vigilance is pure, unspotted by long lapses
in imaginary pleasure or raw instinctive greed,
you will own a simple integrity that penetrates
the layers of nonsense gathered like clouds around the souls
hoping to find themselves surprised at someone's loving touch.

Love and the Source

Though not the ultimate destination, love is the next
step in the return to the Source, our willed evolution's
next encampment. Residing in the Field of Love, the soul
absorbs and enacts God's attention – the substance of love --
till stalwart enough to lift some small portion of God's own
suffering, to abide in pure lightning and not be lost.
Even here in sweet glimpses can be known above the mind
the states and heavens which comprise the cosmos created
for the soul's return. Love is its now, its eternal air.

Love and the Truth

When the truth comes before love is well rooted, it destroys.
Its electric force neuters hope and withers all projects.
There is a time for such destruction: when humanity,
gorged on lies and greed, toxifies the planet and its seed.
But on the scale of friends, lovers, families, neighborhoods
and networks of charity, love must be established first
and practiced, one breath to the next and to the breath of all.

Our insignificance is too deep a hole for the heart
whose great courage and resilience blinks out before the gape
of creation's dark distance. For ages, the heart must make
slow pilgrimage to the Field of Love, and then reside there,
freely giving what is grown. Then and only then can man
bear the shock of truth and shoulder the Absolute's anguish.
Truth devours, but those living in Love's Field are not consumed.

Love and God

Love is the next level up for man, so one is not wrong
to call it God. When a human grows perfected in love,
God will ascend to a new height of being and beckon
that one to follow, to be the transparent observer
of love's activity. But for now, let us be our love.

When my friend's words stumble, let me lift them into my love.
When my friend's pain interrupts, let my love be the soothing.
When my friend doubts, let my love wait calmly for the clearing.
When my friend descends into worry and need, let my love
be the firm reminder of immortality's vantage.

Earth – so stormy and painful in its beauty – is God's school
for the soul to deepen itself in love, to become love
so reliable, so generous that it can dissolve
all the cumbersome mortalities mankind can conjure.
This transformation God has planted in your will to love.

Our love participates in God. It is God reaching down
to Earth, to know it and suffer it and bless its beauty.
When we submit to love's dominion, we no longer need
a name, an estate or a claim of earthly attainment.
We are the air itself, breathed as giving and forgiving.

Love and the Astral Body

Crystallizing an astral body requires the Angels'
best science. The spark of God implanted at conception
is nourished by the balanced cycles of integration
with its host and separation from it. With each movement
in and out, the astral body grows and strengthens, learning
in time to govern the transformation from an Earth life
to an eternal independence in the Field of Love.

How do we experience this movement and rest, this dance
between worlds? On a grand scale, in birth and death and rebirth;
on the smallest scale, in breathing in and out. Between these
are the events of our lives: identification's grip
and release. All the while warmed by Angelic attention,
true consciousness burgeons in deathless substance, maturing
in the human mold but more and more capable of love.

Nor is the miracle complete with the crystallizing
of this new vessel. Even the eternal Field of Love
must be transcended, a yet newer form's subtler being
fashioned by Archangel science. The return does not end
till the beginning is absorbed in the beginningless.
As I write, as you read, love shares its eternal blessing
while love's more conscious observer holds and directs the light.

But If You Can Love

If the lust to own is identity's terminal flaw,
the urge to share may be the fleshbound soul's greatest goodness.
A map for those who come after is not required of you.
It is a dangerous project, too easily suborned
by vanity or the urge to power. So do not feel
compelled to use your talents – to paint, compose, make poems –
unless your poor pen or brush is ordered by an Angel.
Unless your face is turned to God, what you express goes down
the dying universe as do the spreading molecules
you strain to keep. Let all go, aware of its departure.

But if you can love purely – that is, become love itself –
and serve the truth with self-disposing joy, then a record
of your path may be minutely useful. Wayward mankind,
those not yet spiraling up but still recircling the first
of many lives, engrossed in speeding multiplicity,
can in torn twinklings ratify their ultimate return.
How your testimony gets before their eyes is too far
for mind – but let the truth of love and love of truth abide.
Whatever you share in love -- not moist, easy sentiment
but death defying love -- some soul in frightened need can ride.

Let That Be You

Until you see them as souls trapped within bodies, you can't
truly understand people – their tragic struggle to find
and honor the better being they know is there somewhere.
You can't fully appreciate them, admire them, trust them
or forgive them until you accept the depth of their sleep.
They're going to hurt you, and worse, you're going to hurt them.
You and they are grim observers of each other's coma.
Who will wake first and pledge eternal help? Let that be you.

Until you wake, your episodes of love are sporadic.
You may have hours or whole days of elevation, but flesh
revives, reasserts its animal claim, and soon you're back
to calculating, seizing, defending the dirt that draws
your heart and eyes down to the next imagined advantage.
If you live this way, you will waste eternity this way.
If you wake, you will see the prison holding your own kind,
and hear a sweet voice – your own – singing in the key of love.

We in bodies know ourselves by the light of attention.
Awareness of attention is the Presence of the soul,
and the soul known to itself can only love. Love thanks God.
What embodied soul can live this promise? Let that be you.

Marriage

Two young bodies pledge their love and loyalty, knowing not
what drives them to stand before the witnesses assembled.
For a stretch of months, they breathe a common air of pleasure
and dance in the delight of touch, heedless of men or moon.
But in time their wine dilutes to water, the drunken state
retreats before the simple facts, and the warmth in the house
needs painstaking effort and intention. The work begins.

Then come the binding needs of children or promised service
to the city. The pair lifts the burden of providing
and with that weight learns patience and postponement of desire.
This stage is decades long and polishes out the splinters
in their partnership: the private vanities, little lies
and lusts, the idiot hopes their hearts had hidden away.
They emerge dear, in spousal unity smoothed and softened.

They have earned the fulfillment of married love, the perfect
companionship of purified hearts whose compassion comes
unbidden on each breath. How much this love can fortify
the sacred labor of the soul's becoming! Acceptance
of another in selfless love calls the soul to witness
and brings one to the threshold of transformation, ready
for return to God, a departure without a parting.

Come Out and Back

So easy it is to believe the world of the senses.
By early childhood, one's recorded sense experience
is vast and dense enough to bid the mind to tarry there
compulsively and choose a style for personality,
a character to meet the world and charm it, forgetting
fundamental being, losing the truth above the mind.

And what does one get for one's work in the sensory world?
A time-lapsed identity trapped in grim mortality,
a ruthless race to the next imagined pleasure, and rest
stained with longing. What is that state that threatens if you dare
to disbelieve the world? What cleansing absence waits outside
the theatre of mind? Come out to the nothing you've lost.

The key to liberation from this tactile hologram
you long ago made of life is to want nothing from it.
Sight and smell, touch, taste and hearing will still do their duty,
but the character they appeal to must no more use them
for belief. Recollecting what you truly are instead
will summon – through, around and above – original love.

A being freed from flesh lives in and of the Mind of God,
as an obedient power and merciful servant.
The Field of Love wants your Presence! Let God make use of you.

II. *Psalms of Love*

1.   The line you are reading is my pilgrimage. At its end
I am with you and will stay until your heart casts me out.

What have I learned by seeking God in you? The illusion
of individual identity troubles all men.

I can see through you to God but still believe I exist.
What is it in creation that would be other than God?

To join you, to be your lover, draws me closer to God.
The imagined borders of being erode over years.

The source of love reclaims all we have given each other.
No longer two, no more in time, God the pilgrim returns.

2.   There is a finer light than love, but the blessings of love,
its Presence and tender influence, do not know darkness.

The unity of God is the final destination,
but without loving Presence no approach is possible.

A seeker without Presence is trapped in his illusion,
inventing measurements for his progress. He does not love.

A seeker without love remains a seeker. He cannot
surrender the private aspiration of achievement.

The unity of God overtakes one's loving Presence
as perfect light consumes the sun by which one's seeing sees.

3.   As one gets older, nights of love transform from fruit to wine.
Dried to perfume is the syrupy nectar on the chin.

The habits of affection keep the body moderate,
the mind serene. Love sprinkles labor's daily seasoning.

After storms without or within, love collects the debris,
preserving the Present till the heart rebuilds a dwelling.

Love knows its luck to have those who receive its offerings,
who join in weaving a garment of extending meaning.

Love leads the tired body to its rest with comforting notes
sung on easeful breath but clear, so clear – God's own beckoning.

Love accepts death and holds open the conduits closing
in reflexive fear. "Let it come," says love to the great wind.

4.   The individual unhardens and diminishes
as the soul learns how to bestow Earth with gossamer love.

If I don't know how to give you what you want, forgive me.
My love is a deep young river unskilled in providing.

How great is the discovery that the most worthy things
can only be defended by love's ascending freedom.

Love tears on the sharp rocks of the world. With no self-pity
it learns to mend and press on with greater delicacy.

Love is the kind of attention that can learn worthiness
from anything, but it must persist, not hasten or stray.

5.   Not staying long enough for love to waken was the key
      to my defense. "I have to go" was tattooed on my lips.

      When love found me, I did not know I was lost. Thanking God
      seemed too big a gesture. Better to listen to a child.
      Love will not be rushed. It will dig in its paws and resist
      the pull on the leash as it sniffs out the invisible.

      Now I don't go anywhere. I stay here with love and watch
      the turning world before me. Love is preparing something.

      Each day asks a bigger forgiveness, and I can give it
      because there is less and less bone and more understanding.

      I don't expect this to go on forever, just till time
      doesn't matter. Love will say, "You have what you need. Come on."

      Then I will leave this nest astonished that flying results
      from every intention in my heart. What will be my work?

      If one can fly, one can lift. Perhaps another soul needs
      a little upward thrust to reach the next foothold of love.

      Here and now, love is focusing a landscape just below
      this height I'm breathing. I see humans moving things around.

      That's what they do, unaware as I was that love watches.
      Something must interrupt; some gong must sound. One will hear it.

      I heard it. Do you, sir, or you, ma'am? No, you're not doing
      anything wrong. Just listen, up here where love has the sky.

6.   Love has said nothing all day, so these verses will be few.
Sometimes love just wants to sit beside me and do nothing.

Being with love is enough. Each impulse to do crashes
against my breathing, washing up a secret nerve of fear.

Deflected long ago, refused feeling, these little stabs
of energy sank to the bottom. Love can lick them clean.

7.   Love is not above asking for money, not for itself
but for cleaning things the world has forgotten to value.

Cleaning has a cost. Revealing what's under the disguise
of dirt can cause discomfort in the sky that must see it.

Love presses on, begging any little coin, then buying
soap and scrubbing away till the sun observes its own face.

Then one by one they go in a line on the mantel piece,
these nuggets, now unshamed and precious, proud in love's display.

They're worth a fortune. Some say they can buy eternal life,
but love keeps begging, putting the eternal in its place.

8.   There's less to loving than we think because we'd rather think
than love. Which do you do to respond to your own desires?

Thought is the executive suite on the ninety-ninth floor.
Love is a table and two creaky chairs in the lobby.

Thought gets peeved when a perfectly logical plan won't work.
Love changes the diaper and is glad everything's working.

Great universities train our youth in the religion
of thought. We've reverenced the mind since our species stood up.

Love too has its institutions – charities, relief funds –
but love's struggle with Earth's torments is not meant to be won.

I want to graft a rare vine of thought onto love's root stock.
It's a strange, precarious hybrid: its flowers are prayers.

9.   There's a time and a place for everything, but who knows what
it is? Love is the only real order available.

When love is in the crosswalk, people not only don't mind
stopping, they pull their cars to the side and call their mothers.

When love is in charge, confusion doesn't mind stepping out
into the light and showing its splayed eyes, its cubist face.

When love sends the invitation, even the avalanche
pauses to recall that its mess will somehow get cleaned up.

I don't know you, so I can't say I love you, but by God
I do love – I know I do – and you're as here as I am.

10. Don't honor love with a statue. Love is the opposite
of a thing hard and frozen in form, however noble.

The miracle of love is that we live and breathe in it
and can with our fastest attention be aware of it.

We have a faculty that nourishes itself on love
and then blesses Earth with a light in which love flourishes.

But love won't object to its image in cold stone or bronze,
and it needn't be an ideal woman or a cherub.

Whatever utterance or work of art or soft gesture
reminds the soul it is in God makes love happy to be.

So if you want a statue, you might as well build a park
and a city of eternal remembrance – all for love.

11. When everything you've accumulated here is taken
by your last breath, the soul's trajectory comes to a fork:

Back down to buffer the terror – the moon and Earth again –
or up to immolation in the astonishing sun.

Only love can choose the fire; only love accepts the cost,
the shocking cleansing by God's light. By love to love ascend.

Don't look back or heed the siren's call to mortal comfort.
Through all the forms of love's exalted air, press on to God.

12.   If you think you can see the soul of a human being
in the eyes or hear it in the voice, you're imagining.

Not that there isn't a soul within – there is, but so deep,
so vague, so faceless is it in its creeping gestation

that its glow from under layers of personality
and functions cannot be discerned. But love can seek it out.

Love plunges through all the foreign matter to find the soul,
acknowledge it and leave a kiss for it to grow into.

Love knows that all distinctions – yours and mine – do not apply
to souls, that love is one in souls as souls are one in God.

So when a gleam in her eyes or a sweetness in his voice
finds you at home, let unimagined love attend its work.

13.   It doesn't matter who gets the glory because glory
and persons are part of the vanishing downward story.

Stay fixed on the upward revelations which you can know
only in the Field of Love. Every hour vanity leaves

multiple messages urging you to trade the Present
for imagined value and thereby forsake love's foothold.

Don't do it. Let your refusals be rhythmic as raindrops,
by willed attention fusing into one constant cleansing.

Love rises by this effort in an arduous ascent
from here to the precipice to the unseeable height

of completed return. What space can there be for glory
when love fills up far more than all mere single souls can hold?

14.   When you offer a love gift, your lower self feels the loss
        and calculates what it is owed. For it, love is commerce,

        and the interest on its loans is paid in subtle claims
        of influence and alliance. "Take the gift and you're mine."

        The soul sees the same gift as a symbol, a little lens
        to magnify awareness, which is the soul's currency.

        The soul's gift card reads, "Use this token to remember God,
        but do not favor with belief the earthly thoughts it stirs."

        The heart feels both poles of the love gift's meaning and must choose
        again and again the higher intention to profess.

        By such choices does the heart save itself from slavery
        and lightened by what's given learn to fly in finer air.

15.   What love can do is small compared to what it cannot do.
        Ever eye to eye with love, this brute fact obscures the view.

        As the soul learns, passion will expire; then sans wasted flame
        love's fire still burns, subtracted from its person and its name.

        And so love comes to trade desire for God's eternity,
        the permanence not of want or own but of simple be.

16. When it has been blunted or frustrated, love does not sulk
     but seeks a higher companion to keep it from falling.

     As love holds the Present, it has access to Heaven's friends
     and must only ask for the transformation to begin.

     Any Angel witness will do. They all know the secret
     equally well: kissing the truth, one can only ascend.

17. So many find original sin an unjust concept,
     but sin simply means sleep – unconsciousness – and each newborn

     is dropped sleeping and helpless into the parents' taut web
     of cause and effect. For years, sleep is all the child can know.

     When we first awake to be conscious of love, already
     we're in deep debt to time and mechanical patterning.

     The escape – self-remembering and transformation – must
     be searched out, located, mastered and practiced unto death.

     Love is shorthand for all that: it's the strange light on the shore
     of consciousness welcoming us to another cosmos.

     Love becomes cause and effect, the road and the residence.
     You must leave your unjust sleep behind to play in Love's Field.

18.   Personality is like a coating of plastic film.
deflects the world--including love--as it entertains.

We are all in love and don't know it. It is amazing
that we must be instructed in what we would most cherish.

One's essence is not love, but it can lean in and kiss love
and sit quietly content with love and hold love's Presence

with a sensuous touch and in moments of greatest need
drench itself in love to sponge poor burning lips and foreheads.

However needy our bodies are, we're not forbidden
from walking mindfully hand in hand in the Field of Love.

19.   Eyes meet across a room: two souls take an unresisted
plunge into each other's being – all in half a second

done and retracted, making a print on eternity
as the world abruptly speeds to close and suture its wound.

A moment of perfect love – no names, no pasts, no futures.
How fast the jealous illusion-in-common recovers.

20.   If you age well, your love will also. If you grow mellow
and deepen your being as you shrink and slow in your arc,

your love will spread its subtle perfume and complexity
of flavors through the colloquies you visit and address.

Suggest to all you love not to preach, not to waste the heat
in the heart. Ask for help to bear the weight of Angel work

21.   In a potted palm on my porch, a small frog has planted
an outpost of his kind. Now he sings to attract a mate.

His scratchy serenade will more likely make him a meal
than a father, but he bravely persists despite the risk.

"I am here, I am here, I am here. I am here, here, here."
The air rings with his urgency, his firm, one-note promise.

Do not mock this song that knows no otherwise. It is love –
this fine, foolhardy grip on matter life must die to keep.

Up the food chain in my chair I know the Presence of God.
"Here I am, here I am, here I am. Here I am, am, am."

22.   Are you sneaking out to the Field of Love more often now
and staying till the call to leave is unbearably shrill?

If so, then your soul is growing more worthy and defined.
With luck, in some near lifetime, an Angel will spot its glow,

its stubborn radiance in the desert of recurrence –
and a tremor of affection will move eternal life.

Such is the way souls are brought to Conscious School – second birth
and fixed in the upward spiral to Angelic fullness.

No loss in loving, only gain, to you and those you love.
With progress aching slow or breathless fast, love must ascend.

7. Love's Harbor

23. Yes, whirling will unwind the coil a bit, let the soul rise,
    as will yogic postures, fasts, meditations, prayer chanting.

    Each of these practices is a means to a means – a way
    of showing you there is a way, but these are not the way.

    The way is love – not the sentimental human feeling
    but the transformation of oneself in every instant.

    Love is the daring of unlapsed attention, breath to breath
    remembrance of God; love attends failure's ongoing feast

    and forgives all; love bridges the worlds of flesh and spirit;
    love conducts the Presence of God; love marries the moment.

    Do not believe this world of time and death. Find love's footing
    and take the next step, holding in certainty to love's way.

24. Love's sightings and harborings cannot be foretold by codes,
    by logic or by habit. Love is its own law, both bright

    and bewildering. It fills its sails with a self-made breeze
    warmed to power by a cohort sun that dotes upon it.

    Submit to love, though it touch pain, torture patience, or tempt
    great treason. To refuse it, to let your heart flee inland

    when love's sails first appear, flagless and coming in, will seed
    regret and despair of knowing God. Let love's anchoring

    be your new address. God's here to witness your surprise life
    and protect you from mere passion. Obey love's pirate law.

The Second Book of Opportunities

I. Quatrains and Double Fours, Continued

121.   The love for one's child is a blade that can divide the soul.
To one's last breath, some measure of protective will abides
for the babe that chose the shade of one's own heart to live in.
One's child is personhood's most poignant disguise. Look through it.

———

122.   Are you friend or foe? If friend, you'll offer your supporting
shoulder freely, and trust my destiny to the soul's Eye.
If foe, you'll want to steer and drag me into the service
of a righteous idea that has drugged your mind and heart.

———

123.   There's nothing can be done unless done holding hands with God.
My own small purse though deathless cannot buy you one more breath.
So, old flesh, you must let me go. Eternal gratitude
honors you. Your hospitality housed a miracle.

———

124.   The first freedom arrives when the Angels allow themselves
to be discovered, but duty catches up to that joy,
and even their frequent relaxing of the grip of time
is not enough. One wants completion, nothingness in God.

———

125.   When one is seeding a civilization, one must be
as prolific as nature. Much will be lost in the end
that readies the beginning. Do not worry. Throw the seeds.
The Angels themselves are preparing the worthiest ground.

———

126. When the Angels deliver a shock, let it generate
Presence, and when Presence ebbs, let the shock's smoldering core
kindle a grateful heart and renew the effort to be.
Only last give the ashes to the interpreting mind.

———

127. To sense through wonder's opening a world finer than flesh,
to comprehend the invisible and grope and toddle
toward it, to patch together a fragmentary language
from the shocks received: a great transformation has begun.

&

128. The discovery of the soul ensues; the migration
of identity must follow. This the real exodus
from Egypt, the real colonizing of infinite space.
We return to eternal Presence and are welcomed home.

———

129. We are always only a few words away from murder.
To label people subhuman cultivates genocide.
Conscience in human beings must level self-assessment:
the conscious heart knows oneself to be better than no one.

———

130. Even the shortest haircut will not keep the brain quiet.
The chaos of voices competing for your attention
will continue; born salesmen, they will make a currency
of your austerities, a bank account from your chanting.

———

131.   It's June but feels like October; the world's weather's gone mad.
Earth is like a woman convulsing in a swarm of wasps,
and humans the multitude stinging her to misery.
How will the dear planet escape the torment we've become?

&

132.   If you are reading this, you are suffering the answer.
You are living the turmoil of a mother scorned and bound
by terrible necessity. Our kind has made of Earth
a Medea, and we the children her madness shadows.

————

133.   Your finest gown and most skillfully sculpted shoes remain
in the closet. We have entered another age, and things
beautiful and well-made have been stored for the grandchildren.
Poverty rules now. Cheap and clever the prevailing style.

&

134.   Love your friends. Touch them and honor them with small precious thi
that bloom again and again in the light of attention.
Speak softly and openly around the table, holding
the circle, even if the tea is weak, the berries few.

————

135.   All your human parts do only what they've been made to do.
The question's not your human fate but what you are making
of your soul. Look down to see your human destination.
To work on your soul, be aware of yourself looking up.

————

136.	Because the little girl with him required his protection,
	fear had no power over the lad. She moved in wonder,
	delighting in seeing and in the pure experience
	of being. He from up and back, uninterfering watched.

	––––––

137.	Time is droll. The future does not exist, but if it's not
	anticipated, one discovers one foot in the past
	and must chase the Present from deep poverty. Caesar's coin
	must be paid. The game of time must be played. Causes effect.
&

138.	At the same time (and in truth it is always the same time),
	we reside in eternity, the witnesses to all
	being played on the stage before us. The dance of "as if"
	goes on and on, without – praise God in Presence – our belief.

	––––––

139.	Usually an enigma appears in a poem
	by accident, but that's circular, for all accidents
	are enigmas, exposing inadequate mind models,
	and as poems are language, they must be inadequate.
&

140.	So if you enjoy enigmas, you delight in having
	your mind exposed as inadequate. There's hope for your soul,
	for through the hole of the mind's admitted deficiency
	one can see another not accidental dimension.

	––––––

141.   The fly papers of earthly concern come in scented pairs –
right and wrong, profit and loss, security and danger.
It doesn't matter which you stick to – same result, same tears.
What gets you from smell's first notice to the glue's fatal touch?

&

142.   There's a saying in comedy: If you buy the premise,
you'll buy the bit. If in a moment you believe the world
as if it were all there is, you become a dying thing,
your feet stuck, your wingbuds useless to the end – right or wrong.

———

143.   You don't have to be something special; you just have to be.
If you accept what is happening, whether dear or dire,
you will relax into an intelligent functioning
and have the energy left to witness it all – being.

&

144.   So the world stays busy, and you participate in it
and in something else as well: the witnessing dimension,
the awareness not chained to the world, the Presence of God.
To live this way is the aim of life – how one makes a soul.

———

145.   Some days are spent waiting on the brink of an announcement,
an imminent change of great importance. Don't believe it.
The Present doesn't wait, it abides, and what's important
is your being in it whatever your thoughts are doing.

———

146. Man's laws are guidelines: a real law cannot be disobeyed.
Conscience undeveloped – stillborn in anoxic honor
or in fear of punishment – guarantees a wasted life,
an ossuary sealed by expectation of reward.

&

147. Do not exalt a person of authority or book
of statutes. Protect the state of Presence. Whether the cost
be the foreman's favor or the devil's security,
obey first the law that rules the soul's deathless residence.

———

148. If your true work has the appearance of obedience
to human rule, enjoy the silent harvest of your luck.
If in honoring God you seem to disobey, forgive
the noise and loss of liberty you'll have to work within.

———

149. You cannot blame an uninstructed man for worrying.
Never having learned to differentiate his true state
from his thoughts, emotions and instinctive promptings, he takes
his mechanical responses as himself, the hostage.

&

150. It's hard for a hostage to find the soul, get to the end
of what one is not, discover fundamental being.
It's not impossible, but one must want truth beyond hope
and by pitiless inquiry attract higher mercy.

———

151.   The threads of daily business unravel in extremes
        of heat and cold. Unprotected man occupies a range
        of weather so narrow that he looks better to himself
        wrapped head to toe in a deflecting personality.

        ———

152.   Look what's fallen into my begging bowl: a self-help book,
        a daily horoscope, a battered pair of sunglasses,
        a bow tie, a young lawyer's business card, a pencil.
        There's much to wear and think about but no room left for food.

        ———

153.   Many are the substitutes for simple being as time
        turns its back to God: uproarious laughter, victory,
        wealth, a place among the important, patriotism,
        sex, physical fitness, worry and all imagined things.

        ———

154.   I will return to you or stay here working as you wish.
        From an earthly vantage, one cannot gauge a finished life.
        One tallies projects done, friends passed away, body's fatigue,
        mind's embarrassing vacuity – misleading measures.

&

155.   But you with impeccable precision see the level
        of the soul's completion, the count of crystal molecules
        accumulated, the permanence of inclination
        to bear an Angel's burden, and at the perfect moment......

        ———

156.   Don't mince words: human beings own planet Earth. We've staked it,
peopled it, poisoned it to submission. The question now
is how this costly slave will expire – irradiated
to toxic sand or choked on plastic indissolubles.

———

157.   Man has stabbed the dolphin he is riding over the sea,
fleeing from the sharks of his own nature. Now he will drown,
impervious to irony. The double irony –
that life on Earth needs rightly working man – wounds the Angels.

———

158.   We can't trust the stars. They're so far away that by the time
their light reaches us, they may no longer exist as stars.
So focus on the poem, not the poet. Trust the light,
not the candle, the lamp, the sun, an idea of God.

———

159.   Raw sunshine has a way of annihilating worry.
Worry makes us more important (at a horrible price),
but intense light spreading through Nature's expanse keeps us small,
smaller, unagitated, aware of our attention.

———

160.   Men move things around. The thoughts inside their heads become bricks,
and the need for shelter becomes an empire. But then what?
Some rare men witness the expanse of man's activity
and prefer small, still, silent participation in God.

———

161.   Don't try to coax the hermit from his cave. His expertise
        is in resisting the human flow. Leave food at his door.
        Leave poems, soft things to sit on, things with enchanting smells.
        Warn him with plenty that he can't escape the Field of Love.

        ———

162.   Everyone is intriguing given the right attention.
        If you are so deeply in the Present that you're seeing
        the miracles always here, each person is a marvel,
        even one stubbornly convinced of his role in the world.

        ———

163.   Stand firm and with resolve feel the hot fissile energy
        the body is impatient to dispose. Feel all of it.
        After a long moment of insult, what had been poison
        begins to open you, anneal you to new awareness.
&

164.   This is transformation. Indignance, anger and terror
        can become sacred fuel. You're not doing anything
        but refusing to run while the best part of you rises
        on a pure allowing of the world to become a soul.

        ———

165.   As they leave you, setting out audibly into the air,
        the words of Angels placed in your mouth offer surprising
        instruction. The level of your listening determines
        their prophetic reliability. Take care of them.

        ———

166.   The daily tasks are sublime opportunities to be.
       Making the bed, brushing one's teeth, walking the dog – a life
       is mostly made from these activities: how easily
       are they turned to prayer, fused in the heart of transformation.

       _____

167.   Even the Teacher must remember that understanding
       is determined by the context of one's experience
       and knowledge. Vacancies in the known and opacities
       in the mind's mirror hobble what one can give to others.

&

168.   Then is one not to speak of one's visions, visitations
       and transports? Speak with care. These are from abundance funding
       the work of transformation. One must not require belief
       nor misrepresent an interpretation as the truth.

       _____

169.   Russian cosmonauts saw Angels outside their space station.
       The government worked very hard to bury the story.
       If you are granted a vision, the force of denial
       will press within and without. Transform yourself to greet it.

       _____

170.   He wanted to be water, free and life giving to all,
       but he settled for inscrutability and hardened
       into rocky form. What happened? His allegiances dammed
       the flow of self-observation and petrified his heart.

       _____

171.   Voluntary suffering works only a narrow range:
too easy, it generates no friction; but if too hard,
a self-defeating lunacy infects the intention.
Stick with conscious inconvenience that no one can see.

———

172.   The noble seeker's not finding is a poignant drama.
He comes to question his own worthiness, and his powers
of renunciation ebb to an unconvincing frown.
Have nothing to do with the god to which he surrenders.

———

173.   It was not a fork in the road. It was just a milestone
where uncertain mind conspired with unwilling feet to go
no further. He waited there centuries until a child
came walking past with a fish in a bowl. "Come on, old man."

&

174.   He followed the child and in an hour the palace appeared.
"So close," he said. "Why did I wait so long? Am I silly?"
"It wasn't you waiting, so you wouldn't have been welcome."
The child smiled with an ancient benevolence. "Now you are."

———

175.   Do not let your vexations mar your hospitality.
A guest, instructed man or not, should be allowed to drop
his weariness at your threshold and share the benefits
Heaven has given you. Who knows what godsends a guest brings!

———

176. The perch from which you're watching yourself read this was put here
(here being the Mind of God) while time was still a toddler.
That's how long you've been waited for, friend, but beyond measure
is the joy in Heaven your completed soul will witness.

———

177. One cannot say the Absolute and this or that. All "and's"
are comprehended by the Absolute, all included,
including you and me. The Absolute must be fractured
into pieces to get a you or me or anything.

&

178. In our little minds then, the universe is a broken
Absolute still spreading from the shock of its shattering.
The only question is whether you prefer the ride out
to cold ash or the return trip to original love.

———

179. As a vulnerable soul comes to flesh in precious trust,
so a guest comes to your door. A visitation honors
the host and marks the house as reliable to Heaven.
Noted beyond Earth are the promises of host and guest.

———

180. The favor of Heaven is apparent, but the details
of the new civilization the Angels are nursing
is covered and closely held. The adult in the infant
is hard to discern, yet the weatherings of Earth are planned.

———

181.   Human flesh is not the best medium for consciousness.
Flesh distorts the finer frequencies, resists change, tinkers
with what it should be content to marvel at, and exhausts
its guest with animal celebrations and mortal pride.

&

182.   Even the brightest consciousness that bears a human mold
will be compromised, some of its blessings opaque and dimmed.
The mature conscience sees itself in the flaws and weakness
even the best men manifest, the best souls in bodies.

———

183.   If you want a breeze to serve you, make a tunnel open
to the air, a breezeway, a stoa for friendship with God.
Gather there your friends dedicated to highest practice.
Choose a question or a text, each prompting Presence for all.

———

184.   The dogs patrol their routes and daily renew their markings.
Humans the same but more in search of friends. Angels observe,
aching to pour out their blessings of love on the worthy.
Each kind in its being, life moves and watches over Earth.

———

185.   A note found in a corked bottle floating on a wave said,
"As you read this, acknowledge the contribution you've made
to its writing. Connected now beyond all accident,
beyond time and distance, we arise and converge in God."

———

186. Stubborn people circle their disappointments like buzzards,
expecting them to die and at last provide a good meal.
One can starve that way. Disappointments feed on attention
and die only when unwatched. Their bodies are never found.

&

187. That's why you can't have everything you want and Heaven too.
To repeat: desire dissipates attention, and Heaven
opens to the awareness of attention. What you do
with your attention determines the content of your life.

———

188. Plato understood that every individual thing
had splintered from a form back up the Ray of Creation.
Pride in one's identity is a downward condition
and continues downward from Earth to the moon. Who are you?

&

189. You know the answer. Why not take it out and look at it?
Inwardly you know all earthly trappings, relations, roles,
talents, genders, and flesh modes are not you. You are larger,
lighter, less restricted – an awareness of higher worlds.

———

190. Having been reminded, seek the state beyond location,
past a sense of self persisting in otherness to God.
Where awareness leaves the mind behind, is that God, the One?
Such are the sweet refreshments of a trek on Plato's trail.

———

191. Lifting the world on the back of his neck, Atlas soon lost
      the skill of conversation. He imagined dialog,
      but the stress he endured clenched his jaws and tightened his tongue.
      Nor could he lift his head to meet anyone eye to eye.

&

192. At first people were sympathetic. Some even started
      a club for strong ones to carry their own planets around.
      But the teenagers didn't buy in. "Who does that?" they asked.
      When Atlas wandered away, Earth stayed up unassisted.

———

193. What we call coincidence is slivers of fractured time
      reclaiming the unity of higher worlds. The crystal
      rediscovers its perfect geometry, and the light
      returns to unrefraction. Life awakes above our minds.

———

194. The solar eclipse which the country has just turned beneath
      has been a marketing bonanza. For months we've been told
      what products we'll need to watch it and what it all may mean.
      Tourists have scrambled for the few hotel rooms in its path.

&

195. T-shirts will brag, "I watched it all go dark." Millions will pay
      billions to claim a sliver of shadowed identity.
      Among humans anything can be promoted and sold:
      we'll buy whatever distracts us from our incomplete souls.

———

196.   War mongering has officially become a science.
        Major universities advertise advanced degrees.
        Ambitious adolescents will seize the new career path
        as "Collateral Damage Management" firms their transcripts.

&

197.   If this is too bizarre for you, you must be immunized
        against irony. What we cannot prevent must be turned
        to our advantage: adapted genes must have expression.
        Don't resist the future that progress imagines for us.

———

198.   If you've seen mortal combat and killed brothers and sisters,
        know that God has not forgotten you. You have been given
        a crushing weight to mill and parcel out as love to all
        whose need mirrors your burden. God still wants to use your heart.

&

199.   Reading this confronts you with the choice of falling further
        down the universe or committing your return to love:
        choose self-hate and death or the work of remembering God
        and setting each brave breath against the whispers from the past.

———

200.   A dog can get lost in its nose: it can be so deeply
        involved in the olfactory impression of the thing
        on the ground in front of it that the traffic whizzing by
        is as unattended as death. O, pup, come back. Look up!

———

201.   The ring of diet resistant fat around my middle
        is a moat aggressive vanity cannot overleap.
        Thank God I am prevented from believing this body
        to be what I am. This form, this face obscures the mirror.

        ———

202.   Seventy-two minutes of exercise four times a week:
        regular, worthy workouts add good value to one's life.
        They must be both challenging to the body – not extreme –
        and meditative. Conscious rest must mark the other days.

&

203.   Eat less than you want and use sex wisely, remembering
        what it nourishes. Aim the heart at prayerful constancy.
        Express friendship generously and without formula.
        Gratitude to God is the threshold of transcendent love.

        ———

204.   The urgency of greed prompts bad decisions. Wait for God
        to set a fine table and invite you to be seated.
        The beauty of the bounty will surprise you; the design
        will complete itself and part of it your rare contentment.

        ———

205.   In the lifting morning, the long commute dissolves my sleep.
        Sequential prayers at first light hallow the greening rice fields.
        The long trip home at night challenges my weak wakefulness.
        With humble care, I steer round the reaching fingers of dark.

        ———

206.   I can't think about the universe today; there's no room
       in my brain. Talk to me after I've moved all these boxes
       into order and created a pathway of escape.
       People keep sending packages. The doorbell keeps ringing!
&

207.   Tonight after the delivery services have closed,
       I'll meet you under the stars to receive shipments of light
       sent millions of years ago. It seems that to exist means
       having an address where mail piles up. What am I missing?

                        ———

208.   Good manners are never stiff. Lubricated with humble
       understanding of the weight every fumbling human bears –
       the burden of darkness – one's treatment of others always
       presents itself as an opportunity to be kind.
&

209.   Kindness does not dissolve in the downstream of time. It floats
       on unity invisible and by its buoyancy
       returns to God, uncredited, available to all.
       Sometimes clumsy, always poignant, good manners cleanse the heart.

                        ———

210.   One kind of ecstasy is immolation of the heart
       and mind in the coronal light of God. The wise Angels
       may give you this experience but only to instill
       the scale of self-awareness present in a crystal soul.

                        ———

211.   The souls of most people are unfinished and raw, buried
       deep in instinctive sleep. A soul must first be transplanted
       to the good earth of the heart. There when it buds, one will know
       oneself differently, a particle of loving God.

&

212.   The flower of the growing soul is remembrance of God,
       and return its timeless fruit. A mature soul radiates
       a constant witness to the world, in monsoon and in drought,
       a certainty of God, a welcoming of God in you.

       ———

213.   At every opportunity to fill its hands and mouth
       for free, greed suddenly appears, too fast for seasoned thought.
       While calculating storage space, it moves to seize some more
       of whatever has been offered or fallen on the floor.

&

214.   To get proportion re-enshrined, the king himself must be
       disturbed and put in an appearance with a measured rod.
       Experiences, money, food nor goods are safe to show
       till greed is back on bread and water getting used to no.

       ———

215.   Human beings can heroicize their own stubbornness.
       I have seen people build in a flood plain then watch their house
       float away, only to rebuild bigger on the same lot.
       If you inquire, they will brag about their perseverance.

       ———

216.   There are no accidents in a Conscious School. The Angels
        waste nothing, disposing everything intentionally.
        At some point one realizes one is here to observe.
        Thoughts, words, actions – all are knotted in the carpet's design.

        —————

217.   It's one thing to have no records, so myth and history
        overlap, but to have just enough historical fact
        to guarantee uncertainty bespeaks an intention.
        Keen is the precision with which Angels trim our knowing.

        —————

218.   Though there may be tears and stomach wrenching, there is relief
        and breath when the truth's sword edge severs imagination.
        The toxic shapes and tangles of shadowed desire require
        a merciless clearing. Bare the open cuts to the sun.

        —————

219.   Sometimes the shocks grander in scale are easier to bear.
        The external tempests that involve us all in common
        do not rupture one's gut or terrify one's mental scapes
        as much as watching one innocent friend betrayed and mocked.

        —————

220.   I will not trade my little slope of scrubby oak and grass
        for your sweeping mountain views and soothing piney breezes.
        You see, my sky is God's own blue. I cannot look at it
        without remembering God, for it is like no other.

        —————

221. Warning: At whatever level you live your current life,
you are required to choose an organizing principle
worthy of your finest effort – something just out of reach
to give lift to your functions and hallow your use of time.

&

222. Many fine standards are well woven into the culture:
moderation in all things, sound mind in a sound body,
gratitude the foundation. Why not dare the golden one,
the soul's aim: Remember yourself always and everywhere.

_____

223. Some lucky few reach a point of affluence or knowledge
where they shop the civilizations for their next earthlife.
(The dimension in which that crucial selection is made
allows the soul to choose a prior context for its next.)

&

224. This rare possibility – as rare as identity
almost fully shifted to the soul – transforms history
to a grand bazaar and tourism to a grave concern.
But aware or not, we are all preparing our next life.

_____

225. Here I am concerned about scheduling the repair man.
Here I am counting the calories in a piece of pie.
Here I am filling out a form to renew my passport.
Here I am sweeping my own dust off God's porch. Here I am.

226. The passage between the Eye and heart must be cleaned and smoothed,
imagination's poaching channel closed, and on the gate
the hand of worry must unclench. To lose the willed control
of this canal of nourishment is stunting to the soul.

&

227. The current of life energy ascending from its source
is partnered with the sacrificial offering refined
in the heart. To feed the Angel in man, this food must flow
unobstructed through the gate, to the soul's attention go.

———

228. Thought is meant to be an unsecret tool for the pruning
of experience and the application of reason.
When it stays private and becomes a pleasuring refuge,
the lower self has staked a claim and tied your mind to it.

———

229. Peace takes half a life to value, and that's for lucky ones
who don't believe what the brain has cobbled from the senses'
gatherings. "There must be more," people say. Yes, but it takes
a higher faculty to verify it and commit.

&

230. This higher sense makes its Presence known in searing flashes
then in bright episodes, but if by midlife one is not
a seeker of its light ready to become a servant,
one may not attract peace but only sleep and death again.

———

231. In the prayer's beginning and its end, the world is transformed,
but the middle is a struggle needing bold constancy.
Get behind your praying and walk with your eyes wide open.
The great gifts of God may seem a labor to the lower.

———

232. Most people are not sensitive to the labor and stress
of their fantasies. The flexions and diversions required
to feed imagination are over time a burden
on the body, a starving constriction of healthy flow.

&

233. Waking up reclaims the right function for which the body
was designed: the growth of the soul. Unwinding the inner
contortions poaching love for your daydreams frees you to see
fear, anger and grief as energy here to be transformed.

———

234. Sometimes during sleep the body seeks to discharge poison
it has locked away, and the departing contaminants
rise to the brain as grim, alien symbols of horror.
But look! You know these crimes. They scream for the soul's forgiveness

&

235. They want a proper burial like all the mortal spawn
whose chorus of claims is your identity. As they pass
beneath the soul's open Eye of neutral recognition,
you will be more and more of God, and what a morning comes!

———

236. Somewhere back in your infancy, you discovered the need
for a helmet, and you behaved as if you had one on.
Your skull and head muscles hardened into helmet posture,
and so did what you know of the universe and yourself.

&

237. Now the helmet cannot be simply removed. Patiently
you must loosen it from inside and out over a year
or two or more until it jiggles useless on your head.
When at last it falls off, the cosmos reopens for you.

―――

238. All highest mind is in Lord God, but Lord God not in it.
Limitless beyond creation, beyond ability
to conceive is the Absolute, of which all we can know
is a projected image reflected on a droplet.

―――

239. Life could not come from nonlife. Shock the primordial soup
with the perfect charge of lightning, you won't animate it.
Something alive is alive because its matter is fused
with a higher influence: ultimately I mean God.

&

240. The life we experience is God's reaching through matter.
In the case of human beings, we are souls, full droplets
of God becoming longer lasting crystals. All Heaven
rejoices at the finishing – the birth of an Angel.

―――

8. She Creates

II. Occasions

Staying Simple

One level of self-knowledge is recognizing the feel
of personality arising to misrepresent
one's true nature. It's like the innocent man wrongly brought
to trial who must pay the slick lawyer to get him off.
The lawyer cajoles, dodges, misdirects and undermines –
but all for a good cause: to secure the jury's favor
so the man can keep living in that dishonest bubble
of the world's belief about him. To someone with a bit
of light coming in, an infant conscience, it's disgusting,
but a life of simple truth courts merciless extinction.
The world is a brutal place for unprotected children.

Can essence be protected without personality?
Yes, there are two ways. One can be a hermit in a cave
or desert. The danger in that is imagination –
internalizing personality and spending life
talking to oneself. Strangely, one needs help to stay simple.
One needs a remote community of love, aspirants
foreswearing all the things that make lawyers necessary:
lies, negativity, competition, self-importance.
Into such a gathering love and light can come, the soul
can begin to discern itself and be responsible
for the attention holding it in and out of the world.

Away We Go

We can't imagine perfect happiness. There is no way
to describe it that can't be refuted. The mind can piece
together a version from its past experiences
of earthly elations. "Perfect happiness" is a name
in search of a state, a hot air balloon anchored to dirt.

Are we the dirt? Our desire to be individuals –
something other than God – has made us fall out of Heaven.
Separation is a tool for arising from the swamp
of mind, but there is no rising from God, only falling.
Perfect happiness is being in God. Cut the tether.

As we ascend, all our boundaries will disintegrate,
all the constraints of identity: our names, our habits,
our social roles, our genders, our species, our need of flesh.
Nothing limits fundamental being: pure consciousness
is its first creation, the origin of happiness.

Can we live on Earth with a mind serenely organized
to this pyramid? Can we ascend in any moment
to the one capstone and disappear into pure being?
The remembrance of God is not a mental restriction.
Remembering God dissolves restriction. Away we go.

Gone

If you are not absorbed in God, your identity weighs
you down to somewhere and sometime and defines the raw work
of scaling mortal lies. Who are you, friend? Do not answer
until you no longer believe what you would say. Leave it.

Christ on the cross no longer needed a mother, giving
her and his beloved disciple to each other's choked tears.
Christ risen offered nothing that the best woman could touch,
proclaimed unblest the mind anchored to flesh by doubt, then left.

Whatever knot of thought and love perversed has you captured
in its downward cycling, make an ending, a firm holding
on now and nothing else, a taking off from all that mind
has conjured round your name. Be the last word. Then we can leave.

Fire

A fire to the north and east has made the morning hazy
as if the uncertain sun strained to remember itself:
no breathing without tasting smoke, no thoughts without shadows.
So it is when the heart is troubled with a private lie
or a wrong belief. It defends itself destructively,
and a malaise lurks between the will and the love of God.

Hundreds of men – cells trained to danger – have been committed
to fight the flames, but the best they can do is encircle
an acreage of fuel, contain the rage, sacrifice
a zone of farewell to save the forest. New growth will come.
At home where I am, up and away, the smoke disperses
over time, and the pacifying heart reminds the sun.

All This

When you've been swallowed, don't lose God. Don't die inside the fish.
Remember Jonah: stay prayerful and firm in the Present,
even if everything flooding in from your ruined senses
makes you sick, and your lungs are turning inside out sucking
the unreal air. The lower self waited for you to wade
into the polluted sea then made its move, engulfing
your identity, claiming you completely. Don't die here.

Let your mind scrape the lowest depths of yourself for the will
to utter the soul's simplest command: be. Repeat, repeat
and repeat. Let each formulation of that syllable
be more intentional than the last. Let mindfulness sink
its root into the soft belly of darkness; establish
the real separation. A vague nausea will begin
to trouble the monster. Hold on through its wretching spasms.

And when you are vomited forth – ears ringing, eyes burning –
onto the shore of the good Earth, don't spill your gratitude.
Keep it close. Give it silently to God by focusing
your gaze on a single beautiful thing – a bird or branch
standing out against the sky. In the full range of being,
you are all this: the temptation, the belly of darkness,
the surviving mind, the will to return, the light of God.

Everything

Presence is a birthright, not a promise. We must claim it.
We have all the maps and testimonies. We've been well schooled
in the legends, epics, commandments and beatitudes.
We recognize and praise fellow seekers from all ages.
We've learned and practiced the steps in the processional dance.
We receive gifts of attention from the perfected ones.
Yet none of this avails if we will not forsake it all –
everything we clench, cherish, know – abandon it for God.

Not Asked

No invitation to the party. I understand why.
I behave as if I know something, and acting that way
consumes much of the oxygen in a room and offers
in return only verse too hard and sharp-edged to walk on.
Egos within earshot wonder what's worth the cuts and scrapes
their feet and knees will get from trekking across my stanzas.

My poems will need to weather a bit, survive the rise
of poisoned seas and hold against decades of starvation.
In the aftermath, they will seem reliable and firm,
not unmindful of the grayed Earth's residual beauties,
of humans daring Heaven. I admit they are unfit
for today's parties on soft carpets in the languid air
of free verse art, the swelling lava down below unfelt
through comforting soles, the dread Angels' gong not yet sounded.

End Days

There's a vague general alarm that the end days are here:
many match the headlines to their Revelations checklists;
others are proud to have formed a strong hunch that "our species
has overgrown all the checks and balances restraining
its planetary impact," often repeating the phrase.
Even those most comfortable buffer a twinge of guilt
at every plastic bag deposited in the garbage.
We're at the bad smell stage, wondering for just a moment
what could be causing that foul odor as we firmly close
the kitchen window and return to our entertainment,
missing the toxic cloud just now mounting the horizon.

But it's all right. Considering the scale of what's coming,
the best preparations would be as useless as screaming.
As opposed to what Heaven reveals to us, all the thought
that we ourselves produce comes from repackaging the past.
So to clean the planet of our inventions and products,
our monuments and mine scars, our problems and solutions
in some cycle we don't quite fathom, the past must be ripped
out of our minds and annihilated. Most won't survive
the shock, but those who do must transform their ashen longing
into a willed benevolent Presence, thank God, and bless
the good Earth with meek, beautiful children, then disappear.

Adam

If I had the strength to pull away from this temptation
to which my hostage heart is calling me as I watch her
being kidnapped, blinded by the serpent's awful mirror,
I would not be a man but some other kind of being,
perhaps what God intends. I only know this force that pulls
me down to her, enveloping and cancelling the will
to be anything else. What choice is here for me but loss?

Recuperating

Do not be impatient. You do not control this process.
The best you can do is provide a context of nurture.
Keep the ankles relaxed, the lower spine stretched, the breathing
deep and rhythmic, the throat open, the eyes allowed to tear.
The touch from another's hand can heal. Humbly ask for it.

God is here – more a benevolent dusk, enveloping,
not the sudden sun of revelation. The Present lifts
its arms to make an embrace. So many now unneeded
things must be discarded. What you think you are is shrinking.
You must be reduced to real substance, unworried looking

At some point you will make the separation: your body
and mind will be reknit into less important clothing,
and the Presence that you really are, that God is, will move
in these robes from one life defining vantage to the next –
regencrate, loving, a fragrance glad in namelessness.

No, Thanks

The rhetoric of sales having become the dominant
language skill, the price we will pay for a world pervaded
by commerce is a sudden disease: desire exhaustion.
Chronically overstimulated, the want response
will cease to function above survival level. "No, thanks"
will become the universal motto, and though thousands
will still congregate in malls and bazaars – out of habit
and no place else to go – they will stand around listlessly
watching each other, buying nothing. Frightened governments
will recruit the smartest biochemical engineers
to confront this new global pandemic of Triple D
(degenerative desire dysfunction), but the experts
wonder if there will be a market for a cure. No, thanks.

But if we don't want anything, what will keep us busy?
What will challenge attention to make meaning in our lives?
Are we finding ourselves at the onset of a dark age?
What new improved necessity can bridge this interval
in civilization and keep us from self-destruction
till a religion to replace wanting spreads its good news?

Evidence

Just the warning edge of discomfort is necessary
to keep the lower self at bay – a freely chosen chill,
a managed hunger. One must advance the will just one step,
like an Egyptian prince poised in eternal readiness.
Thus is the space for making something worthy created,
taken, and the work of remembering God can begin
by its persistence to affect the material world.

The proud man builds a monument, a stone memorial
to seize a larger share of time than flesh can latch onto,
but the instructed man builds a small guidepost, a stele
on the way out of time and inscribes a few syllables.
What are you building? What permanent thing have you fashioned
from your moments of fragile flight on unimpeded breath?
Return to that project now and now. Steal now from the world.

As you return, leave evidence of God for those coming,
those not yet on Earth and those here whose fitful dreams will break
into wakefulness. Leave a measured piece of string, a jar,
a poem – something tiny and clear in its mystery.
And if you are truly blessed, one among instructed ones,
know that your communions will endow radiant spaces
and summon brave trackers. In your sacred discomfort, sing.

The Day Begins

The children stand beside their tables, breathing in rhythm,
careful not to strain. Once focused and relaxed, they repeat
the invocation delicately voiced by their teacher.
"May I come to know myself, both in this world and beyond,
in thanks, without fear or blame, sharing freely with my friends."
Their voices dress the bells of morning; the day has begun;
the practice of the joy of attention finds its topics.

Small

There is a peace in little tasks, a reassuring scale
in the cleaning of a room, the weeding of a garden.
Doing what we know we can when we can secures the sense
of being worthy servants, prepared for prosperity.

It is the same in our relations with eternity.
The prayer that opens Heaven, that drops the ladder to Earth
for us to climb, requires no special talent from our lips –
only our resolution to join God in proffered peace.
Something in us thinks transcendence must be grand, dramatic,
bought by taming an earthquake or discovered in the dust
of post-Apocalypse. No. All we can bear of glory
sits on the tips of our noses awaiting attention.

What in us favors the distortion into grander feats
than we can dare – visions guaranteed to keep us wishing?
Our real work is small; we have the time, the knowledge, the skill.
Let us be reassured in our little rooms: God abides.

The Demands of Gravity

The flesh falls so easily into habit, and the mind
falls so easily into flesh, that the soul's pure delight
in now gets no attention. The demands of gravity
seem so real, the pressing momenta of obligation
have such force that the pilot light of Presence is snuffed out.
Do you remember now? Can you stop? Can your racing heart
allow itself to bless a single fully Present breath?

Worry is such a huge engine of your mortality
that if you sold it for a piercing prayer or a long look
at the sky, your death would slink off to a pity corner
and leave you to live the miracle right before your Eye.
When you see worry as worry – nothing more – you can know
yourself as something smaller, simpler, lighter – flexible
as dance unfalling in the air, no longer bound down there.

The voice of earthly logic calls you back. "Be practical.
We have responsibilities, the work of livelihood.
We mustn't get behind." It is sincere. It does not lie.
It speaks in honest ignorance and bears the scars of time.
Poor mortal thing, not you. When you return to help it lift
its next projected obstacle, do not forget your soul,
the simple truth of pure being, deathless and delighted.

Hard Conversion

The path of God is the only choice, but one must choose it.
How can one commit to something on the scale of lifetimes?
One must see clearly the end of the cosmos, the cold ash.
And so one turns one's back on the flow of events and seeks
the Source; one changes destinations from the dead nothing
to the living mystery, from labored pleasure to truth,
from then to now. One joins the few turned against the current.

One comes to see that pleasure is a downward chase, a loss
of energy not repaid, that all that one claims to want
has been learned to bolster the denial of one's falling.
One looks at one's habits, one's hopes, the intricate wreckage
one has worked so hard to disguise as home. One calculates
the time imagined, the unlearning to be done, the lies
one must burn. Is there enough life left to reverse it all?

One holds the hand of one above and gives one's other hand
to one below. All move as one in our climbing, holding
each other in our precarious vow. Time collapses.
Each breath, each bold pulse is all the mind can contain of life,
all the heart can hold of love. Joined in the measureless now
of God, we have transformed our choice into eternity.
And you, new readers, now a hand is reaching down for yours.

Fat

The birds are fat. Winter rains much beyond expectation
have brought a bountiful spring, rich in plant and insect life,
and the birds seem unable to override the season's
obligation to eat. The awkward young lilac branches
sink under the sparrows, and the woodpeckers no longer
interrupt what they are sure must be a permanent meal
to warn comrades in neighboring trees about intruders.

The dense green spreading all around me overflows the pools
of my vision, and serenity is carried away
on the flood. It is all too much. Everything knows itself
as an eater and a grower and ignores the brute fact
that it is also food. Everything is being eaten,
but the loud implacable rupture of being devoured
is displaced by the electric elation of plenty.

What besides organic life's constant hunger must I be
to see this closed system from outside it? What has loosened
and spiraled up and out of the circle of birth and death
to know itself apart? I do not disdain abundance
but am mindfully worn out by this recycling dinner.
I can't eat more of this. Beyond satiety I am,
pulled sluggishly toward wonder, an emptiness not to fill.

And Now

This spring is a giant waking from an extended sleep.
Suddenly a huge clumsy energy is descending
upon us, knocking things over and trampling on the fields
and forests. It dominates everything but does not know
what it wants. We are all forced to move, awkward and hoping
for a habit or routine to develop soon. It hurts.

Thus the challenge of needing a new level of being.
We have a shocking sense of sacred task when confronting
an intimidating otherness: not bloody conquest
but embrace, synthesis and self-mastery – for our own
greater becoming. If the monster does not teach us love,
we've risked all for vanity, and victory degrades us.

Agreeing to ascend a mountain shrinks us to single
heartbeats in humble sequence. The mind takes the marriage vow
to the simple second, and one's former imagined life
disperses in the air, replaced by the next single step.
Let us draw strength from the chorus of silent rejoicing:
Our preparing is bearing fruit. Heaven finds us ready.

Which Will It Be?

Foolish lover, do you want more than what is before you?
Do you not know that abandoning everything hoped for,
everything imagined, everything esteemed by the world
does not diminish you but makes consciousness more acute?
You are a mindful observer with nothing real to lose,
that is, when you are anything at all. Which will it be?

Birthing

When one enters labor, one does not know what will be born.
The promptings come unbidden, the mind quiets to listen,
the body abandons its habitual tasks and takes
the position of active surrender. The aperture
enlarges and the suffering breathes its sacred teaching.
The life that emerges is both message and miracle,
out of one yet completely itself, to be cleaned and kissed.

Each such visit of otherness in its travail destroys
a falsehood of the lower nature. The soul is wrenched free
from the flesh grip of what it is not and can only be
the witness of what is. Even the spare humbling honor
of having served vanishes in the power and the glare.
Beyond wonder it is that one can accustom oneself
to creation, but one can. The Present is infinite.

The name your parents gave you claimed a virtue but closed you
to eternity. Forsake that name! Forsake its comforts
and its pains, its longings and its mortal satisfactions.
You are pregnant with a boundless cosmos that would come forth
to breathe and become itself. You need only be Present
to the now and forever of poems and galaxies,
to the Angels midwifing the soul, to the God you are.

Steward is Designed to Fail

When your work is hollow from the waste of the night before,
restrict your expectations and cultivate gratitude.
The lower self suggests reveling in humility,
but its clever self-abasement is not humble, not small.
Rather bring thankfulness to the start of every action,
from getting up from a chair to filling a water glass.
Be quiet, guiltless and small; let the Angels restore you.

Steward is designed to fail. The soul is not the steward.
Prince Gautama is not the Buddha. Jesus is not Christ.
The steward is ascending intention, on scaffolding
that will be erected and dismantled a thousand times
before the soul can levitate at will and know itself
unfailingly as God. If a steward is ruined, brought low,
entreat the Angels to summon a mother's healing love.

At some point after ages of this rise and fall, the soul
claims itself, hatches from the shell of earthly personhood.
Eternal in God, it needs no other designation.
Till then, the art we practice is to urge the Eye to gaze
at the sun and accept the Crown, even as we accept
the moment's smallest talk. As the soul strengthens to return,
so we return to service of its strengthening. Be. Hold.

Sex

Sex is a function of the body but not only that.
In its lowest right use, it clears the valves and corridors
of sense, sweeping out debris, dissolving false conclusions.
It is a tool of health, its need measured by temperament,
not by desire. Used seldom, judiciously, it flushes
the toxins of the lower self's intrusions and restores
the authority of breath from the follies of belief.

As the means of procreation, sex opens the portal
to the realm of souls and must be used with true affection
and complete acceptance of the God spark thus attracted.
It is an honor to usher a soul back to the world,
where through the labor of flesh it can learn and continue
its path of return. One must not begrudge whatever comes
from the sex that invites a soul. It is a dear glory.

Then there is the sex of God, full of danger and delight.
To the degree that it fosters Presence and nurtures it
with love, it is a blessing. But do not confuse Presence
with pleasure or love with passion. Presence exists beyond
pleasure, separate from it, and love surrenders itself
to God, not to passion. The sex of God is not urgent
or selfish or stolen by power. The aim is Presence.

Not Knowing

How does one live with uncertainty? How does one transform
the attack of doubt and anxiety, refuse the lure
of superstitious ritual, keep the frightened mind free
of moral formula? How does one value not knowing?
All the activity of the lower self is to fill
the space of not knowing. All the lies of the lower self
distract us from the terrible beauty of not knowing.

Certainty is the awareness of the Presence of God.
As God is always Present, it is we who must arise,
bring ourselves with effort to a standing place in the light.
What must befall our flesh in the time bound circulation
of matter defeats our poor minds, slips from our mental grip:
step back from the flow of events and from the flow of thoughts.
That you are not those is the beginning of certainty.

The flesh justly fears its unknown fate, but we are not flesh.
In God is eternal being. Be the flesh and suffer
the pain of uncertainty. Be in the Presence of God
and participate in the permanence past all craving.
Be a conscious soul inhabiting flesh in shifting time
and all the delight that human senses can have of Earth
is undeniably yours in this moment's certainty.

More

There's more to this than meets the eye or nose or ears or skin.
There's more to this than mind can find a thought to wrap it in.
There's more to this than all your friends can help you haul away,
and more than all the nanothings piled heaping on your tray.

So this is what I'd purchase if more were most important,
and less could no more threaten with zeroes more redundant
than raindrops on the roof to which enough, enough I say:
Your first sound made the meaning clear; no more of you today.

Awards and Claims

The polite applause for the Lifetime Achievement Award
signals a grim choice: formalin or crematory flame.
Leave that decision to the cleaner who will claim your corpse.

There's a backdoor to this banquet hall, and the kitchen help
will pay no attention as you sneak through and out to find
the only undetermined thing left: the Present moment.

See, what we call the Present is really a special kind
of attention which most only know accidentally
and fleetingly and quickly forget. But you're different.

You've already got the lifetime laurels out of the way,
and your children are safe in their talents and don't need you.
Nothing left to hold you back from the Heaven always here.

Try being aware of your attention. Explore the state
you must will to be – its frequency, depth and duration
stake a claim in eternity for what you truly are.

The Price

There's a hitch in my breathing, like something caught on a hook
in my chest, a subtle clutch impeding the flow of air.
I consciously relax its grip and feel my thoughts disperse
into trusted silence and my eyes widen in wonder,
but quickly there follows a foreboding, a storm warning
saying that if I continue to hold myself open,
there will come a great weeping, a soft flood of warming tears
washing me away: all I think I am will disappear.

Somehow the hitch in breathing formed to keep me from crying,
probably far back in boyhood, but it formed at the loss
of wonder and trust and the thoughtless delight in silence.
Why have I been willing to pay that cost? Who profited?
This control switch on the air moving freely in and out
ensued from a trade with the devil: Take away this pain,
stop these humiliating tears, and my eyes will stay down
in your reach. Brave I'll become and no more look to Heaven.

Now I will reach across time and make a pact with that boy,
but more for you than for him. I would seek Heaven again,
so I can have in me a welcoming place for your love.
I will let all meanings of manhood dissolve and stay small
before the threats of this world, that I may reclaim enough
of wonder to encompass you in the delight I knew
before I sold it for a standing place of honored dirt.
The love you deserve requires Heaven at whatever price.

No Other Way

What is the limit of vigilance? How long can one watch
the gate or listen to a single voice explaining God?
Don't bother thinking of an answer; it doesn't matter.
What matters is that the steward can discern it has reached
its limit and must move to refresh its strained attention
with living prayer, which is like cool water or a sweet breeze.

There is no danger if the heart is glad to be returned
to task and the Eye appears even briefly to approve.
But if you find the gate desolate and resent being
stationed alone or hear more than a few words of complaint
about the presentation, then you are being kidnapped.
A little desperation behind your prayer of escape
is in order, for once you're in the lower self's embrace,
the steward's been bound and gagged and you are...well, not yourself.

The steward is a tool for refining identity
in the organic elements. It is a personage
assembled of desires and skills according to the soul's
instruction over time. It has limits and will break down.
Sometimes a thief gets through the gate. Sometimes the lecture fades.
But there is no other way beyond time and its questions.

Low Comedy

The Angels sometimes lure us into farce, low comedy
that wakes us by dissolving all pretense of dignity.
We stand with broom in hand before a broken pipe gushing
absurdity, flooding the floor, our shoes and socks, our will
to pretend control. Call the plumber; then get the children's
bathtub toys and plant a flag on Heaven's silly island.

And later when we open the door to let out the dog
and in hops or scurries a porch frog or local lizard –
something we know as it darts past that we'll spend half an hour
fumbling to catch and return – we recall the Angels' love
in the room and make a child's game of moving furniture
to rescue the terrified creature from our annoyance.

Steadfastness

The essence of mortality is resistance to change.
If you stay in your good enough house and ignore the mail,
eventually the world quits sending invitations
to the ball, and those few figures you see on the sidewalk
are ghosts, the dreaming dead that don't know they're among the dead.

But why then, you ask rhetorically, is steadfastness
so valued in the moral theatre and sacred books?
Your nap begins immediately and you cannot hear
the Angel answer that steadfastness is not stubbornness
but the constant comprehension of the steadying will.

Consciousness is life and must be willed moment to moment
in perfect adaptive service to the glory of God.
When the body's weight and fractiousness no longer trouble
the conscious will, one may discard the corpse without dying:
one is beyond change. The Presences then sensed are Angels.

Language

So often we have heard of the great value of silence
that we forget to cherish the labored gift of language.

The truth we can know is an energy cloud vibrating
too fast for our denser matters to hold, but a matrix
of words can suggest a form, a network of processes
holding a promise of keen states and high experience
and thereby ready our finer faculties to appear.

Now remember we are conversing across time and space,
perhaps continents or star systems, perhaps centuries
or light years. How supple and adaptive is poetry
in its travel. Liberated from great laws, we fathom
each other's glad greeting and delight in gestures of love.

After ages of preparing near-human flesh to grasp
its intricacies, Angels delivered language to men
and thus made us fit houses for the maturing of souls.
Yes, we often pervert this tool, but the best use of words
can stun us and reveal the threshold of silent Presence.

Can we call it a word, that vessel of original
movement in the Mind of God that brought forth the genesis?

9. Bridging Worlds

New Day

After sustained effort, a brief collapse and a night's rest,
you'll waken with a store of higher fuel. Be careful.
The lower self will want a shopping spree, a rush to spend
the chafing coin that patience knows to hold for higher use.
Not doubting but demanding clarity, the critic mind
asks what higher use may be. Say lifting the struggling heart
of a friend sincerely seeking, capturing a poem
or practicing some art for which you've paid a price of years.

The point is to share your profit through conscious discipline,
in form that firms the will and tones the mind and focuses
the sight so beauty – always here – is apprehensible.
You've earned the right to briefly be an Angel instrument.
If you want more than this, identify the wanting thing.
Step back from it and call its name, unhinge its urgency.
Yes, it is disquieting to wait, and if the pressure
from the fuel's inner ferment splits your skull, let it split.

Godly

It's fine to talk about God, but if God were anything
language could encompass, then your mind would be the cosmos,
and that's a repulsive thought. Maybe it's better to sing
God's praises and enjoy the benefit of the topic
without the greedy mind getting a big piece of the deal..

Perhaps best of all is not to talk or sing about God
or paint or sculpt God or construct God an altar or house,
but most simply to be God. We don't even need the word:
"Be" means "be God" if ideas of God do not intrude
and the silent Presence of all and everything abides.

The Best of You

What stings the lower self most grievously is the failure
of its personalities to arrest another's force.
Next most painful is other personalities' success.
The lower self abides in lawless, predatory dark,
a dire master-or-be-mastered ground of grim encounters.

Feeling this lower world, the heart grows weary, despondent,
reachable for the animal below, and the fuel
the heart with willing beats distills to encounter the soul
falls into grimy hands. Too dull to intervene, the mind
moves from this branch to that, hearing only the louder crows.

Such is the body's life. Is this what you want unto death?
Even if God is a blank for you, a blink in the sky,
an abandoned attention, is there not something in you
that remembers a better beauty, a worthier self?
Be that now, friend. Hold it with prolonged breath. Make it a pledge.

The dirt of all you are not drops away. The best of you,
light and aware, rises. Look up to all that awaits you.
And when the alarm of old personalities below
troubles you, show them your back. Look further up in bold flight.
Be one crossing into the unimaginably real.

One Certain of Eternity

To one certain of eternity there's a heightening
to whatever standing place can be found. The small events
present themselves as types and symbols; time dilates to near
disappearing. The air encircles a grotto of peace.
Each thing is as it is, and as it is, is beautiful.

Will you join me? Put down your instruments of life control.
Free your sight to see. Focus on the silence under all
that can be heard. Relinquish what will happen to your thoughts.
Trust the breath moving in and out to know its own purpose --
its reporting back to Love's Field what it has found in you.

The nature of love is that it overflows. Nothing holds
its flood, washing you away, making worthy everything.
Yet above love, levitating, a witness comes to be.
This we also are, and more beyond, which to our witness
vibrates intimations that will measure new surrenders.

That we fall back to Earth is not a tragedy. The laws
we lift will serve our flight, as we put sequent time in form
that rises like a ladder from the heart. It's not belief
or hope or fancy to be certain of eternity –
higher love's abiding witness. These gifts belong to us.

What is our Work?

What is our work? It is not to improve the heavy world
in which we are embodied, nor to prosper flesh and bone
whose prosperity satisfies a fat self-righteousness.
It is not to serve some human dream, which abstract language
lifts to febrile plausibility. No, this Earth entire
and all our little species does upon it spins in space
to be observed, a sensual metaphor to remind
the soul of its true separate being. Once reminded,
soul begins its work – transformation of experience
into God's awareness -- and thus proceeds eternally.

To Live This Way!

One's moments in the world but not of it – discovering
oneself unhitched and free to go but still in the habits
of freighted flesh – are enlightening, poignant, humbling, strange.

One watches one's friends perform, their labored machinery
bound to an unread script. One's body rumbles to take part,
but the soul's unfettered will is strong enough to refuse.

Oh, to live this way! This is life after death, floating free
but still generous to Earth, a calm selfless monitor.
Now the task: how to direct the superabundant love?

Learning this long work – one's astral duties – takes centuries,
but eternity is measured in attention, not time,
as one masters unbounded expansion and contraction.

When I take the hook of a touch or voice and am reeled back
to the body, let me not forget the loving duties
of the liberated soul: to be, and hold the mirror.

Not Involved

When you observe yourself to be depressed, easily tripped
into self-pity, stuffing anger back down your own throat,
know that your soul is not involved, that you have been swallowed
by the lower self marauding under the moon, knowing
only that its huge mindless hunger is not satisfied.
Such is the creature that consumed Jonah: you are breathing
false air in a stomach. Know that your soul is not involved.

Observe your friends: if their frustrations are too visible,
if more than one of them speaks in strident tones and decries
the purposeless labor of life, then the true cause is not
your own imbalance but a larger influence staining
everything in its wake. The whole canvas has been darkened.
Know that their souls are not involved, and help them be aware
of the abduction that has made hostages of you all.

To be the soul is the solution. Criminality –
in the gut, under the moon, among the planets -- infects
bodies, and healing is a process happening in time.
Retreat to the patience of the soul: the inflammation
will heal or it won't; you will learn to bear the affliction
or it will subside. Leave such things to the wise physicians.
Know that your soul is not involved. It thrives in God's silence.

Daily News

What we call the daily news is a product carefully
crafted on scientific principles to stimulate
exaggerated emotional response. It's gossip
about what we're taught as children to fear and care about
presented with the language cues for adrenal firing.
Will natural selection favor a species living
in semi-permanent alarm? Distraction and relief
have become major industries. Splurge before the ship sinks.

Here's my small alternative. I'm taking just these minutes
to be with you. Let us together find the truth of now
and share what we can of it, reaching above the tumult
of thought that traps us in time. Rightly, language is always
an impoverished prelude to silence. Touch is better.
We are all the same thing – God – unless we break into shards –
hands, eyes, mouths – spinning out, grasping to survive on their own.
Don't attend the sirens of doom. True being is deathless.

Walking

While you walk on Earth, the tempter rides your back, his whisper
audible when your pace goes slack. He urges you to pause
for thought and directs you off the road. He cannot harm one
fixed in purpose, proving by joy the promise of return.

With each breath, let go of all that does not participate
in love, that joy may be distilled in you. There is no need
for more thought, for answers, for permission. Your death and birth
have joined beyond time: the soul's direct instruction begins.

Let Us Find This

I warn you, sometimes when I would pray, all that comes are jokes –
corny constructions chasing punchlines like ecstatic dogs.
What does that say? Perhaps that if one tries too hard, the prayer
turns prey. Honest prayer rises of its own and overbrims
the heart, surprising every part, waking every level,
some high above breath, some so low they know not but to laugh.

Prayer is attention launching itself to Heaven, aware
of the disguises it destroys in its updraft, aware
of its unworthiness, its lack of grace, and yet aware
of God remembered in the now of all else abandoned,
aware of love, of silent mind and nameless more, aware.
Friend, hiding nothing in our search, let us find this to share.

What to Tell a Seeker

If your aim is to get one to join your numbers, I'll leave
to you the devising of a recruitment strategy.
Proselytizing – commerce in souls – is not my concern.
If your aim is to enlighten even for an instant,
to relieve the burden of dark belief in matter's grip,
to remind the soul of its immortal station, say this,
both in words and in your respectful heart's sincere address:

You are a soul wandering in painful fascination,
wasting your light on what cannot satisfy you. Look up!
Strengthen yourself by remembering the Presence of God
as often, as deeply, as enduringly as you can.
Rediscover yourself as undistracted deathless love.

If the ones who hear you want to walk with you, let them come,
sharing costs in kindness, spreading the joy of reminding.

The Embrace of Friends

The order of the wild world derives from how power, speed,
sensory acuity and a talent for hiding
affect breeding and the continual getting of food.
Expect no compassion but also no useless slaughter.

The entry of the human brings new faculties to bear:
as if by magnifying metaphor, the emotions
create a new dimension of sensation; the mind both
extends and encapsulates control over time and space.

And here we are – evolved, acculturated, successful
beyond all reason. We dominate the planet, careless
of the miniscule complexities of the finite web
that holds us up, our progress killing our continuance.

Why have we become so heedless of God that the Presence
is forgotten in our hearts? We are enthralled with ourselves
and think only of the next unnecessary glory
of invention. Expect no compassion in our slaughter.

Children, the Field of Love was to be our inheritance
and still can be if we accept the trial we were born
to bridge. We must pull ourselves back from the brink and hold God
blameless in our hearts and minds, making the embrace of friends.

God's Nothing

Our history is not without cataclysms, blank times
when the whole wall came tumbling down, and one brick would not stay
still upon another. The marauding sun came so close
the borders of everything within our sight vaporized
in the devouring light and our names forgot their reasons.
No confines, no context – all understanding come apart.
We call these episodes of vacant terror "God's nothing."

Both

If we were merely human, we could simply fight and die
and be done with the weighing – letting the moon be nourished.
If we were purely Angels, we could float above the blood
and strengthen will's forbearance by letting the recurring
fate of our cherished human children fall out by the laws.
But we are both flesh and beyond, with each breath cut and snared
by the fishhooks of experience we must not believe.

Your flesh greets mine, and we share a bit of news or gossip
or vain intelligence; our stalwart bellies settle in
and signal our chests to inflate, our minds to take account.
A deal can come from this, an alliance, a slight, a grudge.
Meanwhile in love's ether do our conjoining souls affirm
their single substance, their unity in being, urging
(souls' only power) our hearts to conspire in charity.

Nothing More

Let me not forget that the life of spirit must be lived
directly, now and only now, not treated as knowledge.
Instructed men are nothing more than the dead, nothing more
than stones if our instruction does not bond each breath to God.
Men who know themselves above sleep truly have nothing more
than their work to make a marriage of knowledge and being.

New

The border of understanding – the point at which the veil
is made of chain mail and barb wire – requires transformation.
You may not cross as you are. You must leave all your luggage,
probably your clothes (if they represent you), your license,
wallet, certainly your memberships, affiliations,
beliefs, opinions, feelings, thoughts and habits of posture.

Then you wait, but the waiting isn't waiting: you're working
at purifying your attention – meaning becoming
more and more aware of it and less and less distracted.
When you're ready for what Heaven has to reveal, silence
will have already opened the gate and you'll be elsewhere,
above even the innocent amazement of babies.

Unless you die in that state – and that's another matter –
you'll return to what you left behind – wanting it or not –
and you'll find in your hat or perhaps in your receipts file
a deed to mental acreage and a building permit
so you can erect your new understanding of the world,
your latest mudbrick reconstruction from journeys beyond.

Dying

Dying is important, death is not. People can use help
moving on from organic bodies to some other kind,
but once they have gone, the less clinging we do, the better.

How do we help the dying be born? First, don't make it hard.
Don't communicate fear or worry, don't be disgusted
at their loss of control, don't buffer their pain, don't lament.

Breathe with them through their labor; praise the beauty of their will.
Ride the rhythm of their spasms out and up, out and up.
Attend the silent intervals, your being theirs, theirs yours.

The grip of identity must be loosened for the soul
to move to what it has made of itself. How much better
its passage if consenting, lifted by the love of friends.

Let them take leave. Don't hold them any more than you'd resist
the birth of new life. What have you learned from their departure?
What fearless readiness are you earning, what depth of life?

Wordy Creature

Man is an excerpt, a paragraph in The Great Fable.
Strangely, the whole story consists of one syllable: Be.
Yet each element requires thousands of words to explain
its proud history and significance, its little thrust
in the grand surge. Man's an especially wordy creature.
Language and identity are one and the same for man.
So what can you deduce, O man, about the way back up
the current to the unspeakable source? Liberation
is not handicapped by language, and whatever you are
without words is more real than this poem and all your thoughts.

Birth and All

Birth is a contradictory process: in the womb world,
a fetus reaches a bursting fullness, a completeness
no longer containable, only then in agony
to enter a new dimension of unbearable light
and distance and dependency where everything must be
negotiated from helplessness, a grip on zero.

Then for years the world is a delirium of learning,
an array of feedback loops feverishly constructing
a mind – a growing, strengthening personal replica
of everything, hovering somewhere that seems like above
(the head? the sky?), somehow synthesizing into language
the torrent of sensory deliveries. *It is mine.*

But at some point even as the files keep getting thicker,
the glitches multiply, the program totters toward looming
unreliability. A somber intelligence
arrives to announce the period of maturity,
when growing and falling apart are simultaneous,
and the curtains part on a hanging question: Who am I?

On your answer everything depends. Will you spend what's left
of the organism's time in the faltering senses
protecting old pleasures, in the less and less convincing
versions of the world the slipping mind cobbles together?
Or will you be something untethered, participating
in certain but unnamable being – all, not any?

To be born in God is a contradictory process.
The terror of dying becomes a kind of nourishment
as the dying thing reveals itself as shadow burden.
The work that must go on till final breath – holding aloft
a conscious unbelief – widens into liberation.
The body aches, the mind chatters on. Not these. Everything.

Crossing

There is enough time, time to stop, subtract yourself, step out
of the flow of events and let the stimulations go
without response. They will nuzzle, sigh, beg, pinch and slap you.
Wait them out. There is enough time, enough time to peel off
each stinging thought from the swarm of beliefs your departure
will agitate. Slow your breathing. Above all, do not nod.
Wait for God. God's spark nourishes itself on your silence.

There is enough time, enough time, enough. Eternity
will open around you, above you. You will understand
that all the questions bind you, pull you back into the flow
of mind. You will understand there is nothing to be done
or said or thought. You become as breath, effortless, unowned.
It is clear the life you've left here, life in name and body,
is school for love. You discern you are not alone. Welcome.

Calm

Fear follows the lower self's deceptive agitation,
a misdirecting turbulence of the sacred current
that would rise to nourish the heart and thence to Eye and Crown.
Face them down, these conjurings, not with aggression or spite,
but with the calm of deathless certainty humbly invoked.
Claim the birthright of life in God's service, which cannot die.

No Substitute

How much nonsense rides on the need of mind and hands to do
something – anything – to keep the fear of being nothing
from creeping in. The whole universe is fleeing being
nothing, speeding in an unaware explosion away
from that which no something can hold or make a firm sense of.
That nothing, of course, is God, but the word does not avail –
no substitute of hand or mind for being not a thing.

Solemnity

True solemnity is the reverent attentiveness
that issues from and haloes the effort to be Present.
By what greater greeting can one offer love and welcome?

Intermittently a child at play can feel with relaxed
innocence an envelope of grace, but there will be no
understanding yet, no grateful cognizance of blessing.

The mature soul that has endured the wasteful wanderings
and blind indulgences of flesh and also tasted states
of Angelic elevation and overbrimming love

holds wisdom in restrained delight and delights in wisdom.
It values peace, quiet continuities of movement,
respect and concordant speech that befriends fragile Presence.

Do not mistake a solemn tone for mere formality.
The wise man knows how calm his grasp, how sensitive his touch
must be to hold the cord of Allah in sustaining hands.

Sustenance

We can't live on airplane snacks. Small moments of higher states
are savory but not sufficient to entice the full
persistent lift of attention the steward must shoulder.
Without sustained flights past the lower's reach, the starving grip
of gravity prevails, and the effort to remember
becomes something on a crumpled checklist in a pocket.
We need to desire nothing descending and feed ourselves
accordingly: prayer, beauty, the embrace of companions,
and all the payment we can scrape up. Yes, payment is food:
nothing nourishes like payment we're just now mindful of.

All We Mean

What exactly are we saying? God is here now with us,
in us, as us, as everything. That realization
rises in and wakens the soul and moves identity
out of flesh and time into the soul and eternity.

All that rushes outward clinging wretchedly to matter
for its identity will resist the Presence of God,
which can only be resisted by the suffocation
of consciousness, by a life of forgetting what we are.

When we remember God, we are God. Overbrimming love
cleans the mind of agitation and welcomes the terror
of not being, the truth of not being other than God.
Love is the reach of God calling back the vagrant cosmos.

This poem is all there is to say, all that words can mean.
We carried off by time will live as we remember God
or die as we forget. What are we as these lines induce
our awareness, our denial, our terror, our welcome?

Enough

Horace wrote lovingly of escape to his Sabine farm,
his retreat, his sanctuary of sweet moderation.
There despite some rude slave's occasional impertinence –
which our poet amusingly transformed – he could observe,
trusting his pious heart to nature's unstressed syllables.

Here at my country place, stuck in an age of slavery
more subtle and widespread, I can barely keep the napkin
of land around my house groomed and civilized. Hang the rest.
Whatever's down there in the gulley no longer troubles
my attention and must entertain itself with its cries.

The domain from heart to headtop is all that's truly left
to me, if I'm to believe the Angel indications.
The rest still functions, ever noisome, chairbound and torpid,
but the heart's work of transforming the brute contents of time
has become all important, focusing the readiness

and keeping God's conduit unblocked. The precious return
opens in each moment that will summons into being.
All men seek the good they can see by their limit of light,
and there is no distortion love cannot straighten. God's Eye
sees it all from the balcony of love. That is enough.

This Book

"I can help you," a voice said. "What must I do?" I replied.
"The book is already written, but I can instruct you
in how to access it and bring it here." "And who are you?"
"I am yourself disembodied, a soul now sufficient
after ages of slow development to stand aware
in eternity. I am you in the next dimension.
You are listening to the echo of your own being.

"There is only one danger in this communication:
the impostor will seek to get between my intention
and your hearing and lead you off in imagination.
His whisper is louder than I can be, more alluring.
The best of your mortal identity must be alert,
ready to close the gate on his lies. While we share the state,
I can open the book for you the poet to transcribe."

"We are not new to this collaboration," I noted.
"True, we have labored the passage of hundreds of poems:
you challenged your art; I nurtured deathless identity.
Thus is this book brought forth with full-wakened authority."

Little Psalm

The dew drop on the point of this laurel leaf is the end
of time. The eternity all around it includes me.
I have reached my destination and emptied memory
into God's palm. I will donate my wages to the soul
climbing behind me, who will do likewise until they drop
to Earth and find a prayer waiting to be kissed and wakened.

10. Departure

By Now You Know

If you've been reading this book with Presence, by now you know
that God has written it. The author named on the first page
is but God's instrument, chosen not for his gracefulness
or his precision but for his reliability.

Now remember, you will serve yourself if you quit thinking
of God as a person. God is a state in which our souls,
the Angels and even higher beings participate,
but for which personhood is a troublingly heavy veil.

If you've been reading this book with Presence, by now you know
that God wants your participation, wants you to share love
with the all you see as everything. Thus God's blunt poet
keeps showing up every day and scribing the given lines.

Whether you think of the cosmos we persons reside in
as actual or holographic won't matter to God.
Whether you see yourself as mortal or illusory,
the being of God will transform you into being God.

So come join this dependably repetitive poet
as his pen produces God's repeated revelation:
the state of God is lovingly available to man.
If you've been reading this book with Presence, by now you know.

What is Coming?

The signs have been aligned to the calendar, harmonized
with the simple faith that the laws of Earth that need not be
broken will not be, and the preparation directed
in reverence. What is coming? What great renovation
of the Angels' garden planet is about to begin?
We will fill our barns, organize our neighborhoods, and make
our meagre stockpiles of hard currency, but so many
already do those things better than we, the real issue
can't be mere survival of life and commerce. We must be
ready above the mind for a new measure of mankind.

There will be the challenge of events and their aftermaths.
Those who would carry their souls no further up the ladder –
so many, so many – will fall cursing their spectacles.
Our role must be to protect with Eye and Crown the deathless
unnamable state born here in this mercy of turmoil.

The Book of Intertwinings
of the Sacred and the Practical

I. Prayers and Upturned Sonnets, First Series

Prayer 1

Pinpoint focus without tension; mental effort,
muscular calm: the craft of self-remembering,
of waking the coiled serpent from its sheltered sleep,
luring it out and up to the sun, absorbing
the nourishing lightning, transforming the tempest.
My universe into your universe, O God!

Step Through

One spends years opening the gates; then one must walk through them.
The full, steadfast force of one's life must be redirected
from downward self-protection to a complete commitment
upward to the fearless, compassionate intelligence
that attends self-awareness. One's quietness of action
will ride on a radiant certainty that cannot die.

Step through and beyond like an ancient prince, at once leaving
his father's house and claiming the world, teaching all nations
in every utterance pressed on the one in front of him,
in every silent spurning to be drawn back to mere mind.

Prayer 2

It is so simple and the only thing one has
to do: the willed stride out of imagination
into Presence. May the overwatching Angels
guide my step: make it deft and inconspicuous,
done more often, with deepening understanding,
and held, held with resolve as strong as love is kind.

Only the Soul

With the high heart's recognition of the ladder back up,
one can mount the first rung: the soul's awareness of itself.
The soul acting through the body produces attention,
but the soul's slight withdrawal brings awareness of attention.
Only the soul can have this state. Only the soul can be
aware of itself and know itself as not the body.

Separate from flesh, the soul discovers its existence
in the timeless dimension that we call eternity.
The soul remembers itself, at first a state it can hold
but briefly before the body's gravity reclaims it.

Prayer 3

Let the pages turn by themselves; let the story
unfold. Your job is not the plot – if things could be
different, they would be: yours is the mindfulness,
and if you can, a graciousness of syllables
and gestures. The quality of your witnessing
will progress. Aware attention returns to God.

Running Away

A mistake made too many times becomes necessary.
One will wage war for the right to perpetuate one's lies.
Which among your current misconceptions would you die for?
Identity is first a gamble then an addiction.
Your god is a subtext of your idea of success.
Your brain makes what you see, your heart what you believe. And then?

The universe is running away, and humanity
is trapped in the outward speeding dust. Anything we do
or think from the body outward contributes to the loss.
If time can only flee, what is not of time, not of death?

Prayer 4

When I go out, may I discover something true
and worthy to spend my money on – a seedling
of admired grace, a small gift for a friend, a book
bridging centuries between brothers. And if not,
if Present gaze can light upon no such delight,
may my coins be tight in my purse till I come in.

Temptations

The imagined pleasure of capturing the world's esteem
is the lower self's best tool to rob the sacred ascent
of its fuel. Gluttonies, talk of sweet guilty secrets,
and loud lordly laughter also wait to ambush the climb.
Vagrant mind leaks a toxic gas of drunken songs and sighs.
Dear one, believe in time and you'll bend to these temptations.

You must keep your eyes fixed on the sun, lean into the glare,
blind yourself in its annihilating glory, trading
pleasure for joy, each sequent step more clean of worldly worth.
At the peak, spread your arms to signal God. Your work is done.

Prayer 5

The stronger one's personality, the more laws
it is under. One reason the steward must die
is that it lacks the mineral callous needed
to repel the pain of Earth. The steward observes
both Earth and Heaven, utters a binding contract
between them, then retires in fatal bravery.

The Steward

The embodied principle of action called the steward
matures slowly, scraping itself clean of the world with shards
of wisdom littering the grounds of the temples. At twelve
it is self-aware and craves initiation; the task
of mastery begins. At eighteen it is practicing
discernment between things ascending and things downward faced.

At thirty it is reborn in higher understanding
and committed to a fatal consequence. It lives on
in the world a while, gathering friends and allies, holding
an earth-clumsy certainty, a promising crystal light.

Prayer 6

Worry makes everything worse. It is arthritic
vanity, fear-based nutrition. Leave its low stink.
Who are you to worry anyway? God doesn't.
Do you think by gnawing your own stomach lining
that your brain will achieve a level of control
that Heaven abstains from? Be as quiet as God.

Male and Female

In some scriptures, the mind is steward, the heart is consort.
In others, the heart as passive mother births the steward
as a principle of action which dies delivering
man to the brink of conscious being, God's promised kingdom.
Adam and Eve, Jesus and one or another Mary,
Odysseus and Penelope – always the same union.

Male and female must unite to reverse the refraction
of God into humans. And ever waiting in disguise
is the lower self, armed with alarms and seduction songs
and thousands of mouths counseling division and divorce.

Prayer 7

The lower self is more than instinct though less good.
Instinct serves its brute purpose on Earth: appalling
to the heart, yet it keeps a pitiless balance.
The lower self knows no such bounds. Born in a wound
of abandonment, its intelligence is turned
against God's love. It imagines that God can fail.

Insult

The reflex to fight back against abuse jerks to a halt
at the end of the steward's choke chain. True action can breathe
and take its certain steps only when raw reactiveness
retreats and slow memory of principle moves to fill
the baffled space. Why is this happening? Absorb the shock,
steady the nerves, awake to what Heaven is allowing.

This unknown field in which one finds oneself is a matrix
of karmas, a tapestry weaving itself of matter
and time. Forsake those threads of being that must be used here.
Forgive yourself. Forgive the one trapped in hate. Forgive God.

Prayer 8

Each train coming into the station promises
a life less burdened, a wondrous destination.
All aboard! But they're all lies – imagination –
plumped to evoke longing and keep me traveling.
I pray for the strength to watch them arrive and go
while I stay, standing still among the swarming crowds.

Abduction

I'd like to report an abduction. A smooth gang of thoughts
wearing the alluring clothes of intelligent questions
have kidnapped Peace, put a hood over its head to give it
an identity, and driven off down the karmic road.
The dispatcher said, "All I can do is record the time
and take a description. You'll have to imagine the rest."

It's backward. The laws here exist to propagate more laws.
This happens often enough for me to know not to count
the losses but to return to God's house, strip off my name,
and not answer the door without God standing beside me.

Prayer 9

Let me not be shocked when kindness is rejected,
cursed for interfering or twisted into crime.
When wounded or afraid, the instinctive part clamps
the transit of trust in a febrile assessment
of damage while the lower self, judging kindness
as weakness, begins to calculate advantage.

Deposed

The instinctive element and lower self overlap
but are not the same. The former's purpose is survival –
of the organism itself, yes, but more profoundly
of its coded endowment, its version of the species.
The latter is a personality, a thing of learned
lies and stealth which exists to subvert the soul's purpose here.

Not always was our species suitable to house a soul.
Ages under Angels' care were needed. But when souls came,
bringing their immortal work, the mortal intelligence
was deposed and from it split a shadow of rebellion.

Prayer 10

To separate from fury, one must surrender
what has been insulted – the false self, so firmly
imagined and defended by one's inner talk.
Without it, one is small, naked, easily hurt,
but free of Earth, forgiving, bonding with any
who aspire to embrace the Presence here for each.

Barking

I should see the expression of destructive emotions
as the barking of a dog – a primitive behavior
venting a potent energy, an obsolete response
robbing fine fuel from the newer aim to know oneself.
And if I hold back the bark, there is that fuel ready
for the kiln of acceptance to fire into consciousness.

I would become the vessel with an iridescent glaze
surprising the eye and holding the kindled attention
of the man who earnestly went to the window to see
if in the darkness he could know why the dog was barking.

Prayer 11

Dear Angels, I would not be a judge in your land.
Too often have I seen my poor intelligence
crippled by impatience, and what wisdom I have
clouded by the testimony of impostors.
Teach me to wait, to let your purposes come clear,
truth's arriving water refreshing the Present.

Rough to Touch

Earth is pleasing to the eyes but rough to the touch. It chafes
the soul's sensitivities and shocks the finer justice
we have brought with us for our sojourn here. We must refine
earthly wildness, clean and dress it in the sweet symmetry
and poignant water flow of gardens. Pathways must be trimmed
and honored to allow our passage to each other's hearts.

The sky above the mountain ridge takes us out of ourselves
and lets the soul breathe, but the daily dirt will deaden us
if we don't make from it the numbered bricks of remembrance.
Yes, Earth has wondrous beauties, and yes, Earth must be transformed.

Prayer 12

We are dense creatures slow to feel and understand;
otherwise, life here would not need to generate
such a surplus of suffering to elicit
our compassion. The genocide, the poisoning
of the river, the starved dog hiding in the weeds:
we act from our level of consciousness, O Lord.

If God

For the woman and child who must daily carry water
and the man who must dig for salt, the wearying labor
of living shrinks the understanding of human purpose.
Labor has always been required, but grim toil not feeding
the ascent of self-knowledge will finally crush the heart
and ratify the lower self's stealthy intelligence.

Our work must be in light of God, then in God and through God
to all we touch. Work done to stay alive wears out our time
and leaves us empty handed on return. The chance to come
to Earth to work is precious if God is not forgotten.

Prayer 13

Let me not think reason to be infallible.
Reasoning is always premised, and premises
lose track of themselves and sleep in trusted foliage.
True certainty is a mystic state, a province
of the soul, and the soul must know itself to be
certain of certainty and not trapped in reason.

The Law

Because it must be written down, the law is better known
by the lower self than by the higher heart, which appeals
to spirit and immortal purpose. Language was given
to man as a staircase out of darkness, but the knowledge
of language – how it veils the truth or serves to reveal it –
is, as is all knowledge, a tool of the user's value.

No human version of the law dare be made absolute.
By the discretion of judges – a tender, fragile touch –
is justice balanced. Mercy is dangerous, but more so
is its lack. A well-ordered darkness is still hell. Be wise.

Prayer 14

They call to you, O Lord, these most desperate thoughts
begging for annihilation in a greater
consciousness. Our lies hate themselves, and hope to be
extinguished – such is the tragic mortal limit
of holiness, such is our greatest suffering.
God, may this human mind not be everlasting.

Karma

Destiny is what happens. It is living on the cliff
of karma, giving your identity to gravity.
As long as you are you, the only triumph you can have
is attaining some specific ledge or peak, some landmark
of designated value. Then your mind must get to work
finding the next thing: the great struggle of "then what?" Then what?

The mind is not free. Give your identity back to God.
The mind will try to sneak out like a gas under a door,
but the will of God's awareness can retrieve it, keep it
from recondensing into karma and reclaiming you.

Prayer 15

To have been chosen to support the Angels' work
on Earth is the highest honor. When chosen ones of those
complete a life, the rest are both bereft and glad.
After the call to radiant life, what is earned
in each appearance here is at each departure
made permanent. The great return accumulates.

Don't Waste It

What is it that believes that bodies aren't supposed to ache?
I keep thinking something's wrong, that the pain is a signal,
but the truth is I'm more awake with pain than without it.
It's not consuming or unbearable. It's worrisome,
and that's the real problem: I'm allowing what can make me
more conscious to be diverted into useless worry.

What a loss it is to waste the myriad sufferings
of Earth when with a brief concession – "Yes, God, as you will" –
we can transform them into heart-tempering gratitude
and be more mindful of the accumulating return.

Prayer 16

Nothing any teacher can say, no poetry
however beautiful, no well-turned rhetoric
has the tensile strength in its laced geometry
to bind one's own experience to ideas
not verified and not understood. One must live
and own the truth that makes the fine words rise, O Lord.

Language

When speaking Italian, it's impossible not to rhyme.
Alliterations pour forth unintended from the mouths
of Englishmen, and Americans turn the five beat line
to four deliberate drawls. Each language has devices
of character, and the cacophony we hear on Earth
is, when unentangled, smart strands of living poetry.

Language is a gift for straightening the stunned budding soul
discovering itself in a body on Earth. Each word –
no, each syllable – can be an offering to a state
closer to the self-remembered soul's self-possessed silence.

Prayer 17

If slow death by ten thousand irritations be
my fate, O Lord, may I be Present to each one,
feeling each cut, each abrasion of personhood
till only energy remains. The soul survives
when everything that can be hurt has burned away,
everything that interferes with the will of God.

The Difference

The Angels know what's coming yet hold their Godly Presence
undisturbed. However horrific the phase of events,
Angel identity is not stolen or distorted.
If human identity stampedes in the briefest gusts
and is abandoned to animal fury in a storm,
the self-aware attention of the Angels never blinks.

Therein is the difference, the defining human task:
to bring a fragile, febrile watch weighted with fleshly fear
to constancy unmoved by thorn or thunder – possible
only in Love's Field where abiding Angels welcome us.

Prayer 18

Don't believe your thoughts. They bend the truth as the stars
bend light. Nothing in space or time exists unbent.
The simple nows of your awareness can travel
the universe without passports. Invisible
is their witness, beyond belief, unrefracted.
Let's pray by being Present, the all and nothing.

Not Enough

The curious heart's pressing restlessness races ahead
with half sentences and poorly formulated questions
while the frail intellect's ancient sundial calculates
shadows by a monument in a manicured park. Stop.
What you feel as you is a play of forces varying
in speed and power, functioning without authority.

It is not enough to be full of hearty energy,
sure of your mind's precision, healthy to a peachy glow,
proud of your real estate's location. It is not enough.
Where is the awareness above these mortal conditions?

Prayer 19

I should not address you, O Lord, who needs nothing
from me. Rather I should offer my prayers to those
who would know the same miracles I have witnessed.
Come, all of you whose vision is darkened by laws
of your own making or consent, hear my appeal:
drop the proud logics defending your ignorance.

Into Which We've Fallen

We don't have time: time has us and we must get free of it,
step out of the frame, become nothing to the clasping minds –
including our own – that make us into poor measurements.
"I am" may not be followed by another syllable
without a lie coming to mind and submitting to time.
No mere words can justly answer the question, "Who are you?"

The Present is not time. It is the awareness of God,
the participation in God, fundamental being.
The rest is hallucination, torture and amusement
into which we've fallen. Unto death? No, far beyond that.

Prayer 20

Lord, let me not relax into belief's soft bed.
The hypnotic power in ritual, the ease
of repetition, the knee-jerk pride of having
a ready answer, the assurance of the group
and of status within the group – let none of these
seduce me out of love into blind believing.

Opening the Mouth to Bark

Personhood – one's body, name, and all that social living
has stuck to them – should be the soul's alert companion dog.
But the gravity of Earth makes me forget what I am,
and instead I become the canine, barking and whining
for the attention that ends in a treat. Confirmed as dog –
I mean person – I will howl all night at mortality.

Why one would want to be a dog is the reliable
mystery of planet Earth. Angels establish things here
in such a way that the incarnate soul forgets itself
and leaves identity – who am I? – to animal flesh.

Prayer 21

We must put in our time; the will must instigate
the body's movements, and the work must be sincere.
However abiding is the soul's attention –
always more or less than believed – the soul cannot
strengthen without the counterforce of things governed
by gravity and duration. Accept this fact.

Here

The highest moments we have ever had, the most streamlined
advances free from laws of time and death are reminders
of the next level to which we bring our eternal work.
All that we aim to be here is the excellence required
to go on with the conscious task. What ends here is a scale
of understanding and a distilling of readiness.

All that is of Earth in our identities, in our love,
in our service to beauty and our will to be transformed
must drop away so the labor of light can continue.
We are becoming the necessity of this passage.

Prayer 22

What good is prayer to one who does good to feel good?
To him, prayer is the donkey trained to pull the cart
of his pleasure, his luggage of benevolence.
But do not judge. We are all actors stuck in roles
we like until we see ourselves and realize
an observer is closer to the truth of God.

Ballet

Off to the city to see the ballet: three hours each way,
a contest to find parking, tickets costing three months' worth
of satellite television, a meal more craft than food,
our backs in dull, chronic ache from the relentless sitting.
Such is pilgrimage in our age. We know our sins enough
to still seek plenary indulgence when it comes in reach.

But when she is in the air, lifted by her sleek steward,
her body disciplined for years to this moment in art,
she invites God to bend to kiss her slender upturned hands –
the vast hall now a pendant portal of absolving awe.

Prayer 23

Do not believe in a personage or worship
human beings. The Angels make no such demand.
Rather lend your labor and your heart to visions
that inform and sustain your own. There is a wise
old motto: everything that rises must converge.
The certainty of love abides above persons.

Roles

Perhaps you wanted something interactive and instead
got a lecture; or you desired a transparent crystal
of perfect form and got an opaque accumulation
of twisted wisdoms. However botched the delivery,
however repetitive and droning, it's up to us
to extract the gold – to find God in the rabbit droppings.

The one appointed teacher – for the day or for the age –
is a tool, and probably better blunt than marvelous.
We want our soil tilled not sung to, planted not entertained.
When neither we nor teacher believes the roles, God abides.

Prayer 24

May my soul's love somehow extend to every friend
of every friend of mine. Thus may the multitude
be fed and the risking reach of every high heart
find and hold sufficient bread to keep it reaching.
If one labors long enough in a web of love,
one comes to see past the border of time, to God.

Religion

The religions of the world work very well for one's heart
if sincerely practiced without belief. The flimsy veil
of belief is all that hides the well from the parched seeker.
Believe and you are fogged in the mindless anesthesia
of ritual and symbol, driven by greed for reward.
Rather observe and shrink not from eternity's threshold.

The awareness of attention is the unending work,
and the acceptance of one's true scale is humility.
If you school your heart to hold this practice, all the symbols
undrape and you participate in God. That's all there is.

Prayer 25

As anger is the desire to own and command,
so peace is the transformation beyond needing.
As anger requires the corruption of the will,
so in peace simple being suffices the will.
As anger broods and only releases itself
in violence, we remember peace with this prayer.

Negotiation

Resolve the differences: synthesize a shared square inch
from contending arguments and go no further till all
see and agree that there is, however tiny, one stitch.
Then all that's needed is a deep desire to preserve it.
The rest of the negotiation follows on patience
and forbearance, virtues learned holding the Present's clear truth.

Only the touch of peace reveals the disease of power.
The truth is not an argument; it is not defended
but held dear, not advanced but freely offered, not taken
but revealed by the soul. All unity begins with it.

Prayer 26

What is the point of saying "O Lord" in a prayer?
What is being addressed? An imagined father?
The inconceivable Absolute? The cosmos?
The Angels collectively? One's own conscious self?
A distant pole symbolizing transformation?
O Lord, let this prayer pour out to be examined.

Let No Thought Follow

Language is the way in and way out of the labyrinth.
The word of God enters the headspace only to be trapped
by the lower self's throat grip, made to mate and multiply
through the whole range of thought, then left to spent forgetfulness.
Identity in the world is the dreamsong of language,
one word after another driving the spell unto death.

To escape, one must pare the words to single syllables,
link them in a line that logic can't distort, make the last
the fulfillment of the first, and speak them with the whole mouth.
Then let no thought follow you past the threshold of silence.

Prayer 27

What becomes of unwelcome love? Is it wasted?
Does it droop like flesh and perish in exhaustion?
No, love turned away leaves an eternal fragrance
then returns home to God. Its trace is always here
for the remembering soul waking from mistake
to find and follow. Love holds eternity's door.

Opposing

We need not regard opposing force as an enemy.
Feeling that force and continuing – head up, eyes open –
requires prolonged will resilient in its aim but does not
necessitate battle: winners, losers, triumph, defeat.
Transformation means we have risen above the struggle
of mere opposites to a restored unity with God.

In truth, without an energy opposing us, our aim
cannot turn back to God. It remains imaginary,
proud of its free ride down the passage to its cosmic end.
One who challenges your heart can be your loyal servant.

Prayer 28

Get on the donkey, ride for a time, then get off.
Let me remember that such is life here on Earth.
Each donkey is assigned but still needs wisest care
(one gets nowhere without it); the route is nuanced,
intricate, but fixed by the illusion of choice.
The aim: to be a conscious rider, a blessing.

Drink, Taste, Feel

The milk from your mother's breast protects you yet binds your life
to Earth and the approval of your kind. As you are weaned
from her, you must seek nourishment beyond Earth's provision
and a truth beyond the consensus of human beings.
What is the way out of the closed system of birth and death?
What is the transformation one must travel to know God?

Only in the Present does God nurture the soul. A life
journeyed from here to here, in a dimension unnoticed
by human eyes, develops from the work of drawing out
awareness from attention. Drink, taste, feel the love of God.

11. Pyramids

Prayer 29

Life is best when nothing is wanted from the world,
from friends, even from the overwatching Angels.
In the contentment of the Eye and Crown, one dwells
in eternity, out of reach of grasping hands,
even one's own. Let me remember that a thing
desired signifies a fall already taken.

Vessel

A human is a broken vessel identifying
with its largest shard, taking a name, polishing a slick
reflective surface for the world. Early on in a life,
hope for reunion capitulates to some nepenthe –
success, responsibility, pleasure, noble failure.
They're all the same drug, and all have the same destination.

At some point, death interrupts, and one either believes it
and drops below zero or sees through it and starts to breathe
a different dimension, an awareness of being,
a resident emptiness ready for God's new vessel.

Prayer 30

Life on Earth is a drama to distract the Self.
From fundamental being, one can only love
the performers here and without leverage urge
their unbelief. This benevolent attention
is all one has to offer here, all one is here.
I try to be that loving attention to you.

Answers

You want answers. What is this? Why is that? With the logic
of words you have dug a little hole, and you want more words
to fill it. Here's your answer: you're residing in your throat.
Try this. Just look: no words. Hold pure looking for one minute.
You'll notice the throat start to tighten – a clamor of words
and voices demanding attention, pulling you back down.

You see, all your questions, however earnest or noble
are throat fillers. Above them is pure looking which can use
the high heart's tender music to propose the Eye's Presence.
And above that? Ah, there you go, wanting answers again.

Prayer 31

The mother knows in advance the death of the son.
The son has learned his part and purified his words.
The movement out of the world's fog can now begin.
The first step is steep, but the instruction takes hold.
At the most precarious point, the clarity
of Heaven offers itself for the completion.

Heaven

What more do you want of Heaven than this very moment?
Do not let your wanting misplace what you already have.
Wanting is the force of distortion, gravity's dark pull
that deviates matter and bends light. Your identity
is made of wanting, the result of everything below
offering an imaginary crown that fits so well.

Heaven is eternal welcome. There is nothing to want,
nothing needing a name, nothing to change in the belief
of a better idea. Since your beginning – your fall
into time and wanting – Heaven has prompted your return.

Prayer 32

As God is the object of all prepositions,
the language of prayer must always be redundant,
every word already understood. Then why pray?
A prayer is a little play of humility:
a self-devised character acutely aware
of character's bleak limits seeks something finer.

What Are You?

What are you but the point at which higher worlds penetrate
lower ones? As you descend deeper, you acquire a name,
a baggage of mental filings and associations
and layerings of matter organized into functions.
Here you stay until the highest in you is recognized,
purified and transformed into a finer vehicle.

The "I am" rises and starts a timeless, measureless work
on being, the becoming of borderless consciousness.
So when asked what about a human being can be real,
say transformation into God, the unending welcome.

Prayer 33

Creation is propelled out and out to expire
in cold ash unless this word and every next one
finds you Present, and unless you give your handhold
to one reaching for the understanding you earned
when handheld by those above. You can't climb alone,
so join this prayer from us who cannot deny God.

Only True Work

Heaven will test your discernment. Beware the arguments
that claim you've already arrived, that underestimate
the obdurate reach of the lower self to kidnap you
back into time and identity. You are only God
when remembering to be, and a price of sympathy
must be paid at each ascending level of creation.

Being is all we know of the Absolute. That we are
included in being is self-evident, but only
true work engenders transformation, which must be sustained
and fed by the will to draw awareness from attention.

Prayer 34

God, grant me not so much relief that I forget
the pain that humans manufacture for themselves.
Even as I learn myself to know you, let me
forgive till my last breath the ignorance that binds
the human heart, and when you take me, may the grain
of true compassion be an abundant harvest.

At Last

When you discard something to enjoy your freedom from it,
offer it for sale to one who might find value in it:
that is, a climber who can use the remnant nourishment.
The things you've kept too long, the things for which no buyers call,
leave them where they can be found by the most desperate lives.
Shameless naked cleverness will claim the currency there.

At last when you've removed yourself from all that matters here,
the climb will seem a weightless wonder; your last temptation
will again be that hard self-ownership which held you back
the last time, the last thousand times, you stood at God's threshold.

Prayer 35

True prayer is awareness rising from attention.
Whether petition or praise is the intention,
whether wonder or contrition the expression,
words become prayer only when the heart overflows
and its fine perfume quickens higher sense and wakes
the soul whose residence in God affirms itself.

A True Teacher

That which is not held open struggles to tighten and close.
At one pole of human being is a fully opened
aperture to God, at the other a marble statue
locked in an airless room. Our lives go back and forth between,
moment by moment, response by response, until the will
to leave ourselves moves and seeks, recognizes and submits.

The fear of loss protects the vault of chalk at the dark end
of your corridor. No true teacher desires anything
from you: your dependency would be a pathetic debt
binding you both. A true teacher opens your will to God.

Prayer 36

Wholeheartedness is not stupid and unbridled.
To give unreservedly, to be lit by love
and delight while residing in this sharp-edged world
requires the understanding that can only root
in one's remembered retreats to eternity.
The heart is as whole as one's remembrance of God.

How Many Baubles?

Actually, seeking out awareness is returning –
advancing by retreat. When the garage is full of stuff,
most people rent storage or construct another garage.
The true seeker walks away leaving the key in the lock.
Thus one's true self departs from the karma of personhood,
self-subtracting from what is owned or subject to desire.

Unnecessary suffering is precisely the weight
of manufactured identity. How many baubles
can hang from the branches of the Christmas tree, whose beauty
unadorned in the grove joined you in praise when you found it?

Prayer 37

Universal is the need for God's attention.
Do not let me forget that man's idolatries
spring from the urge to stand in the approving light
of something higher. If he has no certainty
of God, he veils his lacking with desire and hope.
What can we do? Love is God's attention unveiled.

Communicating

One never has to outright lie, but often outright truth
does its own damage. Asked if he'd given men of Athens
the best laws, Solon replied, "The best that they could receive."
Social intercourse is the activity of fragments
unaware of their edges and shapes, hoping to cohere
in meaningful contribution. If only hope were love.

Communication's greatest skill is preparing others
to welcome the truth, a task impossible without love.
The Angels, who reside in love, must work beyond themselves
to usher our hearts to the vestibule of gratitude.

Prayer 38

What are we to do with shocks clearly from Heaven
but unclear in their meaning? Make the noble pledge.
Awaken and hold and let your readiness fill
the uncertain space between you and the Angels.
Let the mystery above move through your high heart
and out to the world as a blessing. Patience. Be.

Dear Friend

Dear friend, what else can I do with you but tell you the truth?
Your mind teems and breeds and would be soothed, dampened by water
and restrained by remembrance. Your heart is sick with belief.
Such are the afflictions of personhood fleeing the source.
Best return to the Angel perch and watch. If boredom stirs,
expose the expectations of its own rude vanity.

If a vine is not directed with intention, it snarls
and strangles. So a child will have attention, happily
from loving eyes, but deprived, will settle for destruction.
Thus our hearts and minds prosper in the Presence of the soul.

Prayer 39

When I upstarted this work, O Lord, I mistook
your Presence for an interruption on my path
to accomplishment. It took a long time to learn
that the aim is to know you, to be overwhelmed
by the now your Presence ignites, to realign
my tiny cosmos to the state of your being.

Decades In

In its earliest stages, a civilization grows
slowly: tree by tree, house by house, pond by pond, crop by crop.
And slowly grow the souls of its citizens, listening
to the Teacher over the noise in their minds, collecting
energies around a remembered purpose, reminding
each other to be the seeds of wakefulness in good earth.

Decades in, houses in order, traditions layering,
the written work commences. Testaments proliferate,
mythic allegories sprout and spread and need winnowing.
The Teacher becomes a story explained in young cities.

Prayer 40

Keep me out of self-pity while I pay the price
you have demanded, Lord. Keep me humble, holding
to the right edge of the road. I have grown so old
that everything now is painful, yet you require
me utterly new, as yet unshadowed by thought.
I am discarded to reveal a new being.

Two Ends at Once

To live breath by daring breath through a delicate passage
revealing the body's frailty shudders the standing place
of one's identity. One must move, but why? What am I?
If the senses stop, am I here at all? Am I a mind
awaiting the onset of infinite silent darkness?
How do I exist – as a soul, a synergy, a dream?

Approach the question from two ends at once: what you are not
and what you would be. Eliminating all the products
of the body – thoughts, feelings, needs – refines self-awareness
while you struggle beyond ideas to discover God.

Prayer 41

Lord, may my better parts verify and each day
reconfirm that Earth life's most astounding treasures
cannot satisfy the soul. To have God Present
as one moves through Earth's palace of wonders keeps rein
on the heart and braces the mind. Do not let me
settle for the beauties that stir my poor senses.

If We Could

The truth of beauty is clear: there is an elevation
of the heart, a liberation of ascending order.
However skeptic and contained, the mind cannot deny
a brighter being has appeared, a patent radiance.
But the beauty of truth, not so. So many truthful things
are harsh, abrasive, twisted, cruel. Where's the beauty here?

If we could see things as they are, without the distortions
that mind and heart inured to customary morals make –
or more profoundly, that the human prejudice installs –
we would know that in God's Eye, all that is is beautiful.

Prayer 42

Teach me not to trust answers that the eager mind
serves up in profusion. What does it want? What prize
does it get for delivering the right response?
To be of higher use, the mind must be tutored
to parsimony and partnered to a conscience:
thus molecule by molecule a crystal grows.

Watch Dog

My dog is learning to be a watchdog, taking great pride
in her weighty role. She looks out of my office window,
poised in vigilant observation of the yard and street.
There's just one problem: she responds with adrenal fury
to just about anything. She lacks the discernment earned
over time by an intelligent, overriding heart.

There's potential here. She's superb at alarm. Her bark stuns
the ears, her teeth slash the air, her whole body strains to launch.
At some point she'll tire of this wasted battle mode. She'll learn
to wait, assess, control the gate of her bold attention.

Prayer 43

The aim of watching the mind is to exhaust it
into disappearing so that the luminous
background totality, which is God, manifests
unobstructed. Lord, may you hold my attention,
for as soon as I am charmed by the appearance
of some worldly problem's solution, all is lost.

Sex, Money, Power

Humans will do anything for sex, money or power.
If one doesn't get you, another will. Is it not strange
how much meaning we manufacture around those forces?
Together they form a knot of accomplishment, a noose,
and we mistake the esteemed strangulation for success.
We'll sell off our breath to further the lie of personhood.

Freedom begins with unbelieving the world one's senses
have cobbled together, with observing without judgment
the parade of roles and costumes, with detaching desire
from the death grip of this alluring planet's jealousy.

Prayer 44

Some prayers want deliverance, some prayers want favor.
This prayer wants you here beside me, above the gap
in time and space, aware of your attention, pure.
The love connecting us is more real than my feet
against the ground, and the sounds in my ears are not
sufficient distraction to break the bond we share.

Love

Love is an energy field, the living soul a planet
must respire to host organic life. Love, in fact, is life,
and life is the operation of love. Like consciousness,
of which it is one eternal scale, love is inclusive
and more and more and more available to each and all.
Though God is yet more, it is not wrong to say God is love.

Thus with advancing purity does recognition move
to pleased relation, then to affinity and sharing
of a world reconstructed in mutual mind; at last
to unity, the residence in love that blesses God.

Prayer 45

We know ourselves by our experience, O Lord;
thus our souls, always here but so subtle and mute,
are long forgotten under the brute sensory
onslaught of life and the oxygen depleting
crowd of our own responding thoughts. My attention,
where is it now? What is this awareness rising?

Apparent

In a human, the conscious soul rides an elevator
between darkened catacomb levels and the sweeping views
of the higher floors. The car doesn't stay anywhere long.
It is programed to obey each strong summons, not to care
what nurtures its invisible, secret rider. The soul
must somehow make apparent its being, its otherness.

The captive must infiltrate the more delicate functions
of the upper floors, praise the fragile brilliance of their light,
favor their view of the sky. The soul must create a pole
of fine attention serving its awareness of beyond.

Prayer 46

For the soul to develop, the heart must commit
to the art of transformation and the selfless
labor of refining the fuel for that art.
O Lord, I cannot address you without feeling
the urgency of this work, without discerning
that this is what you want from and for your children.

The Heart's Role

The Earth's abrasive beauty is a conflict for the heart.
From a height, looking across ethereal sweeps of light,
the heart is almost satisfied, almost content to stay.
But the hard ground, the scraping bark of the tangled branches,
the bruising stones – all are reminders of Earth's oppression.
Deeply must the heart pay for what it offers to the soul.

The heart knows it is a prisoner: its only freedom
is purchasing the soul's nourishment; its only reward
is knowing the soul attains deliverance that the Earth
can't seize. Thus the heart bears its role in the soul's completion.

Prayer 47

Each new burial of the developing soul
back into human form requires the same appeal:
the soul's supplication of the heart's sacrifice.
Only the heart can set a table where the soul
can be nourished. Only the heart can weave the robe
of secret virtue then accept so great a loss.

Please

The heart is the captive soul's only ally in escape.
Tirelessly the soul must send its influence to the heart,
support its clumsy early tries at vague self-sacrifice,
open the intuition to invisible advance,
direct attention to the beautiful, praise compassion.
Then the rare willing heart becomes the image of the soul.

From the rooftop garden, the vantage hints at boundlessness.
Here the soul must genuflect and make proposal, beseech
from its child-mother the greatest mercy. "You may not leave,
but with your nurture I can claim my birthright. Please help me."

Prayer 48

O Lord, do not let me settle for mere delight,
even the joy of higher states that you confer
by your appearance here within. Rather make me
an instrument – of truth beyond the glad garden
and of wisdom encompassing beauty's blisses –
as you observe this young soul's self-discovery.

Portrait

No need to overdo your work of art. This picture life
has been traced out for you. (You chose it before you were fused
to flesh, though that memory will release itself to you
only in grains of earned discovery.) It is enough
to hold the aim of offering God each painted moment,
of presenting your life's portrait framed in new awareness.

You cannot do more than God, and all history belongs
to Heaven, even down to the tombstones. You gain nothing
from the conspicuous, everything from the connection
to the invisible, each brushstroke of remembering.

Prayer 49

Anger is shame armed with inflammable fuel.
Shame is identification with injustice –
committing it, feeling its boot, watching its pain.
Lord, we cannot expect mere human hearts to rise
above injustice; thus shame and anger smolder,
igniting wherever the wind touches mankind.

Only the Heart

Taking the morality out of one's view of the world
requires one's heart to observe without judgment the blind rush
of forces leaving murder, torture and ruin in its wake.
Moral rule is a paper rope attempting to restrain
brute animal vitality. Only the heart holding
open the door to Heaven has the strength needed to watch.

Higher Love wants nothing, does nothing unnecessary.
Only the heart unshaken by unpittied suffering
has the attentive power able to bear this rough world's
constant cry for the all-forgiving kiss of Higher Love.

Prayer 50

Hush. Your life is a movie in four dimensions.
Watch it play as you feel your responses to cues
rise and deliver themselves as audible speech
and patterned movement and rolling commentaries
of thought. You'd never have entered the theater
if you were not sure the film would end. You chose this.

Regarding the Earthsuit

This aging machine is a cacophony of pressures
to be balanced and managed. There's work I still want to get
from its creaky upliftings and attenuated flights.
Its noises are beyond embarrassing, but on rare days
a worthy music still comes forth from its proud frequencies.
When it stops humming, I'll stop listening and be ready.

And how do you regard your earthsuit? Is it a carcass,
a wingless angel, a sack of ashes or a temple?
No matter. With the approval of Heaven, you chose it
as best fitting the task of its resident. Remember?

Prayer 51

Underneath the well worded prayers of petition
lurks the weak kneed poverty of collapsing will.
To answer the prayer for ourselves, we must relearn
that everything is bearable in this moment,
and in this, and in this, till time disintegrates
and our being rejoins what God has made perfect.

This Flesh, These Thoughts

The body doesn't ache, it is an ache: such is the strange
mercy of the Angels. Life here is bruised and snuffable
else we believe it. If we insist on an organic
identity, there is no injustice in our ending.
We are a span of constant change, pounded and shaped like dough,
then eaten. Without pain there's no inference of lasting.

What are we then if not this battered flesh, these troubled thoughts?
Note that a distance lies between the seer and the seeing,
between awareness and the moving mind. Trace the return
to pure observation, prior to body and name. Be.

Prayer 52

As our sensory measures are so imprecise
and the scope of reality our fragile brains
construct is so suspect, we're often overwhelmed
and driven into mute muddle. Let me focus
on what is before me, this single impression.
If I see it truly, I can verify God.

Healing

Much of the human past seems golden because there were not
enough of us to do much damage. Now there are billions,
all making smoke and sewage and dumping deathless plastic.
Before a wound – or Earth – can heal itself, the diseased flesh
must be scraped away. We have become that flesh and must be
debrided, so our astonishing garbage can decay.

The most hopeful envision these decades as a grim race
between the polluters and the sustainers, a contest
that can still be won. No, but a sustaining awareness
will survive among the few of our kind scattered around.

Prayer 53

I will not pray for power, but give me the strength
to take the clear sequent step toward transformation.
The aim to change the world is audacious folly.
To use the world to reclaim the Self is God's will.
I know my little light cannot illuminate
the darkness. To see one step ahead is enough.

The Sword

Pulling the sword from the stone will be your fated surprise,
but it's only the beginning. You must learn to use it,
to master its jabs and swoops and thrusts until you've become
one with its power, a dedicated role. Step by step
drive the trespassers back into the sea from which they came.
Then comes the quiet work and its discovery of peace.

Your city prospers, but it also must return to Earth.
The souls of your friends mature and are ready to bequeath
their names and houses to the forest children. Take the sword
from the mantel. Cast it in the lake of weaponless will.

Prayer 54

Why are you reading this prayer? Do you expect proof
of a higher order to distill before you?
Do you understand that the "Lord" now here addressed
is something we share, something we are, all we are?
Consciousness of what truly is is the purpose
of prayer. O Lord, O friend, we are not separate.

Starry Sky

I breathe the starry sky my eyes traverse in unowned calm,
and you and I though seeming separate are one in God.
May understanding bless and liberate experience,
removing without ceremony the smart formulas
and customized contraptions that abuse geometry
and fix borders where souls reside in timeless loving peace.

The passage down creation from the Source is a clutching
decline, an ongoing collapse, a mortal plummeting
driven by gravity and buffered by the waste products
of identity – distinction, status, ownership, pride.

Prayer 55

Friend, the next thought must be refused, and then the next...
No longer let your orders come from a throat tired
of talking to your brain, but from the single Eye
that sees and knows. Then every keen perception forms
a praising prayer to the God you are becoming.
You are a blessing to the world passing through you.

Let Go

A somber sky drives my happiness more deeply within.
I enfold it and become radiant, a pregnancy
that turns hunger into love and thoughts into prophecies.
Use me now, use me if you have any doubts to dissolve,
any lingering bitterness to discharge and transform.
Then we can climb together, leaving our earthly stations.

Above the moist womb of clouds, above the six atmospheres –
each of finer air and light less shadowing than the last –
is the infinite which needs nothing from us. What we hold
we can let go, even the illusion of being two.

Prayer 56

I do not want the peace of poverty, the peace
of resignation, of helplessness, of sleeping.
I want the peace that crowds the I out of wanting
and melts the wanting from being, the peace that makes
mirth of this poor prayer, the peace so fundamental
it needs nothing to meditate on or yield to.

Toward the End

There are many things to fear, but death isn't one of them.
Remember, Socrates proved one can't fear death: not having
an actual memory of it, a man imagines
a multicourse meal of grim tortures fear can feast upon.
If you insist on fear, fear decrepitude: lungs that pump
at half capacity, fingers in knots, a vaguing brain.

If you want clarity up through the moment of your death,
you must leave impressions neutral, unbiased. Vacating
the congested head will help it breathe. Roost above the mere
machinery: watch till watching has become departure.

Prayer 57

All the effort of prayer is to find in the heart
the vibration of attention which rends the veil.
Then the words can cough and quit, the thoughts can retire,
the mind's crude scaffolding can go back in the box.
The activity and the content become fused
in the awareness of God, the pure nothing else.

Hold Open

Your watchfulness must be so acute that you are alarmed
at imagination's whispered request for permission.
No! No, you may not go on. And here in the shocking gap
between your refusal and the arrested fantasy
is the real, offering its clarity for the taking.
How long can you stand here relaxed and open-eyed with God?

Pressing against every opening of being, the world
will urge a return to the normalcy of trance, the flow
of thought and action you have dared to suspend. Don't believe.
Breather of light, your eyelids hold open the crypt's dark door.

Prayer 58

If you are aware of yourself in the Present,
you are aware of God. It is this awareness,
not your personhood nor any mere idea
of a deity that establishes the real
beyond all containment and welcomes the many
home to the One. You are God's self-remembering.

Nails

There are no accidents, only limited perspectives.
The misstep resulting in the foot sprain followed the law
of attention, and the seismic shaking splitting the ground
holding your city has been preparing for centuries.
Reality is far vaster than our understanding:
our plans are experiments with shivers of remembrance.

Even the Absolute agrees to creation's movement.
Until all borders of identity have been dissolved
and we are reabsorbed in God, we'll be creation's nails
holding the house together as galaxies shift orbits.

Prayer 59

Stop. Say the words of not doing. Not doing. Stop.
See how the mind opposes the will. Not thinking
feels like death to the mind. Not wanting feels like death
to the flesh. Not doing feels like death to the one
you imagine yourself to be, and so it is.
But you've been praying for this. Here is real prayer. Stop.

Minus All

All the desperate faithful of the old dispensations
have wrenched their beliefs to the breaking point. Blank responses
in heart and mind echo the pain of coming extinction.
Where does one find identity if nothing in the world
is true and personhood is a claim no longer counted?
In the scorched fission of all you think you know, what are you?

Vacate your address in the scheme of things. Remember life
before your current alias, your talents, your gender,
your reluctant wonder at becoming flesh – life without
history, location, language. Minus all, what are you?

Prayer 60

Let us not breed ourselves beyond the heart's talent
for mercy. As population burgeons, the laws
governing the people become less flexible,
and the breath of their institutions grinds and groans.
Individuals only know their roles in crowds.
Let us measure success by the soul's open road.

Sex

Sex holds humans in its coiled grip and lends the lower self
a tool of great power. That thrill confuses heart and mind,
interposing a veil so pleasuring to the body,
so invigorating to vanity, that seeing it
for what it is is barely possible. It is the urge
to life in flesh, a swollen river mocking its levees.

And yet the soul has higher right to redirect this force
out of the flood of eager sensation, through the portal
of compassion, past imagination's great divergence
to the married generosity of deathless being.

II. *Prayers and Upturned Sonnets, Second Series*

Prayer 61

Aging will chase down even the most urgent life,
seize its throat and stop the heart's mission to the brain.
Do not let me be the man shocked at this breakdown.
Let me watch from behind the curtain as the throne
topples and the dependents gasp in vacancy.
The castle loses language, falls to ruin. I am.

Slipping the Grip

Most human lives are lost to the mechanical forces
driving the universe outward: fear, the will to power,
dominance, greed, lust – all the plot's usual propellants.
To have true value, which for us means the growth of the soul,
a man must inwardly attend, planting identity
in a nameless self-awareness that slips the grip of flesh.

We must do what the Absolute is doing, nothing less:
having created the mirror of mind, apprehended
all its possibilities, witnessed its fatality,
we must retract ourselves into God, back beyond all cause.

Prayer 62

Let me not be the coiled instinct's self-absorbed heat,
the heart self-defrauded by belief, the vain mind
content with its own counterfeits. These deceptions
make us human by default, not by real purpose.
True human use is as a turbulent mirror
in which the soul sees itself in waking shudders.

More is Required

The man of mere faith must not be allowed to discover
the enormity of his task. What he trusts of Heaven
is true but only on a scale of work and suffering
that will melt the brain and wither the heart. Human lifetimes
measure the soul's great return as thimbles do the ocean,
as reflected gleams on dust light the forgetting cosmos.

More is required of us than faith or hope, and charity
to be of use must wrench the gut, threaten its ownership.
We must ascend and hold the most mindful peak on which breath
can still be mastered, and in that state do our daily work.

Prayer 63

A deep crackling cough from a few rows behind me
offers the reminder, and I gladly take it.
Pardon me, Lord, my state was drooping toward belief
till that gravelly human sound admonished me.
I'd wonder whether you arranged the whole vignette,
but such smooth thoughts would yet again divert my aim.

The Single Truth

Often have I caught myself stalking an unneeded treat,
heard myself propounding some hasty made hypothesis
to hold a group's attention, found myself in a rubble
of vain wishes down a long detour from the simple truth.
Snapped awake by Heaven's luck, I know authentic being,
but why do I carry so much draining indebtedness?

I am: the rest is a lie of the stomach, of the heart,
of the mind, of the culture, of the species adapting.
The first step into space and time summoned into movement
all the possibles circling the single truth eternal.

Prayer 64

Every true prayer is a pyramid, a rising
to the point, a conscious scaling of the thousands
of human impulses promoting their brief names.
Find good earth, square it off and by conscious lifting
make of stones a map out of time, a great promise
of perfect attention attainable in God.

Seed

The greatest thing that one can do for a sleeping human
is to offer the news that it's possible to awake.
If that knowledge penetrates to the embryonic soul,
it will smolder there for lifetimes and at some point combust
into a flame of conscious destination, a value
and reason for every breath, a hold on eternity.

Matter in space time races outward to ash, having spent
itself in heedless flight; but brunting the current, the soul
in its return to the Source crystallizes its purpose.
Knowing this makes one an indestructible seed of God.

Prayer 65

Tell us, O Lord, the kind of god that could allow
this world's atrocities. Until the suffering
here is comprehensible, love forgets itself
or hides in the shadow of fear. What are you, Lord?
Perhaps the better question is what we must be
to know the truth, the state before all responses.

Do Not Be Fooled

Do not be fooled. "I am" is all that can be truly known.
The rest is navigation of illusion, a mapping
of an ever shifting hologram, made deeper, denser,
and more convincing by our belief. Hold the energy
of awareness back. Don't let what is higher dissipate
by pursuing the lower: be available to God.

See the uraeus on the ancient crown. The bird attests
to infinite sky, to the infinite patience of God.
The serpent must be brought to bear, to know satisfaction
only in its rising gift: such is the lift into flight.

Prayer 66

What kind of prayer makes sense in this situation?
A petition? A loud plea? A supplication
whispered from a lowbent posture of helplessness?
If the aim is to participate in you, God,
the only prayer worth salt is the firm reminder
that in Presence all's one without need of address.

Inflection Point

"I am" is an inflection point: above it is boundless,
nameless being; below it are cascading, cheapening
fragments of identity, a cataract of language.
I reach out to you and without meaning to involve us
in the lie that we are two. Above urgent neediness,
above even the noblest respect, we're already one.

"Am" – the Absolute's only prompt – the creation itself.
"I" – the reflexive reference "am" creates, the first name.
Thus the mirror – the Mind of God, from which all else descends
in time – produces images, reflections of being.

Prayer 67

Whether we like it or not, Lord, we have no choice
but to be friends. Though the depth of my small duty
mocks the vastness of your burden, I am nothing
not of you, and you can only ask the service
of my highest self-conception. Lord, we are one
on a sliding scale of being, all and only.

Only

We are allowed to put down our burdens that we may choose
to pick them up again. Such is the Angels' artistry
in the dimension of time. They move us in a sequence
that by intervals suggests forever till we're ready
for eternity. Have you reached peace with never being
untasked, with continuing to trek back and up to God?

When time lies dead by exhaustion, all sequence is unmasked:
you're not a beast of burden, a human under a load,
a soul gestating in a human body, a seedspark
of God informing a soul. There is only God, All One.

Prayer 68

A man of rare savant insanity was asked,
"How did you come to understand that you were God?"
"Easy," he replied. "I was able to observe
that each time I prayed, I was talking to myself.
Who else then could I be? All that was left to do
was to take responsibility for being."

Eros

Eros is full of mischief and hates being put to work.
Because he can run ahead of time, his acts seem random,
and our explanations of the passions he goads from us
fail to catch up, panting and wheezing, pooped in their logic.
When we faint and come to, we find our pockets half-empty
of money we've spent on unchosen karmic transactions.

In the background echoes his rude giggling. The only way
to handle him is to feel his arrows without response,
burn without squirming, till all resistance – to anything –
is neutralized. Then he will obey and call God for you.

Prayer 69

Lord, I ask not for glorious appearances,
no broad displays of power or sweet affection.
Rather stay aloof. At the edge of your Presence
I can live a life of meaning, infusing time
with the awareness of eternity. Your love
transforms my heart. No other proof can matter now.

Above Each Mirrored Self

Being a multiplicity – a few fruits, many thorns –
I know too well that all the wary eyes around me plot
in shadow even as they prize the sun. Trust in Allah
I remind myself as I double lock my fat camel
behind steel doors. What but self-hatred makes a misanthrope,
and as self-hatred roots in shame, how can I love this form?

The purity of Angels manifests in infinite
forgiveness, yet I grudge my own flesh for its sticky grip.
Look up! Look up! Above each mirrored self I move among
levitates the same real being, the same flesh-tethered soul.

Prayer 70

Lord, have patience with my dangerous wondering.
I cannot help but ask what strategy comes next
when all the slights to vanity and all the prompts
to cry injustice are seen for what they are – tricks
to raise the fever that fuels transformation.
What's next when only you are left at the chessboard?

The Clinging

The clinging to personhood blinds us to the infinite.
The body's entrails coil around a false identity
whose fumes pollute the heart and drag it down. The heart would sing
a sweet refrain, "I am yours, Lord," but the world's gravity
is strong as stone. The heart goes to sleep in belief, and life
dreams itself as a person marked for death, clutching a name.

What are the borders of your dream of life? What property
do you claim and defend? When you think of work unfinished,
all markings erased, things no longer owned, what terror floods
into the space where breath used to be? What is this being?

Prayer 71

The phrase "O Lord" comes forth too easily, O Lord,
as if one were talking to some other being,
not the encompassing One. Or am I calling
to some level of my own attention, rousing
my mind from the grand illusion to the Presence
that ready self-awareness is now summoning?

Harvest

As you know yourself, you know God. If you know some splinters,
tastes, beliefs, earthly practices, edges of relation –
then God will be a fragment to you, a blunt mystery,
receding into the distance as you age and harden.
If you know yourself in the Present and can hold the state,
then God will be the Presence – timeless, infinite, certain.

You only exist as a joyful labor ascending
to God or as a plummeting, a thing just before death.
Now is decision, an equilibrium between breaths.
Will you harvest your attention or let the wind take it?

Prayer 72

Let me not ask for more than is possible now
as these words appear left to right across this page.
Move this pen as you move the universe, O Lord,
in the harmony behind what the struggling mind
reconstructs from the shards that the senses retrieve.
Let me understand the real city from these ruins.

Till

Much of personality is engendered to buffer
the feeling of something missing – a loss, an open wound,
the promise which lured essence back to Earth again .... broken.
We come to each new life with innocence restored, scars healed
and transformed by the soul's witnessing will, but each new life
brings new hurt, new responses, and consigns us strange new names.

Your name, your claim of individuation, is what forms
like a crust on your being. This bruised skin of vanity
and sorrow must be scraped away, now or after each death,
till slow growing wisdom forgives everything forever.

Prayer 73

I pray for the strength to serve the Heaven I've been
given to know. If my vision proves distorted
and riddled with vanity's rot, may the Angels
in their mercy disabuse me of illusion.
If it costs annihilation, I seek the truth.
Worse than death is living knowingly without it.

The Truth

The truth is always a revelation. Though vanity
believes it can deduce what must be, we form premises
and reason from within the corked bottle of our functions.
Sometimes it seems we created the future to allow
room for our predictions; in our counterfeit certainty
of tomorrow's rain, we remain time's self-praising puppets.

We have the higher faculties to apprehend the truth,
but Angels overwatch their development, maintaining
a humbling pressure on these apertures, guaranteeing
their readiness when time fumbles or at last drops our strings.

Prayer 74

What is that part that cannot bear my helplessness?
The heartbeat, the breathing, the lawless cleverness
of a mind driven by an empty stomach – none
of these do I control, yet a stubborn, bitter
thing within demands allegiance to the fiction.
Attention to you, Lord, is the will's true province.

The Great Array

As your final identity is indestructible,
you will at some point lay aside your fear. Just be patient.
Until then everything is change. Mastering one rhythm,
you are confronted by another, a calamity
for the illusion that personhood can know the cosmos.
Here's a hint: it's not about knowing, it's about being.

You are the cosmos, but as long as you're planted in time,
you'll see things sequentially – one thing after another.
Climb out of the flowerpot of personhood and you'll see
time, change and fear in the great array you no longer need.

Prayer 75

Our reviving tenderness for innocent life
is at once salvation and illusion, O Lord.
The climb out of the deep stone quarry of ourselves
back up to purity is so fraught with failure
that in the first rim of light perceived we expect
the goal. Not so, but in new radiance, press on.

The Truth of Nothingness

Scrubbing the common toilet, kissing the dead leper's hand,
sleeping with the pigs – we prefer any affirmation
of flesh, however putrid, to the interrogation
of personhood's reality. To regard our precious
selves to be mere unattended response, behavior bound
by shared belief, is to fathom the truth of nothingness.

Yet through self-cancellation being survives, purified.
There is no imagining the absence of awareness.
God's name or your own designates the same final being
in which all participate. Pig, person, God – stop clinging.

Prayer 76

When one finds oneself puzzled and confused, thank God
for the opportunity to rise above thought.
The brain jams as too many parts send messages,
each wanting to be the solution, the answer.
With everything at a hot standstill, suddenly
the wordless sky, always here aware, can appear.

Not Lost

Are you ready for the one truth that will burst your knowing,
for the answer at the end of all possible problems?
The opposite of being is identification.
To be, you must first let the world go, including the world
inside – your thoughts and feelings. Then you must let go the sense
of being other than God. There is no other than God.

That's it: say goodbye to the world and to all otherness.
Toss the mask, make the last weightless step over the threshold
of the costume shop out to love and terror and vision
of totality. God is not hindered. God is not lost.

Prayer 77

How to protect the truth without fighting for it?
Remember that the knowledge you have been given
through experience is a trust from the Angels,
a polish cloth for love, not a grant of franchise
for self-righteousness. When attacked, let your anger
pale before a holding greater than personhood.

Life

What to do with the bewildering requests from people
who are so enrapt in their projects that they cannot see
your disengagement? Be kind. Offer them something poignant
that does not partake of your higher energies. Keep God
in the closet and observe the machinery of life
and death stuck in its exhilarating earthbound struggle.

Of course, your high heart longs to free them, to take them with you
out of time, but as they are not seeking liberation,
they could not receive it. You could open the prison door,
beaming, but they'd motion you in to join their game of cards.

Prayer 78

I pray for grace to make bearable the piercing
deliverance I bring: we are nothing that we think
we are, and thought itself has been evolved for Earth,
not for Heaven. Like upright posture, handiness,
and complex speech, thought advantages our species,
but souls flower from more fundamental being.

Before Words

Signs are corruptible. Bringing them out of the bright glare
to interpret them usually involves some cobbling
of associations, some folding and stretching to make
the seams fit. We end up with a manufactured meaning
where before had been a shock propelling a brief transport
beyond meaning, a state before the beginning of words.

So when we read a sign, we have enslaved it, made it work
for us rather than on us. There is a mathematics
to this that lets our readings make money often enough
to drive us to keep reading. The Angels hold and move us.

Prayer 79

"I am not worthy" is a self-evident claim,
as all the illusory identities named
by that pronoun are poor substitutes for being
truly, namelessly Present. Self-remembering
supersedes names and transcends all forms and values,
all measurements of worthiness that I can make.

And Then We Go

The soul is given time on Earth to recognize and be
itself in every situation, and thus to strengthen
to Angelic being. Back and forth we go for ages –
giving ourselves away and then reclaiming what was lost
until the state of truth returns as easily as breath
resumes when our talking stops. Then the taste for Earth is gone.

And then we go, equipped by our labors here with a form
and body suitable to interstellar distances
and tasks done at the speed of light. The ultimate master
of our service is the one unchanging destination.

Prayer 80

How to make prayer pure? If prayer attends a desire,
then purity is a willingness to accept
the consequences of desire. If prayer is praise,
then purity is elevating gratitude
above the mire of judgment. If prayer is Presence,
then purity is imagination forsworn.

The Original

What life can be made by you who find only starvation
in your culture and customs? Find the first floor of Heaven;
there you discern a new kind of being, a discipline
of states worth serving, whose daring ancient loom unifies
and sanctifies the torn web of earthly experience.
No more warfare of values; no more salvation by blood.

You must hold the original diamond from which all
our light here below has fallen fractured. You must return
to the impeccable first thought that made the Mind of God.
Here is your own and only home, the first and last address.

Prayer 81

Lord, sometimes our share of your being is much more
than we can bear, and we must open the sluices
or become rubble under the flood. Remind us
that a man needs more than himself to be himself.
Friends keep us from breaking, and the contributions
of each build the city where men can complete souls.

The Luckiest

Once you have found a community of practitioners
of the ancient science of awareness and verified
its connection to Heaven, there is nowhere else to go.
Even the least of them will struggle nobly against lies
and cravings while the best will upraise you with their Presence.
Their love is all a truly ready soul seeks here on Earth.

Though individual, the path to Heaven cannot be
walked alone. One is always helped and helping, and the luck
of one's condition can be measured by the devotion
of those with whom one works. The luckiest work with Angels.

Prayer 82

Angels, keep me small, with functions humbly focused
on the task before me, in soul's awareness full.
To taste a bite of food or hear the gait latch lift
is enough to fill eternity. No matter
how the measuring mind would stretch itself to fill
sacred emptiness, let me abide here with you.

Focus

Do not begrudge the way your time is spent if God is here,
and if God is here, who's escorting whom doesn't matter.
Let the laws – Cause and Effect, for example – governing
what they govern, govern, and focus on the miracle –
that God is here. "But what if God is not here?" asks a voice
from well below your balcony. "What if we're on our own?"

That that voice belongs to God, as does your high balcony,
as does the whole theater is the ultimate answer.
God is playing all the parts in this play, including you,
so how can God not be here? Focus on the miracle.

Prayer 83

Knowledge is defined in dependability –
be it an hypothesis whose consummation
is a reliable measurement, or a prayer
which every time sincerely attended unmasks
itself as God's eternal love. What we count on
opens the reality we will occupy.

With Bodies

Ultimately we are not individual beings,
but the veils of separateness that must be discarded
include everything but God. Whatever God is, I am,
and you are, but see, already I've made three out of one.
Just talking about what I am deepens the illusion.
All bodies – carnal, astral, whatever – host this problem.

The practical way is to remember God with each breath.
Remembering God, watch all the rest working itself out.
Marvel at all the strange debris your caring gets caught on
as you swim upstream back to the Source, remembering God.

Prayer 84

When time has taken everything back – the meaning
of work, desire's familiar moorings, the focus
of pain, the hair, the teeth – let the path of return
be straight, O Lord, not tempted by a mind still proud.
Let time have everything that love never needed,
nor certainty required, nor peace relied upon.

Homeward Flight

The universe ends at exhaustion's empty horizon.
For that measure, where and when mean exactly the same thing.
If you prefer, think of it as God's full satisfaction
of possibility. Those attending God – namely us –
have already begun the homeward flight – the gathering
into our being of all that will return self-aware.

The first willed movement in God's mind gave birth to time and space,
and everything proud and unsurrendered to God stays there
to the end. Turning back to God frees what we truly are
for friendship's fusion. Clasp a hand above and below you.

Prayer 85

Serve your lower self and lose civilization.
Serve the web of social programing and you're dead
to love and higher reason, but a comfy corpse,
well-liked, welcome to speak at the table, no threat.
Serve God and you cling to the raft of the Present,
too far out to rescue, unreal to the tourists.

Man's Morality

Man's morality is a substitute for consciousness.
A truly conscious human is focused on the Present,
far seeing, sensitive to the pain of others, steady
in renouncing the waves of sentiment, comprehending
of the limits of life here on Earth. Such a one breathes in
the remembrance of God and breathes out loving certainty.

But as most humans live and move in sleep, they must rely
on codes and precedents, traditions, credentialed experts,
and the measure of the turmoil in their own chests and guts –
whatever obscures from the sun a shared cloud to hide in.

12. Eclipse

Prayer 86

Justice is unity, yet judging separates.
To seek justice we must not judge: we must embrace.
Nothing that happens is not part of us, nothing
can be denied or God goes with it, and we're left
intact in partiality, safe prisoners
framing our images. Please God, don't believe us.

Justice

Justice can only really be justice when limited
to a specific case. Generalize a legal frame,
a tradition of decades, precedents, and many strands
of messy, uncut karma wriggle free from the picture.
Retribution, vengeance – that's what can be done in man's time.
True justice accompanies creation's return to God.

So what can an individual who wants justice do?
Forgive, forgive, forgive. Do not make more interference.
At once is the universe expanding and returning.
Be aware in which direction your desire takes you now.

Prayer 87

What can I know of God but self-knowledge? All else
advances the illusion of all else, the hope
of not having to discover the need to love
unreservedly what is already perfect.
Let me by repeated exposure to the truth –
more often, longer, deeper – live in God aware.

Not Two Things

You cannot change the world. All its distresses contribute
to its equilibrium. A constant of suffering
is required to leave open the strange possibility
of discovering an unimaginable witness
in ourselves, a Presence at home in remembering God.
The world must churn and threaten even as the soul does not.

Yet they're not two things. They are one obeying the one law
of self-aware inclusion. To split things and make borders
is to foster illusion. If you'd profit from false work,
you are not yourself but a rich patron of the unreal.

Prayer 88

What lures the immature soul down here, pulls it through
the inflection point between spirit and matter
and traps it in a womb? What loud unwisdom keeps
calling it until it believes the name? Waking
means to realize one has once again been duped.
Immortality's for those tired of being born.

Polishing

Personhood is a level of descent each spark of God
must make many times before its next station of service
is accomplished and conferred. Many dips into bodies
are needed before flesh can be seen as it is and known.
The cloth of "I am" must polish the mirror patiently
for ages before the world becomes at last apparent.

Do not worry. Whether you have just begun your return
or have been watching many lifetimes, this light-enhancing,
moment-making, self-remembering work will bring you home.
Be glad for everything that must be dropped along the way.

Prayer 89

Please do not tempt me with belief. I am too weak,
too undiscerning. Help me keep watch on that part –
the naïve heart's unquestioned trust in harmony –
that in kindness or self-sacrifice would settle
for what dispassionate intellect would reject.
Belief is the tyrannous rule of partial truth.

Understanding

Yes, this work is based on understanding, but what is that?
Must everything be scissored and combed in sequential strands
of cause and effect? Must all the jigsawed squares and circles
in an image be counted, coded, mapped? Must we drag down
Heaven and squeeze it back through formatory mind to find
a way to talk about it? This is not understanding.

Understanding is participating in God, being
a point aware in the all aware, a nameless knowing.
Measurement and words are found on the downslope of the state
and are used to inflate the functions with time and purpose.

Prayer 90

In the next dimension, the soul can move through time
as bodies in this dimension can move through space.
How many levels of liberation appear
before we see the illusion of everything
that is not you, O God? If anything is real,
it is only real in your being. That is all.

A Step Down

I don't know how to say it more simply, so please listen:
Identification is suffering and vice versa.
One can only purchase identity by selling God –
and anything we buy distorts true being, the "I am."
Attach an adjective or noun – I am intelligent,
I am an American – and the great longing begins.

See, identity is partiality, a step down,
a hole in the sacred fabric that the worming self claims
and occupies with sleep and lies and weighty thoughts. The heart,
aching to be free of this condition, cries to Heaven.

Prayer 91

Angels, the first urge is still to fight your insults,
your stupid indignities and slapstick bruisings.
You know my loyalty: why do you persevere
in mocking this poor form? Do I still need kicking?
The torments you devise would be cruel were I
the flesh and personality you're targeting.

Soul

A near instantaneous electronic connection
with the whole world won't make you more conscious if you insist
on maintaining your current identity. The software
that you know as your social self will never be able
to keep up with the data flow, and toxic edema
from habitual emotions and brainlock will result.

There's no shortcutting the old fashioned way to make a soul:
transform earthly identity to awareness of God;
master the Angel property of loving expansion;
extend yourself as abounding love to everything here.

Prayer 92

All teachers, even those who employ fewer words
than sense requires, re-repeat the keystone message
of the great arch they construct above time and mind.
Back and forth they walk in their students' brains, clearing
a clean and weedless path that cannot be unseen,
that their students' prayers – yes, this one – can always find.

The Grandchildren

The founders have done their work; the fuel has combusted
to a steady flame of transformation. Now the children
will assume the practices – the Teacher's artful lessons –
and foster roots of tradition: a civilization
of conscious love, a welcoming to those who recognize
the possibility budding under the doom at hand.

The next generation, the grandchildren, now newly born
or waiting to be born, will pay the greatest price: the pain
maimed Earth requires in compensation. Yet many young souls
yearn to be offered these roles. What promise has been given?

Prayer 93

Despise worship, for worship of any teacher
is the compound of idiocy and weakness.
No true teacher wants to be loved in effigy,
a likeness of the fleshly form turned to symbol.
Confront the Angels themselves, not some focal point
of their influence. Worship does not share with love.

Signs

The biggest problem with the Angels is their penmanship.
Their signs are murky, smudged, often not legible at all.
And when they can be decoded, they're full of private puns
and allusions to subtle sights and sounds they directed
our attention to years ago. At their smallest notice,
thought stops; we rise in ready obedience: Here I am.

But too often nothing comes that makes for honest action.
Perhaps we're meant to settle for the passage out of thought
to Present hold, and the clear order we crave – Do this now –
means little in the dimension they long to share with us.

Prayer 94

When one asks for Angels' help, one must be willing
to watch without prejudice. Seeking higher help
differs from requesting a specific favor
that human reason has brought forth from the layers
of logic and association pressuring
our shadowed minds. Face it, we don't know what we need.

What Now, God?

Here's the situation: You're lost at sea, treading water,
close to drowning; each desperate gulp of air feels final.
Suddenly a rope drops from the sky, its source beyond sight.
As soon as you grab it, the waves begin to roil and churn,
growing in depth and power. You must hoist your body out,
gripping the rope with arms and legs. Thirty feet up, you pause.

Here you are, a dripping carcass clinging to a sky rope.
This alone is a miracle. Heaven has gone fishing
and you're the lucky catch, but Heaven won't just reel you in.
"What now, God?" you cry. The answer comes from your being: Climb.

Prayer 95

May Heaven let me remember what is now seen:
that all prayers arise from the longing to return
to God, to renounce the folly of distinction.
In God there is no difference, and the striving
for identity is stilled. Who would barter God
for a shard of broken being? Not I. Not you.

Beyond

Dancing in the Field of Love is not the end of being.
There is yet your response to terror – to all the monsters
in the dark of mind, creatures with the faces of your crimes;
and to the apocalypse of Earth, man, and all meaning.
How will you give yourself to the Unnameable's command
to navigate and colonize empty, infinite space?

In learning right attention, humble labor, forgiveness
of your debtors and renunciation's art, you have earned
a room with a balcony over a sunlit garden.
You may stay as long as you wish, but there is more beyond.

Prayer 96

Asking the Angels for anything is wanting
the world to be different. Granting the request
increases the suffering of the Absolute.
Amazingly, humans sometimes get what they want:
so great is the love riding Heaven's attention.
May this prayer find itself in God's own awareness.

Privacy

If you try to bring the world to the truth that God is one,
you will be called a heretic. The world prefers many –
many names, ideas, territories, classes, movements –
and the world wants some distance from God, enough to allow
an "I and Thou." The world's conspiracy of privacy –
our pretending there's a yours and mine – dare not be challenged.

And so we live on in words and numbers, defending claims
to the real estate of ourselves, measured, titled, storied,
the huge inductive distance from us to God untraveled.
The world can't comprehend one who'd leave the many for God.

Prayer 97

The lower self claims to abhor dependency
because it prizes the illusion of being
individual. The crystal soul humbly shrinks
to breathe the love of its infinite relations
and offer blessings well down creation's free fall.
There is no exclusion in God, only welcome.

No Goodbye

How to sever identification with the Teacher?
First, one proceeds only when one's soul has fully ripened,
gestated to a bold love bearing a ready sweetness.
One need not change addresses or hats; one's tasks will accord
with everything one has learned: there is no rebellion here;
the sack which ruptures and dies in the night is need, not love.

And the air that fills one's lungs is suffused with gratitude;
and the vessel of one's heart overbrims with certainty;
and one's awareness is a lens of perfect clarity.
Now, only now, can one be oneself in higher service.

Prayer 98

The knowledge entrusted to us is not reward
but a planting, the growth of being its harvest.
We need stability, roots pushed into good earth,
to dare the awe of the sun and digest the light.
We're civilization's deathless food, nourishing
human souls to bear the attention of Angels.

Your Book

These words in lines compounding to a book are why I'm here.
Life and labor; liftings up to love; failures; filterings
from the world's sordid streams; friendships; knowledge of the wisdom
of the ancients; and small, precious wisdoms earned here and now –
all are measured, blended, heated to a vapor and breathed
by a deepening soul guided by strange Angel promptings.

Thus what you read. And why? Because its time is here, and you
are here, and now as always is time ordered and resolved
by truths revealed from eternity. Why me? I'm the one
in your mirror. When you read this, you know you've written it.

Prayer 99

May I not forget that the energy coursing
in my spine now is mine to purpose and to turn
upward to God. I do not need to give my nerves
to some new experience, some manic pursuit,
and no earthly loyalty has a mother's claim
to the attention fashioning this Present prayer.

Higher Note

To find a higher note, tighten the string till it responds
to the shadow of your finger. Many times it will break
before balancing itself one breath over the threshold,
but when there, it awaits and repays all sincerity,
all real effort, with heavenly clarity in a sound
that orders the worlds above and below, echoing God.

You will not have the fine attention tightening requires,
the calm to see the string's vibrations at the breaking point,
unless you can abstain from the draining, stillborn pleasures
of crude pelvic rhythms that would mindlessly pound the ground.

Prayer 100

Let us purify this prayer of worldly desire,
of the bent half-lives of victory or defeat,
of all imagined fruits, of weighty ownership,
of all that would stand defiant of God's embrace.
The red and blue flowers by the Gate of Nothing
are the last temptation. Let us leave them blooming.

Not Bound

The formless intellect pervades and silently observes
all things, understanding non-assertion's higher duty.
It sees things as they are: the exchange of form and chaos,
identities coming into being and dissolving.
Not the lowest passions nor the saint's highest sacrifice
can tempt it from its infinite, ever abiding watch.

All emotions of the mother heart, even those that call
the soul to its balcony, fail to hold formless being.
Noble as forms can be, the truth is not bound to their laws,
and knowing itself at last, will not be anything else.

Prayer 101

Teach me to wait, to have respect for slow designs
developing over days while my buzzing nerves
would flee the Present for any instant action.
Everything has its ripening, its perfect point
of cosmic service, and taken prematurely
what could be delicious dies bitter in the mouth.

School Now

Each true School has its ripening, a radiance of years –
less than a handful – in which the flowers proliferate
and the fruit comes forth as a marvel to the world and dies
as the enduring food for centuries. The Teacher's tree
soars to mysterious completion, and the great branches
weave the entire sky into a garment clothing the sun.

If you are alive in that time, you have a tolerance
for wonder that Angels are relying on. Pray for strength
to hold what you have verified as the dissolution
that follows close behind a birth leaves Earth empty of love.

Prayer 102

Let me absorb and not react, take deep within
the welcoming heart what would roil the lower coil
and make the mind expel a storm of argument.
I would know what is. Only the bladed stair mounts
Heavenward, each breath a step, each step a sharp edge
gleaming with reflected light sustaining the soul.

13. Lives

Whatever Men Would Do

Knowledge is responsibility, and higher knowledge
drives one to Gethsemane where one finally accepts
the night mob's arrest. From then, how long it takes to kill you
really doesn't matter. You eat death. The taste of its fruit
overcomes the bloody alarm in your throat. The reward
of being rises deathless from whatever men would do.

You have earned the right to love them as they are. Their candles,
choking in each personal cloud of fear and bitterness,
are not obscured to you and can be addressed, unified.
Your work spawns a flame by which you can read the universe.

Prayer 103

On its way back to God, a forming soul must brunt
the outward and descending rush of brute matter.
Collisions are inevitable; reversals
and long delays breed a self-possessing patience.
Near the end, the abrading medium becomes
a fine polish raising a pearly radiance.

Are You Ready?

What in you resents, lies or exults in others' failures?
These are the actions of your miserable prisoner.
Your compassion for him is generous, but you must stay
out of earshot. Attention to his voice keeps him alive.
When his screams stop echoing through the corridors, you'll know
he's dying the good death he always secretly longed for.

And you, now having prepared the way for awakening,
what is your good death? Having climbed every stair to the roof,
having held the rhythm of breath against all temptation,
are you now ready for the borderless being of God?

Prayer 104

Let me be earnest, not stained with thought's advantage.
Let me not grow fat on accomplishment, nor starve
on cleverness, but be nourished by wordless breath
and clear-eyed witness. I know I can be tempted;
I know I can be drawn away. Let me value
being free of everything observed and passing.

The Mind of God

Greater than the mind of the body is the Mind of God.
You are both, but when you are your best, you are witnessing
the small human mind and thus participating in God's.
Pathetic is the irony of identifying
with mortal mind – the fear of death in the already dead.
There's no identifying with God's mind: it simply is.

The bordered mind is made of language and symbols. One frees
oneself by being ever aware of the plastic veil
symbols and words cast over the actual to refract
it into meaning. No meaning limits the Mind of God.

Prayer 105

I must ride personhood till it no further goes –
its questions turned inside out, littering the road
of pilgrimage; its view of the shrine too shadowed.
Then what? O Lord, all I am is you, no other,
and when as now I pray, it is your voice singing
your song in the cool garden of your universe.

Both

Be the mind actual or virtual, it stands between
soul and body. Some would have it the child of the high heart,
brought by years of discipline to readiness and virtue.
Some have it as the rebel lord of the senses' chaos,
the "I am" corrupted and reimagined as "I want."
Both steward and lower self claim identity in mind.

Both must be surrendered if the spark – the only certain
unimaginary being – would make return to God.
"Only through me," the steward asserts; the lower self whines,
"I'm your only life." Send them thank you notes from beyond thought.

Prayer 106

The most daring way to pray for humility
is to exalt yourself and trust the balancing
art of bright Heaven to remind you why you're here.
A better way is to serve the souls of others
with superhuman patience. Let me not forget
that true humility is patient beyond form.

The Bow

Why do the Angels bow to teach us who are trapped in time?
Standing in eternity, they cannot say no to those
whose sincere voices rise from their circles of suffering.
To hold them in awareness and say nothing will suffice:
silence is a form of teaching as the aspirant learns
from his own echoes – but outright refusal is not love.

That which is not love does not exist in eternity.
Even the Absolute abides by one law: the self-love
that must make the universe. Everything else must return
to that love, renouncing what would be a separate thing.

Prayer 107

From below, crystallizing an astral body
seems an accomplishment, but from above it is
a responsibility to oneself as God.
Identification is belief in the light
which personality refracts for its own ends.
Let me love the duty of unrefracted light.

Not Different

The awareness trapped in a person strains to separate
from all here below – the laws of denser matters – and fly
home to God. This return is done in stages – out and back,
incarnation and liberation – until a vessel
of the next order is fashioned, a bright identity
subject only to the lighter laws governing the stars.

But even then the process continues. Behind the mind's
words and images, beyond all Angel identities,
is the great destination, the final discovery,
the last unattainment: we are not different from God.

Prayer 108

Even as petition, prayer is always the call
to oneself to be more. "Let the circumstances
have less potency over my being, O Lord."
The Lord is the Higher Self. In short, prayer asks God
to be God more definitely: the human fog
dispersed, certainty makes all hazards bearable.

Detached

I am not indifferent to your suffering; I am
detached from your desires. If you begged plaintively enough,
my hand would grope in my pocket for a coin, but the one
I truly am would be watching bodies interacting –
my overwhelmed heart reacting to a cry of hunger.
Both bodies then go the way of bodies, love not discerned.

When one does not identify with the toxic turmoil
of human desire and pursuit, love emerges – the real
always here – and your soul and mine recognize each other,
being instantly free of the yours and mine illusion.

Prayer 109

I do not need to know humility by name.
Rather by fitted experience let me learn
a fitting use in eternity's boundlessness,
and let the logistics of above and below
be lost along with all reliance on belief.
Now, God, in this prayer of simple being, I am.

Balanced

The only problem is the problem of identity.
Who am I? Even a middling poet knows he is not
the body, the hand holding the pen, or the brain combing
the gravel of memory from which these words and phrases
rise like steam. Nothing in sensory attention can hold
the "I am" – this awareness out of time, balanced between.

"Between what?" you ask, with fear's intruding entitlement.
Between the Mind of God in which the "I am" is a glint
reflected in the mirror, a spark apparent for probes
and poems – between this and the Nothing, Nothing and this.

Prayer 110

Sometimes your own neighborhood appears alien;
luckily the dog knows the way home and won't care
if there's a fuddled mind at your end of the leash.
Let your confusion be an accidental prayer,
a stumbling onto the vast grounds of God's estate.
Don't panic. Breathe. Explore. Stay till you're dragged away.

Nameless Here

The way couples grow together as they age, distilling
a fragrance from their patient dying, is love returning
to the source of love, immune to the descent of matter.
Thus these words in lines forget their boundaries and become
your breath, your mind, the mortar of your heart's understanding.
Let them gather in you what would rise and return to God.

All the words you call yourself name falling things, things speeding
out to an inconceivable end that mankind will spend
all its pride to calculate. Let them go. Stay nameless here,
aware of levitation, aware of God, God, aware.

Prayer 111

The heart center opens like overripe fruit bursts –
death by superabundance, a deluge of love.
Let all controls and containments be washed away,
borders drowned, identities swallowed by the surge.
This is how the cross is conquered, how the crypt stone
is rolled away, how one is eternally born.

Your Living

If the soul needs more time with human form, then it will take
another body and another. Having crystallized
the being of one cosmos, it moves on to inhabit
and absorb the next. With each quantum increase in being,
the soul fills more of the Absolute's mirror. When it knows
itself as its own creator, creation is complete.

How long is the infancy that so limits you, my friend?
When will you acquiesce to namelessness, the eternal
watching of outward change? When will responsibility
for God's self-knowing become the purpose of your breathing?

Prayer 112

The first thought is pure: I am. Everything coming
after is an image, and if believed, a lie.
The mind needs reminding with each breath, with each breath.
Let us return to the source of thought – the mirror
whose surface faces all, being's first awareness,
the discovery of God – and keep it holy.

The Limit

The aim is not to clench against the loss of anything.
Let God have it back, even whatever directs this hand
with a pen in it. The illusion of authorship laughs
as it divests itself. The illusion of personhood
shrinks toward abandonment. God appears but is instantly
recognized and instantly forsakes all recognition.

Your stripping away begins as an act of love – ridding
all your interference from what without you simply is.
Then the first laws of being assert themselves: what is willed
must be, and God, being God, must will what's in the mirror.

Prayer 113

At long last we stop believing we are bodies.
We know ourselves as conscious beings and can drop
the swollen sack of the world's responses carried
since birth. What we used to be is now a grotto
we move in and out of like young waves exploring
the unbounded and coming quickly back, O Lord.

Trusting the Angels

What does it mean to trust the Angels? I don't want to speak
in polite generalities: positive attitude,
reverence, acceptance – all right facing but still too vague
for this discussion. I'm talking about specific signs,
injunctions that higher centers instantly understand.
To trust the Angels means to obey such signs exactly.

When an omen appears and you get it with clarity,
you have been given a precise map for your advancement.
Your obedience measures your reception of this gift.
The logic arising to oppose is the grip of Earth.

Prayer 114

Lord, let these eyes forget my kind, the freight of flesh
be disengendered. Let these ears forget all names.
Let the stern chiselings of personhood erode
and mind itself surrender to the elements.
If I exist, may I be unbounded being
sharing you perfectly with all and everything.

The Picture One is Seeing

The distance between the thorny world – which includes one's thoughts –
and the fragile light of self-observation is a space
the soul requires. Though astonishing in its brute beauty,
the world is too rough and calloused. It is shaped by its scars.
An awareness of not being it – including one's thoughts –
must be perseveringly nursed, mothered with attention.

Then after many lives a crystal of self becomes part
of every view, every vista. The chaos that had been
becomes the picture one is seeing. Finally one has
something to trade upon return to all-embracing God.

Prayer 115

Do not let a poem or a prayer make me miss
an opportunity to greet a child of light
with my love. To be a mirror for another
even for an instant is to make a portal
to eternity, something the best of poems
and prayers can do but weakly as a distant star.

To Myself

Stored fat goes rancid. Well used fat supports earthly delight.
Catalogued knowledge returns to dust. Self-knowledge finds God.
Searching for the answer can become its own profession.
Seeing what is before one is the answer of answers.
If your child were sick, you'd be fearless of the cost of cure.
The soul you are suffocates while you hide rocks in your throat.

Who are you? Supply me a noun and I'll show you the mask
you've made of it. Give me a picture, I'll locate the wall.
Who are you? Your mind's objections to the question are not
infinite, but God is infinitely Present and kind.

Prayer 116

When one finds oneself in a cloud of angry wasps,
one is grateful to have mastered the discipline
of disappearing. Thank you, Angels, for guiding
my training, but as much as I'd cherish making
a poem of praise, I need to put this parting
skill to work. Stingers are finding my ears. Adieu.

One's Own Departure

In the womb of a thick clouded sky, one waits, concentrates,
draws oneself in to a point, the inside out of pursuit,
the bliss of limitation, awareness wanting nothing.
Dress for warmth, move from necessity, postpone the pleasure
of distinction, withhold charm. Let the base of the spine hum
with potency, its current only for the Eye and Crown.

It's strange, but we have bodies so that one day self-knowledge
will not need them. They are servants of their own departure,
and we are what will remain to observe small spinning Earth,
as the cloudy galaxies move past this perfect stillness.

Prayer 117

Angels, I accept your verdict as a blessing.
The favor I sought was wrong footed or ill timed.
That I would petition you at all for something
in this shadow world contravenes my best knowledge,
the gold extracted from a life of instruction.
The sting of the nothing denied me spurs return.

What You Are Now

Enough pain wrings the silliness out of one. Suicide
becomes an option; but that's all one really wants – to hold
a final wild card against God's incomprehensible
cruelty. Each new attack is like climbing a rock face
in an avalanche. The aim through and between the spasms
is to get one's mind above it all. The body is pulp.

The only thing to be gained is a floor of survival –
hours then days of not dying. At some point, a flash crosses
what's left of one – the consciousness: there is no death, nothing
left to hammer out. What you are now, you are forever.

Prayer 118

The aim, Lord, is to know your voice when I hear it,
feel its subtle vibration arresting the spin
of Earth, creating a rent in spacetime's fabric....
Then to act – to shake off the dust from attention
and establish the breath of awareness, to be
ready for whatever you dare. Thus comes this prayer.

No Hiding from You

Angels, as there is no hiding from you, no privacy,
there is no imaginary worthiness to uphold.
Everything wrapping the "I am," everything credited
to this flesh or tattooed on it or issuing from it,
every inane formation of psychological stuff –
you must tolerate it all and not forget what to love.

I am beyond gratitude, wondering what discipline
you had to master in the time since your last earthsuit lost
its meaning. What training did you undergo to possess
patience on a scale of the stars for this provoking child?

Prayer 119

Did God ask Abraham to sacrifice Isaac?
Abraham thought so until a higher vision
supplanted what he had been seeing. What Isaac
represented had to be given up to God.
Lord, the world I gauge is a stubborn illusion,
but only your mercy soothes the pain of leaving.

Scale

Arjuna looks at impending slaughter and sees nothing
but harm. Krishna assures him that right action produces
no harm and that duty bids him fight and kill his brethren.
To the steward Arjuna, the battlefield circumscribes
what is real; in Krishna's Eye, the doomed individuals
are not real as death is not real as God alone is real.

To learn that one is God, that the soul and God are the same,
transforms duty. The soul sees events proceed as they must
according to the governing law. Glory and heartbreak
enact a scale of vision. No scale encompasses God.

Prayer 120

This is a daring height to which you've summoned me,
O Lord, demanding I remain myself though blind
and deaf in this jetstream of gusts beyond duty.
To what I've left below, I appear ungracious,
but there's no rude rebel here, just a slave praising
your majesty in a raw, disappearing voice.

Gazing at the Sun

There is no daintiness left in me, no delicacy,
no love for shimmering things. Enough of precious beauties.
These prizes – so long to gain, their materials so long
to master – no longer satisfy. The aging salon
in which they're celebrated invokes an understanding
of God all too comfortable, a sagging abundance.

The next level demands a revelation terrible
in its power, a solemn procession through chaos, doubt
and death to an all surviving certainty that gazes
openly at the sun, fearing not the dissolution.